PIPE FITTINGS

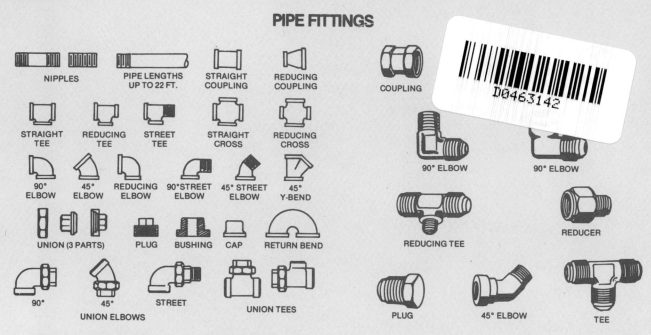

NIPPLES — PIPE LENGTHS UP TO 22 FT. — STRAIGHT COUPLING — REDUCING COUPLING — COUPLING

STRAIGHT TEE — REDUCING TEE — STREET TEE — STRAIGHT CROSS — REDUCING CROSS

90° ELBOW — 45° ELBOW — REDUCING ELBOW — 90° STREET ELBOW — 45° STREET ELBOW — 45° Y-BEND — 90° ELBOW — 90° ELBOW

UNION (3 PARTS) — PLUG — BUSHING — CAP — RETURN BEND — REDUCING TEE — REDUCER

90° — 45° UNION ELBOWS — STREET — UNION TEES — PLUG — 45° ELBOW — TEE

Here are the common steel pipe fittings. Nipples are simply short lengths of pipe threaded on both ends. Reducing fittings join two different sizes of pipe.

Compression fittings of the flared-tube type are the easiest for the novice to handle when working with copper tubing.

STANDARD STEEL PIPE
(All Dimensions in Inches)

Nominal Size	Outside Diameter	Inside Diameter	Nominal Size	Outside Diameter	Inside Diameter
⅛	0.405	0.269	1	1.315	1.049
¼	0.540	0.364	1¼	1.660	1.380
⅜	0.675	0.493	1½	1.900	1.610
½	0.840	0.622	2	2.375	2.067
¾	1.050	0.824	2½	2.875	2.469

SQUARE MEASURE
144 sq in = 1 sq ft
9 sq ft = 1 sq yd
272.25 sq ft = 1 sq rod
160 sq rods = 1 acre

VOLUME MEASURE
1728 cu in = 1 cu ft
27 cu ft = 1 cu yd

MEASURES OF CAPACITY
1 cup = 8 fl oz
2 cups = 1 pint
2 pints = 1 quart
4 quarts = 1 gallon
2 gallons = 1 peck
4 pecks = 1 bushel

WOOD SCREWS

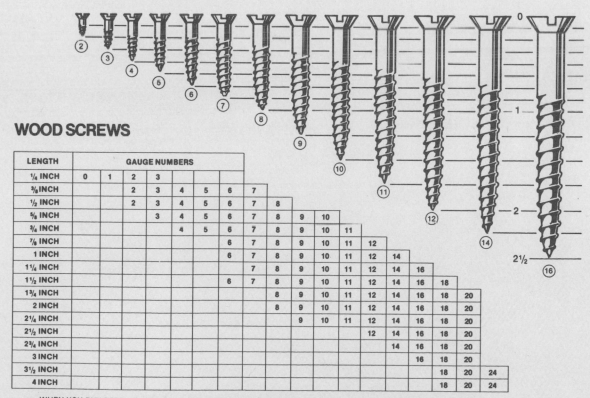

LENGTH	GAUGE NUMBERS																
	0	1	2	3	4	5	6	7	8	9	10	11	12	14	16	18	20	24
¼ INCH	0	1	2	3														
⅜ INCH			2	3	4	5	6	7										
½ INCH			2	3	4	5	6	7	8									
⅝ INCH				3	4	5	6	7	8	9	10							
¾ INCH					4	5	6	7	8	9	10	11						
⅞ INCH							6	7	8	9	10	11	12					
1 INCH							6	7	8	9	10	11	12	14				
1¼ INCH								7	8	9	10	11	12	14	16			
1½ INCH							6	7	8	9	10	11	12	14	16	18		
1¾ INCH									8	9	10	11	12	14	16	18	20	
2 INCH									8	9	10	11	12	14	16	18	20	
2¼ INCH										9	10	11	12	14	16	18	20	
2½ INCH													12	14	16	18	20	
2¾ INCH														14	16	18	20	
3 INCH															16	18	20	
3½ INCH																18	20	24
4 INCH																18	20	24

WHEN YOU BUY SCREWS, SPECIFY (1) LENGTH, (2) GAUGE NUMBER, (3) TYPE OF HEAD—FLAT, ROUND, OR OVAL, (4) MATERIAL—STEEL, BRASS, BRONZE, ETC., (5) FINISH—BRIGHT, STEEL BLUED, CADMIUM, NICKEL, OR CHROMIUM PLATED.

Popular Mechanics Guide to Do-It-Yourself Materials

POPULAR MECHANICS GUIDE TO
DO-IT-YOURSELF MATERIALS

Richard V. Nunn

Hearst Books
New York

Library of Congress Cataloging in Publication Data

Nunn, Richard V.
  Popular mechanics guide to do-it-yourself materials.

  Includes index.
  1. Building materials—Amateurs' manuals. 2. Dwellings—Maintenance and repair—Amateurs' manuals. I. Popular mechanics (New York, N.Y.) II. Title.
TA403.4.N86   691   82-1083
ISBN 0-87851-150-4   AACR2

10   9   8   7   6   5   4   3   2   1

PRINTED IN THE UNITED STATES OF AMERICA

CONTENTS

INTRODUCTION

Once upon a time most of the nation's lumberyards and hardware stores seemed to be staffed with friendly older men who had file-cabinet minds crammed full of home repair information. When something went wrong in your house you could always ask one of these gentlemen to analyze the problem and come up with the right part or tool to fix it.

Times change.

Many lumberyards and hardware stores have become home center stores in establishments dedicated to self-service, one-stop shopping: every product for any need. Even drug stores and grocery stores have begun to stock repair products. This marketing approach was demanded by the changing buying patterns of the consumer, and for economic reasons: You get more for your money by serving yourself—if, of course, what you serve yourself is the right product. Many retailers are still staffed with one or two people who know the answers to your home repair problems, but you can have trouble finding them.

Nowadays, you're usually on your own when trouble strikes. What happens is this: First, you hope that the problem will go away; then, as things go from bad to worse, something has to be done. The difficulty you face is not so much making the repair as finding the right part or tool to use and getting enough knowledge to do the job properly.

That's what this book is all about.

The **Popular Mechanics Guide to Do-It-Yourself Materials** was written and illustrated to help you find the right product for the job, and to give you the basic idea of how to use that product.

The first time you open this book you'll see that most of the chapters and product categories are organized into these sections:
- What It Is
- Where It's Used
- How It's Graded
- How It's Sold
- Special Orders

By scanning these sections, you'll get a broad view of the subjects each chapter covers, and the range of products available. Take time to thumb through the entire chapter that deals with the subject you're interested in, rather than going first to the index for specific information. This way you'll soon see how products and problems relate to one another, and you'll learn how to find the specific item you need quickly.

Someone has estimated that there are 500,000 building products on the market. This figure is probably conservative. To show every product would take a book the size of the Manhattan telephone directory. This book, obviously, is not that complete. What it does contain are all the basic products used in residential building construction today. And although a book cannot completely replace that knowledgeable person at the lumberyard or hardware store, it can relieve much of the frustration of finding what you need among all those packaged goods hanging on hooks and stacked in bins by giving you some very important information before you go shopping. This **Guide** lists the sizes, shapes, colors, ingredients, formulas, and some how-to information about every material and product you're likely to need for home repairs and improvements. It also explains the names and terms used to label and describe these items in the stores; this nomenclature is sometimes misleading and very often confusing.

This is a how-to-buy-it book. By using the information you'll find here, you can ask for and get what you need—even if you can't see it on the hooks or in the bins. By making you a wiser and better buyer, it will save you a great deal of time and money. If you follow the suggestions you find here, you are likely to come home from the first trip to the store with the right product for the job at hand.

The **Popular Mechanics Guide to Do-It-Yourself Materials** is *not* simply a guide to new products. In the fast-changing world of home repair and improvement products, such a guide would be out of date the day it was printed. This book does not recommend any commercial products; brand and manufacturer names have been left out whenever possible.

At the store you will find several similar items from which to choose, and your needs and budget will determine the decision. Product quality is not rated, although there are references to the quality standards used to classify materials. Prices are usually not mentioned, either, but you will find information *about* prices. For example, a product that originates on the West Coast (redwood, for example) may cost less there than on the East Coast; plastic pipe is less expensive than copper pipe; a doorbell costs less than a solid brass knocker.

The kinds of stores where you most likely will find the item you want are mentioned. Try as they might, home center stores can't stock all of those 500,000 items. But if you can find what you need at another kind of store (a plumbing specialty shop that caters to the professional plumber or builder, for example), this is pointed out. If you are not able to locate the product anywhere in your buying area, we've listed manufacturers who may be able to help. No attempt was made to single out any specific manufacturer; those listed are mentioned because they are the ones most likely to know the answers and be willing to pass on the information. The retailers where you shop probably can add other names to the list.

Do-it-yourselfers spent $52 billion in a recent year on home repair and improvement. Your share of this constantly growing investment is probably greater than you realize. The **Popular Mechanics Guide to Do-It-Yourself Materials** is dedicated to helping you get the greatest value out of your expenditure, to keeping your home running smoothly and comfortably, and to adding to your leisure-time enjoyment.

1

LUMBER AND BOARDS

Lumber is the general term for most building materials made from wood. However the type of lumber, its size and grade, and its usage can be anything but what the term would imply. The communication gap is in the nomenclature of the industry; you need to know its idiosyncrasies to be a smart buyer who will save money and time.

What it is

Dimension lumber is either hardwood or softwood that has been cut to a nominal thickness of 2 inches and a width of 2 inches or more.

Board is either hardwood or softwood that has been cut to a nominal thickness of 1 inch and a width of 3 inches or more.

Strips are usually softwood that have been cut to a nominal thickness of 1 inch and a width of less than 3 inches. Strips are called "furring" or, in some cases, "clear strip," "appearance boards," or "trim," especially if the grade of the wood is B or better.

Posts are square and have a nomi-nal size of 4×4 and 6×6 inches.

Timbers are at least 5 inches or larger in the smallest dimension. There are no standard nominal sizes. However, the actual size of timbers is ½ inch smaller than any stated nominal size. That is, a 6×8 timber actually measures 7½ inches wide by 5½ inches thick.

Shiplap are boards that have been cut with rabbeted (notched) edges.

Matched lumber has edges and/or ends cut in a tongue-and-groove pattern. The sizes vary.

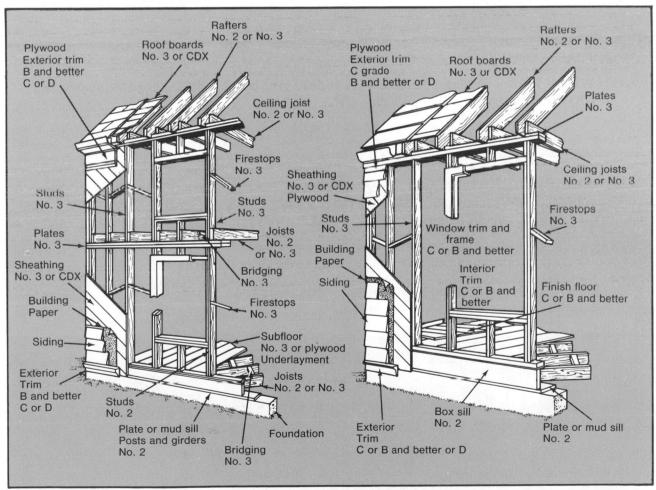

What material goes where? Lumber grades are important in construction because of the strength and stability that various grades offer. Typical one- and two-story house framing is illus-trated as a grade selector. When you buy material, pick the lowest grade that will do the job that you want it to do; i.e., don't buy Select when No. 2 Common is adequate. Framing lumber generally is manufactured from pine, hemlock, fir, and spruce. Finish lum-ber is usually pine or fir, as well as the hardwoods such as oak, maple, and mahogany.

Where it's used

Dimension lumber and boards are used in almost all aspects of building construction, including high rises.

Strips, posts, timbers, shiplap, and matched lumber could be considered "specialties"; they are used for specific components in building construction such as siding, bearing posts and beams, flooring, roof decking, and bracing.

Unraveling the nomenclature still further, *hardwood* is not necessarily hard and *softwood* is not necessarily soft. In fact, some softwood is harder than some woods classified as hardwoods. For example, fir is harder than cedar, yet both are classed as softwoods.

To help you make a selection for the job at hand, here is a general classification of construction stock available at most building-material retailers that cater to the do-it-yourself market.

BOARDS. The wood species choice may be limited to pine with, possibly, spruce and fir. You also may find cedar (plentiful in the East and South), redwood (primarily in the West), and cypress (mainly in the South). However, these woods almost always cost more than pine, spruce, and fir, which are competitively priced.

The grade range will be Nos. 1, 2, 3, and 4 Common, with No. 1 and No. 3 Common the standard stock. You may be able to buy all species in Select Lumber, which will be graded B and better, C, and D. Most often, these grades will appear under the category *appearance boards,* that are intended for projects that will show. You can expect to pay higher prices for the better appearance.

Boards are used for paneling, shelving, trim molding, underlayment,

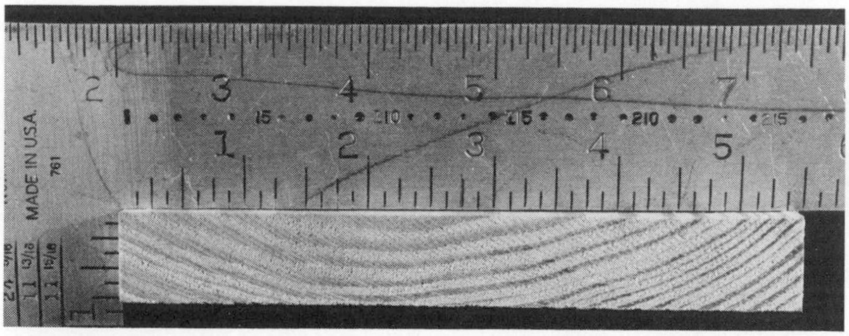

Boards, like dimension lumber, measure less than nominal size. This is a 1×6, which actually measures $3/4$ inch thick by $5\frac{1}{2}$ inches wide. *Lengths* of boards and dimension lumber are standard: usually 6, 8, 10, 12, 16, 18, 20, and 22 feet (actual, not nominal).

sheathing, siding, flooring, decks, fences, cabinets, subflooring, casing, linings, soffits, facia, baseboards, jambs, headers, stair risers, bracing, concrete forms, sills, window stools, walks, and planters.

Sizes are standard and are listed below. Lengths are fairly standard: 4, 6, 8, 10, and 12 feet. The 8- and 10-footers may be considered as normal stock items.

Special board sizes sometimes are stocked. These include $5/4$ (five-quarter) boards, $1\frac{1}{16}$-inch thick, in various widths, and laminated boards that vary in thickness from $3/4$ to $1\frac{1}{16}$ and $1\frac{1}{4}$ inches to widths of 12 to 18 inches or more. Laminated boards are similar to butcher blocks in construction, that is, edge-glued and surfaced smooth all sides.

Nominal Size of Boards	Actual Size
1×4	$3/4 \times 3\frac{1}{2}$ in.
1×6	$3/4 \times 5\frac{1}{2}$ in.
1×8	$3/4 \times 7\frac{1}{4}$ in.
1×10	$3/4 \times 9\frac{1}{4}$ in.
1×12	$3/4 \times 11\frac{1}{4}$ in.

DIMENSION LUMBER. The wood species used include spruce and pine and, perhaps, fir. Redwood, cypress, and cedar are seldom stocked in dimension lumber, although these are common in post dimensions.

Studs (2×3s and 2×4s) usually are white or yellow pine and sometimes spruce. The structural framing (2×6s, 2×8s, 2×10s) is usually spruce and fir. This wood has superior strength and workability.

For interior, non–load-bearing walls, 2×3s may be used if local codes permit. The 2×3s are less expensive than 2×4s; however, there are considerations: Standard $3\frac{1}{2}$-inch insulation will not fit between 2×3 studs, and some electrical junction boxes can't be used between 2×3s.

If your project calls for studs more than 10 feet long, you should use light framing or structural light framing with these grades: construction, standard and better, and select structural.

Dimension lumber is used for rafters, joists, studs, sills, fencing, retaining walls, posts, concrete forms, steps,

Stud Stamps

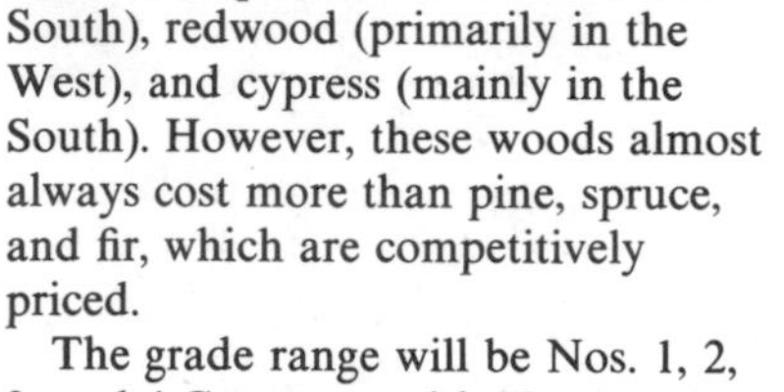

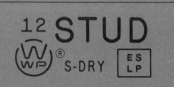

Most studs—2×4s—carry grade stamps that contain a wealth of information about the product. These stamps are applied by the Western Wood Products Association (WWPA or WWP) and the Southern Pine Inspection Bureau (SPIB). The West Coast Lumber Inspection Bureau (WCLIB) also grades western lumber and its stamps contain similar data.

The grade stamp reproduced here shows that the stud was manufactured or milled at Mill No. 12, which follows Western Wood Products Association (WWP) standards. The word "STUD" identifies the 2×4 as "stud grade." "S-DRY" means that the stud was dried to a moisture level of 19 percent or less. The letters in the little box, "ES" and "LP", mean the wood is either Engelmann spruce or Lodgepole pine. These two woods have the same grading characteristics.

Douglas fir and larch species also are combined and are stamped, DOUG FIR-L. HEM-FIR is included with the fir species. If the wood is stamped WW (White Woods), it means that the species can be fir, pine, Engelmann spruce, and hemlock.

Most building measurements are in 16-inch increments—or multiples of 8 inches. For example, studs are set 16 inches on center (O.C.). In some applications, framing goes 24 inches and 32 inches O.C. Most building materials are also made to match this measuring system. Four-foot-wide sheet materials, for example, can be

backed by four framing members 16 inches O.C., or three members 24 inches O.C. To measure centers, work from the same-side faces of the material, as shown. This measurement equals the distance from the center of one stud to the center of the next stud, or "16 inches on center."

Otherwise, the chemicals used in treating the wood may bleed through the paint film and show.

SHELVING. Precut particleboard is replacing softwood shelving boards in the marketplace, because particleboard is knotfree and dimensionally stable, and is usually priced lower than its softwood cousin. Particleboard takes finishes well; its raw edges may be covered with veneer tape or the voids filled with wood putty and sanded.

Particleboard shelving is available in ¾-inch thicknesses, 8-, 10-, and 12-inch widths (actual size), and in 4-, 6-, and 8-foot lengths; all these are stock items.

Another replacement for softwood shelving boards is prefinished shelving in solid colors, wood veneer coverings, and various wood grain laminates. Its cost is competitive with softwood shelving and particleboard when you consider the value added to the products. Sizes range from ¾-inch thicknesses to widths of 4 to 10 inches. Lengths are 2, 4, 6, and 8 feet. Prefinished shelving is a stock item in most stores.

decks, flooring, beams, columns, window stools, threshholds, fire blocking, braces, walks, headers, bridging, rails, and ridge poles.

Sizes are standard and listed below. Studs are standard in two lengths: 7 and 8 feet. Standard lengths of other dimension lumber are 6, 8, 10, 12, and 16 feet. Eight-, 10-, and 12-footers may be considered as a stock item.

Nominal Size of Dimension Lumber	Actual Size
2×2	1½ × 1½ in.
2×3	1½ × 2½ in.
2×4	1½ × 3½ in.
2×6	1½ × 5½ in.
2×8	1½ × 7¼ in.
2×10	1½ × 9¼ in.
2×12	1½ × 11¼ in.

PRESSURE-TREATED. Dimension lumber and boards are treated under high pressure with a chemical—usually copper naphthenate or pentachlorophenol—to make the wood resistant to rot. A newcomer to the building materials market, pressure-treated lumber is available in most of the standard sizes at a slightly higher price.

The higher cost, however, may be worth it, since the material usually is No. 1 Common grade—instead of No. 3—with the rot-resistant advantage for basement remodeling and exterior construction where moisture and water are always present.

If you intend to paint pressure-treated lumber in an exterior application, let the wood weather for four to six months before paint is applied.

POSTS. The wood species used are cedar or fir; spruce and redwood are sometimes available. The grade almost always will be No. 1. You may be able to buy posts that are pressure-treated; cedar, redwood, and cypress posts, which are naturally rot-resistant, and don't need this chemical treatment to withstand moisture and water.

Posts are used for structural framing, braces, supports, fencing, retaining walls, walks, and landscaping purposes. Standard sizes are 4×4 (3½ × 3½ inches actual) and 6×6 (5½ × 5½ inches actual) in stock lengths of 4, 6, 8, and 10 feet. Twelve- and 16-footers are milled, but they may be hard to locate.

TIMBERS. The wood species used are fir, oak, and pine, and, sometimes, spruce. Pine timbers, which resemble a small railroad tie, may be pressure-treated—or just treated—with creosote. The grade generally is No. 1, although No. 2 and 3 grades might be found in pine timbers.

Timbers are used for structural framing and applications similar to posts. Standard sizes are 6×8 (5½ × 7½ inches actual) in lengths of 6 and 8 feet. Longer lengths are sometimes available, depending on the retailer's stocking practices.

Dimension lumber actually measures less than its nominal size would indicate. For example, this piece is called a 2×6, but it actually measures 1½ inches thick by 5½ inches wide. You must plan your use of material by its actual measurements even though you buy it in nominal sizes.

LANDSCAPING TIES. These are usually spruce or fir posts that have been pressure-treated to withstand moisture. They differ in shape from regular posts: the edges are rounded slightly to form an oval rather than a square or rectangle. The faces, however, have about a 3-inch-wide flat surface to which boards and dimension lumber can be solidly fastened.

The actual size of ties can vary; 4×6 inches could be considered standard with 6- and 8-foot lengths also standard. If you want size consistency, take your tape measure to the store and pick-and-choose, if the retailer will permit.

Landscaping ties are designed for use as fence posts, retaining walls, braces, some structural framing applications, and, as the name implies: landscaping ties.

SHIPLAP. The wood species used are fir, spruce, and pine. The edges are milled with a rabbet, or notch, that is, either with or without a reveal, or slight offset, on the face of the boards when they are fitted tightly together and fastened.

Shiplap is generally used for underlayment and sheathing. It also makes a suitable surface for siding, flooring, decking, walks, retaining walls, fencing, and some landscaping applications.

The rabbets provide a standard ⅜-inch lap of the boards that may be applied to framing vertically, horizontally, or diagonally in about a 45° configuration.

How it's graded

All *lumber*—dimension, boards, trim and molding, plywood, and so on—is graded as to quality (appearance) and strength. The wood also falls into two classifications: softwood and hardwood. Generally, softwoods are less expensive than hardwoods, and the better the quality of the wood, the more you can expect to pay for it.

As you might expect, the lumber industry has a set of terms that applies to various grades.

Softwood building materials are manufactured from evergreen trees that are cone-bearing (pine, spruce, and fir trees). Since softwood is plentiful throughout the United States, it usually is less expensive than hardwood. There are two notable exceptions: redwood and cedar usually cost more. However, if you live in the western states, redwood prices may be affordable because you are next to the source of supply and shipping costs are lower. Cedar wood is also less costly where it is milled in the West and South.

Hardwood building materials are manufactured from trees that shed their leaves annually (oak, maple, walnut, poplar). Hardwood is not plentiful; therefore, it is fairly expensive to buy, even if you live next to a lumber manufacturer that mills it.

Hardwood seldom is used as a framing material, with the exception of oak in some areas. Use of hardwood is almost limited to furniture and cabinet products and some trim applications. The more expensive paneling boards are skinned on their faces with hardwood veneers, but most of the affordable paneling today is a plastic laminate that resembles

Those Letters and Numbers

Although they're not too common anymore—especially at home centers—boards and dimension lumber may have a designation such as S4S, S1E, S2S, etc. These letters and numbers are easy to decode: "S" means "surfaced." "E" means "edge." The numbers—1, 2, 3, and 4—refer to the number of surfaces "cut" or "squared."

For example, a board marked "S4S" means that it has been cut or squared on the faces and edges: "surfaced 4 sides." A board marked "S1E," means that the board has been cut or squared on one edge: "surfaced 1 edge." A board marked "S1S1E" means "surfaced 1 side and 1 edge."

Selection Guide for Basic Woods

NAME	HARDNESS	STRENGTH	STABILITY	GLUING	NAILING
Ash	Medium	Medium	Good	Fair	Good
Birch	Hard	Good	Good	Fair	Poor
Cherry	Medium	Medium	Good	Good	Fair
Cottonwood	Soft	Poor	Fair	Good	Good
Cypress	Soft	Medium	Good	Fair	Fair
Gum (Red)	Medium	Medium	Poor	Good	Good
Hickory	Hard	Good	Good	Poor	Good
Mahogany	Medium	Medium	Good	Good	Good
Mahogany (Ph.)	Medium	Good	Good	Good	Good
Maple (Hard)	Hard	Good	Good	Fair	Poor
Maple (Soft)	Medium	Medium	Fair	Good	Fair
Oak (Red)	Hard	Good	Good	Good	Good
Oak (White)	Hard	Good	Good	Good	Good
Pine (White)	Soft	Poor	Good	Good	Good
Pine (Yellow)	Hard	Good	Fair	Fair	Poor
Poplar	Soft	Poor	Good	Good	Good
Redwood	Soft	Fair	Good	Good	Good
Walnut	Medium	Good	Good	Good	Fair

Strength: Composite value for all species. "Fair" is strong enough for most jobs.

Nailing: Composite value for all species; indicates the resistance to splitting when nailed.

Stability: Most woods are stable if properly seasoned.

fine hardwoods. The reproductions are so perfect, it's difficult to tell the real thing from laminate.

Most home centers don't stock hardwoods, with the possible exception of oak and birch, but you often can buy hardwoods at lumber dealers that cater to the professional, or at cabinet and millwork shops.

Sizes of hardwood materials (thickness and width) are the same as for softwoods. For example, a 1×4 piece of hardwood actually will measure ¾ ×3½ inches just as its 1×4 softwood counterpart. Lengths are also standard. Hardwood moldings and trim are similar to softwood, but the lengths almost always are random—not consistent.

Grades of softwoods range from Select to No. 5, which is the lowest grade.

The piece of stock being graded

End grain of boards and dimension lumber indicates the likelihood of warping, twisting, and cupping. Indefinite grain (top) tends to cup and warp. Vertical grain (center) will have minor shrinkage and will stay tight in joints. Flat grain (bottom) offers a smooth, matched, or random face grain.

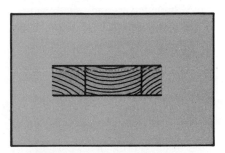

Alternating grain patterns when you assemble stock tends to balance the stress of the wood so the wood shrinks and swells in unison, or as a single "unit." If you alternate the grain, the joints will stay tighter and faces will stay flatter.

must meet only the lowest requirements of the grading rule. Because of this, quality variances are often found. Some of the wood will check out better than the grade specs, while other pieces will be at the low end of the grade. The low end, however, may not be bad enough to drop it into the next lowest grade specification.

Defects and other characteristics also affect wood grading; these include knots, checks, wood decay, pitch, splits, stains, warps, cups, and crooks.

No. 1 grade clear softwood is the best grade. It sometimes is specified as A grade. This wood should be selected for use where appearance, strength, and finishing qualities are top priority.

No. 2 grade softwood will show some minor defects, but one side will be clear. This grade is often referred to as "common."

No. 1 and 2 grades are select stock. The industry subdivides both:

B-grade and better may have very tiny blemishes, usually on one face.
C-grade has very small, but tight, knots and possibly some sap streaks. It can include heart and sap wood in the piece.
D-grade will have imperfections, but they can be hidden with paint.

There is still another subdivision:

No. 1 grade Common can have small to medium knots and minor blemishes. The knots are tight. This material is ideal for a see-through, clear finish. An example of application would be a knotty-pine paneled wall.
No. 2 grade Common has larger knots, but they are tight. You can apply a clear finish to the material, if you want a rustic look, or you can paint it to hide the knots. No. 2 is good for rough paneling and floors where appearance is not primary.
No. 3 grade Common is knotty, and some of the knots may be loose. The stock may be used for shelving, sheathing, and subflooring, or where appearance is not important—such as in a rustic look.
No. 4 grade Common has lots of loose knots. It is really utility stock for use as temporary siding and some concrete forms.

No. 5 grade has limited strength and poor appearance. For many retailers, No. 5 is not even a stock item.

Some species of pine lumber—usually trees grown in Idaho—have special grades. The select grades are classed as *supreme, choice,* and *quality.* The common grades—Nos. 1 through 5—are *colonial, sterling, standard, utility,* and *industrial.* Some retailers use these terms in advertising rather than No. 1, 2, 3, etc.

Hardwood grading is easier to understand. Hardwood is generally available in three grades. They are:

Firsts and seconds. Top quality hardwood used for cabinetmaking and furniture pieces. The grade often is referred to as FAS, for "firsts and seconds."

Warping or cupping occurs in unseasoned (green) wood or material that has been subjected to moisture over a long period of time. You can see twists like this by sighting down the lumber like a rifle. Avoid using warped material since it seldom can be straightened through either moisture and weight treatments or by nailing.

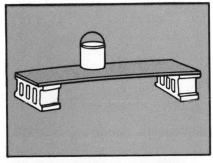

Bent boards and some dimension lumber can be straightened by weighting the material, as illustrated. Before applying the weight, wet the board on all surfaces with water. If you store lumber, stack it in tiers, with each tier at right angles to the one below; separate each tier with strips of 1×2s so air can circulate around the material.

Select. Slightly less quality than FAS, but good enough for cabinets, furniture, built-ins, and other "show" applications.

No. 1 Common. Some knots, splits, sap pockets, discoloration, and other blemishes, but still good enough for appearance jobs. One face usually is acceptable.

Dry and green lumber may be considered for noncritical applications, although most dimension lumber and boards are "dry."

If the wood has a Western Wood Products Association (WWPA) grade stamp on it, the stamp will give you the degree of dryness:

S-DRY on the stamp means that the moisture content in the wood does not exceed 19 percent. If the stamp reads MC-15 the moisture content does not exceed 15 percent. S-GRN means the wood has more than 19 percent moisture content.

The Southern Pine Inspection Bureau (SPIB) and the West Coast Lumber Inspection Bureau (WCLIB) have similar grade stamps that give the same basic information.

Stress-graded lumber is structural material that is stamped with the load it will support.

How it's sold

In most home centers, dimension lumber and boards are sold by the *piece*. For example, a 2×4×8 is usually stamped "$2.44," or some such price.

At building material outlets catering to the professional, dimension lumber and boards probably will be sold by the *board foot*. A board foot is a quantity of lumber that measures 1 inch thick, 12 inches wide, and 12

Sizes of Unseasoned (Green) Lumber

NOMINAL SIZE	ACTUAL SIZE
1×4	$^{28}/_{32} \times 3^9/_{16}$ in.
1×6	$^{28}/_{32} \times 5^5/_{8}$ in.
1×8	$^{28}/_{32} \times 7^1/_{2}$ in.
1×10	$^{28}/_{32} \times 9^1/_{2}$ in.
1×12	$^{28}/_{32} \times 11^1/_{2}$ in.
2×4	$1^9/_{16} \times 3^9/_{16}$ in.
2×6	$1^9/_{16} \times 5^5/_{8}$ in.
2×8	$1^9/_{16} \times 7^1/_{2}$ in.
2×10	$1^9/_{16} \times 9^1/_{2}$ in.
2×12	$1^9/_{16} \times 11^1/_{2}$ in.

Board Foot Calculator

Many sizes of lumber are sold by the *board foot*. This chart gives board foot measurements for most common sizes. For example, a piece of 2×4 that's 10 feet long contains 6⅔ board feet. The formula for finding the number of board feet in any piece is: thickness (in inches) × width (in feet) × length (in feet). Other sizes are sold by the *linear foot*, that is, by the length of the piece in feet.

NOMINAL DIMENSION OF STOCK	LENGTH OF STOCK (in feet)					
	8	10	12	14	16	18
1×2	(sold only by piece or by linear foot)					
1×3	(sold only by piece or by linear foot)					
1×4	2⅔	3⅓	4	4⅔	5⅓	6
1×6	4	5	6	7	8	9
1×8	5⅓	6⅔	8	9⅓	10⅔	12
1×10	6⅔	8⅓	10	11⅔	13⅓	15
1×12	8	10	12	14	16	18
2×2	(sold only by piece or by linear foot)					
2×3	(sold only by piece or by linear foot)					
2×4	5⅓	6⅔	8	9⅓	10⅔	12
2×6	8	10	12	14	16	18
2×8	10⅔	13⅓	16	18⅔	21⅓	24
2×10	13⅓	16⅔	20	23⅓	26⅔	30
2×12	16	20	24	28	32	36

inches long. The thickness and width are nominal measurements, not actual size.

Both home centers and building materials outlets sell moldings and trim pieces by the *linear foot*, that is, the actual measurement of the length of the stock.

Hardwood may be sold by the piece or board foot, depending on where you buy it. Home centers generally sell it by the piece, lumberyards by the board foot.

Posts and timbers are sold by the piece; matched lumber and shiplap are sold by the board foot at lumberyards and by the piece at most home center stores.

Laminated boards are sold by the piece. Furring strips and trim boards are sold by the piece and sometimes by the linear foot. Dimension lumber—2×2s and 2×3s—often is sold by the linear foot.

When you must order lumber, instead of piece-picking it yourself out of a bin or rack, follow this specifying procedure:

State the number of pieces you want. Then state the size in thickness, width, and length. Then give details.

For example, "I want 2 pieces of 1×6×8, No. 1 Common white pine, if possible. If not, No. 2 or 3 Common white pine."

Ordering this way will help the salesperson fill the order faster and better without confusion and misunderstanding.

Special order

Say you want two pieces of 1×10×12 No. 1 select pine, and the retailer doesn't stock it. You ask the retailer if he will special-order it for you, and he refuses. To understand the refusal, you should understand home center vs. building material selling. Home centers, which cater basically to the do-it-yourselfer, use inventory controls to show the retailer which products don't sell or sell slowly. These items are not stocked to eliminate inventory cost. Also, home centers are big-volume buyers and usually purchase directly from the manufacturer in large quantities to take advantage of discounts. These retailers seldom buy on a piece basis.

Building material stores—the old-fashioned lumberyard type—cater more to the professional who buys in large quantity, not by piece. Also, the building material retailer generally does business through a wholesale building material supplier, rather than directly with the manufacturer. This way, the store keeps down its inventory overhead, orders only as needed (the pros seldom need two skids of 2×4s at a minute's notice), and buys selectively in small quantities. Therefore, the home center may have large quantities of certain items at a low price (which save you money), while the building material outlet may be able to special order your 1×10×12 No. 1 Select pine. You will have to wait for the order, and you will pay a premium for the material. You probably will even have to pay transportation costs on such a small quantity.

If you can't get the material you want at a home center or a building material outlet, you may have two more local sources: a wholesale building material distributor and a cabinet/millwork shop.

Neither the distributor nor the cabinet/millwork shop are in the retail lumber business as such. However, if your purchase is a small one and you let them know your buying problem, they may sell you the material. You'll find firms like these listed in the telephone book advertising pages.

SALVAGE HOUSE PARTS. If you reside in a pre-1920 house, you probably have difficulty finding repair and replacement parts for building components such as trim, molding, windows doors, stair spindles, porch columns, etc. Many of these house parts are no longer manufactured; duplication can be costly because the parts have to be specially milled by a cabinet shop.

The best places to look for these out-of-stock items are lumber salvage yards and sites where buildings are being torn down.

Prices usually are negotiable, especially at wrecking sites. See the foreman to make arrangements.

Both places also can be bargain outlets for used lumber. Although the material may look dirty, dusty, and worn, it usually is solid stuff below the grime. Best yet, it is thoroughly seasoned, so warping and twisting are no longer problems.

IF IT'S ADVERTISED AS . . .	IT ALSO CAN BE . . .
Southern white pine	Loblolly pine, Pitch pine, Longleaf pine, Virginia pine, Slash pine, Shortleaf pine
Norway pine	Red pine
Northern white pine	Eastern pine
White fir	California red fir, Noble fir, Grand fir, Pacific silver fir
Mahogany	Philippine mahogany
Oak	Red oak, White oak
Yellow Poplar	Poplar, Tulip poplar, Tulipwood, Hickory poplar
Alaska cedar	Cedar, Yellow cypress
Tupelo	Water tupelo, Black gum, Sour gum, Ogeechee plum
Hickory (true)	Shagbark, Pignut, Shellbark, Mockernut
Butternut	White walnut, Oilnut
Basswood	Linden, Linn, Beetree
Cottonwood	Swamp cottonwood, Swamp poplar, Balsam
Eastern Spruce	Black spruce, White spruce, Blue spruce, Engelmann spruce, Red spruce
Cypress	Pond cypress, Bald cypress

Note: Wood identified as one of the following species will be only that species. Lodgepole pine, Ponderosa pine, Sugar pine, Western larch, Redwood, Sitka spruce

You often can find fine hardwoods at wrecking sites: walnut, cherry, maple, ash, gum, mahogany. Other good buys can include fireplace fronts, antique ceramic tile, solid brass lighting and plumbing fixtures, builders' hardware, wide pine flooring, railings, door and window hardware.

CUTTING AND LOADING. Some lumber retailers will cut materials to size for you free (if the order is large enough) or for a small fee. The retailers usually will not let you do the cutting yourself because of insurance regulations.

Many retailers do not have cutting facilities. However, some have a public hand saw that you can use to size

the material for loading into a car.

Many retailers will load the material into or onto your vehicle, but they will not tie down or secure the materials. You are asked to do this. The reason is insurance regulations. If they tie down the load and the load blows off the car or spills onto the road, they can be held liable for any damages. If you fasten it down and the load spills, you are liable for the damages.

Free materials delivery is almost a thing of the past—especially in large cities. The cost of running a truck is prohibitive. However, some retailers will deliver goods within a specific area—such as a 25-mile radius of the store—for a fee.

Plywood: The Almost Perfect Building Material

What it is

Perhaps the most versatile building material available on the market, plywood is a face (not edge) laminate of an odd number of wood veneers or plies (3 to 9) that are crisscrossed for strength and bonded with an exterior or interior waterproof/water-resistant adhesive. Since each ply is laminated with the wood grain running perpendicular to the joining ply, the material is dimensionally stable with a high resistance to warping, expansion, and contraction.

Plywood also is resistant to splitting, warping, chipping, cracking, cupping crumbling, and rot. The adhesive that binds it together is so tough that the wood will break before the adhesive.

Where it's used

Plywood is a great cover-all and cover-up. It may be used as the base or substructure of a building, serving as the framing as well as the finishing material. For example, plywood paneling may be used to finish off stud framing, or it may be nailed to floor joists as a subflooring over which carpeting or resilient tile or sheet material will be installed. Plywood with a hardwood face, such as walnut, birch, or cherry, is often used for built-ins and cabinet fronts—or for entire cabinets.

Typical uses include sheathing, subflooring, furniture pieces, cabinets, wall paneling, fencing, built-ins, countertop base, siding, roofing, boats and other marine use, shelving, molding, screening, doors, framing, furring, and concrete forming.

Veneer core plywood is the most common; the number of plies ranges from 3 to 9.

There are two disadvantages to plywood, but both can be readily and satisfactorily overcome. Plywood has a tendency to delaminate—simply come unglued—when subjected to moisture over a long period of time. The raw edges of the material also can present a problem to the do-it-yourselfer. Delamination can be deterred, if not completely stopped, by applying water-resistant finishes such as paint to the surface. Edges can be hidden with wood putty, veneer tape, and various molding treatments. In long spans, butted edges can be covered with bevels or a molding overlay.

How it's graded

To assure consistant quality, most plywood is manufactured to standards adopted by the American Plywood Association (APA). Individual sheets of the material are stamped with the APA mark, if the sheets qualify (see grade stamp illustration). The stamp usually appears on the back face of the panel and sometimes on the edge of the panel.

In order to read the stamp you have to know the meaning of three words: face, back, and grade.

Face refers to the quality of the top layer of veneer on the face side of the panel—the surface that usually is seen. This is noted by a letter: A, B, C, D.

Back refers to the quality of the bottom side or layer of the veneer on the back side of the panel. This also is noted by a letter: A, B, C, D.

Grade refers to the adhesive and is marked *Exterior* or *Interior*. This simply means that Exterior grade, which is intended for outdoor use, plywood has a waterproof adhesive bonding the plies together. Interior grade, which is intended for indoor use, plywood has a moisture-resistant adhesive bonding the plies together. The word *type* is sometimes used instead of grade.

On some panels, such as sheathing, you may find numbers such as 48/24 and 24/0. The first number indicates the maximum spacing in inches between rafters for roof decks, and the

second number indicates maximum spacing in inches between floor joists for subflooring. If the second number is 0, this indicates that the panel is not to be used for subflooring.

Other nomenclature worth knowing includes *Classification of Species, CDX,* and *MDO.* A Classification table can be found in this chapter. CDX is a sheathing grade of plywood and is sold as sheathing grade. The faces (C) and the backs (D) of this material have large knots and knotholes and splits. The X refers to the exterior glue bond. MDO translates as Medium Dense Overlay. This is plywood that has a glass-smooth fiber face bonded to the top veneer. The fiber is impregnated with resin. This panel is excellent for use wherever you want a super-smooth finished surface.

The letter symbols that describe plywood faces follow:

A Super smooth and paintable. Any repairs have been neatly made. Natural finishes may be used in less demanding application.

B Veneers are solid with circular repair plugs; tight knots are permitted in the surface.

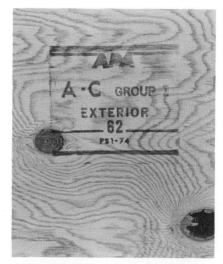

APA grade stamps are inked so the ink may be removed with sandpaper. Some plywood edges are stamped to avoid inking the face surfaces. Symbols are explained in the text.

Plywood Appearance and Use Selector

INTERIOR USE

Interior Grade	Face	Back	Inner Plies	Uses
A-A	A	A	D	Cabinets, furniture, built-ins where both sides will show.
A-B	A	B	D	Substitute for A-A. Back is smooth, solid. May be used for paneling; built-ins.
A-D	A	D	D	Face is "perfect"; back is rough, knotty. Paneling; countertops; accent panels.
B-D	B	D	D	Utility grade. Shelving, drawers, underlayment, cabinet sides.
C-D	C	D	D	Structural use; sheathing; some framing, general rough-in building.
Underlayment	C-Plugged	D	C/D	Underlayment for carpeting, tile; some sheathing and framing; rough-ins.

EXTERIOR USE

Exterior Grade	Face	Back	Inner Plies	Uses
A-A	A	A	C	Where appearance of both sides is important. Screening; fencing; doors; accents.
A-B	A	B	C	Substitute for A-A. Back is smooth, solid.
A-C	A	C	C	A is good finish side. Fences, soffits, building panels; accents; screening, doors.
B-B	B	B	C	Rough-texture screening; concrete forms.
C-C	C	C	C	Rough construction.
MDO	B	B/C	C/D	For very smooth and fine finishing.
C-C Plugged	C	C	C	Subflooring; backing for coverings; base for smooth pigmented finishes.
CDX	C	C	C/D	Rough and knotty. Utility grade. Some sheathing applications.

The plywood grading system and core differences

Plywood is basically priced by the quality of the top veneers—face and back—and of the inner plies or core. This is done to give you a wide selection.

For example, plywood with an A face and an A back would not be used as roof sheathing because both the quality and the price are too high for the job. Conversely, CDX plywood—a sheathing—wouldn't be used for cabinet fronts; its appearance is not good enough.

The American Plywood Association (APA) grade stamp shown here provides you with information about the quality of the panel.

For example, "A-C" describes the faces of the panel. The good face is A; the back face is C. The wood is any one or a combination of species from Group 1 as shown in the Species Chart. "Exterior" means the panel has a waterproof adhesive bond and may be used outdoors or where there is a high level of humidity or moisture. PS 1-74 is the grade standard by which the panel was manufactured. The 000 number in the drawing would be the number of the plywood mill where the panel was manufactured.

Note the "C" face of the panel pictured. The specifications call for "veneer with knots and knotholes to 2½ inches. Limited splits are permitted."

Cores—veneer, particleboard, and lumber—can affect pricing. Lumber cores almost always add to the price of the panel. Veneer and particleboard cores are priced about the same, although particleboard generally costs more than veneer.

For expert cabinet work, all cores usually are covered with veneer tape or molding, or stain-finished to match the face or back veneers. A quality carpenter's adhesive or contact cement is used to apply the veneer tape if the tape isn't self-sticking.

C The veneer has knotholes up to 1 inch in diameter. Knotholes of ½ inch and larger are permitted if the total width of all knots and knotholes within a specified section does not exceed certain limits. Limited splits are permitted in the surface. In exterior-type plywood, minimum veneer is permitted.

C-Plugged This has an improved C-face veneer, with the splits limited to ⅛ inch in width and knotholes and borer holes limited to ¼ by ½ inches.

D The veneer has knots and knotholes to 2½ inches in width and ½ inch larger under specified limits. Limited splits are permitted.

N This is generally a special order, natural finish veneer; many retailers do not stock it. It is select all heartwood or all sapwood and is free of open defects, but some repairs are permitted.

How it's sold

All retailers who sell plywood stock *softwood-faced* plywood. Some retailers carry *hardwood-faced* plywood. Softwood-faced plywood has a face and back veneers of soft wood such as fir and pine. Hardwood-faced plywood has a face and back veneers of hardwood such as walnut, birch, cherry, and oak. Many retailers stock only birch-faced hardwood plywood, along with a wide selection of softwood-faced plywood. You may have to special-order other hardwood species, or shop around for them. You'll most likely find hardwood-faced plywood at a millwork or cabinet shop or at retailers who cater mainly to the professional.

Hardwood-faced plywood is graded differently than softwood-faced plywood and is sold accordingly. The grades:

Custom grade (No. 1) is free of knots, patches and plugs.

Good grade (No. 2) has tight, smoothly cut veneer. The joints are evenly matched so the grain runs the same.

Sound grade (No. 3) doesn't have open defects, but the veneer may not be matched as No. 2. The veneer may also have mineral streaks and stains.

Utility grade (No. 4) has discolorations.

Reject grade (No. 5) can have 2-inch diameter knotholes and ½-inch splits.

You can buy almost any grade combination of face and back veneers

---

The Minimum Bending Radii for Fir Plywood

These are average values and apply only for areas of clear, straight grain. A panel can rupture at a longer radius than shown in the chart because of short grain in the panel. If patches are present, the radii may be considerably longer.

PANEL THICKNESS (IN.)	APPROX. MIN. BEND ACROSS GRAIN	APPROX. MIN. BEND PARALLEL GRAIN
¼	15 in.	24 in.
⅜	36 in.	54 in.
½	6 ft.	8 ft.
⅝	8 ft.	10 ft.
¾	10 ft.	12 ft.

---

in the standard grades. The combinations include 1-1, 1-4, 1-2, 1-3, 2-4, and 2-3. The price of the panel depends on the species of wood, the quality of veneer, and the core of the panel.

The wood sandwiched between the face and back veneers of plywood is called a *core*. The most common core is veneer core. Two other cores are manufactured: particleboard (composite) and lumber.

Veneer cores are a series (from 3 to 9) of laminated veneers.

Particleboard cores are manufactured from resin-coated wood particles, such as sawdust, that are heat-pressed into sheets. The veneers are laminated to these sheets.

Lumber cores have a series of laminated veneers. The center core is made of solid wood strips that are edge-gluded together, much like the solid core in an exterior door.

Particleboard and lumber cores are not always available at many home center stores and other lumber outlets. The material sometimes can be

---

Classification of Plywood Panel Species

The standard plywood panels you buy at most home centers and building-material outlets are manufactured from more than 70 different species of wood. The grade stamp on the panel lists the group number of the species. The numbers range from 1 to 5. The woods are classified in the group by their stiffness and strength. The lower the group number, the

greater the stiffness and strength of the panel.

Although the groups are based on strength and stiffness, the group numbers do not always affect the unit pricing of the panel.

Plywood is sold on the commodity market and therefore is subject to price differences during the year.

GROUP 1		GROUP 2	GROUP 3	GROUP 4	GROUP 5
Apitong	Cedar, Port Orford	Maple, Black	Alder, Red	Aspen	Basswood
Beech,	Cypress	Mengkulang	Birch, Paper	Bigtooth	Fir, Balsam
American	Douglas Fir	Meranti, Red	Cedar, Alaska	Quaking	Poplar, Balsam
Birch	Fir	Mersawa	Fir, Subalpine	Cativo	
Sweet	California Red	Pine	Hemlock, Eastern	Cedar	
Yellow	Grand	Pond	Maple, Bigleaf	Incense	
Douglas Fir	Noble	Red	Pine	Western Red	
Kapur	Pacific Silver	Virginia	Jack	Cottonwood	
Keruing	White	Western White	Lodgepole	Eastern	
Larch, Western	Hemlock, Western	Spruce	Ponderosa	Black (Western	
Maple, Sugar	Lauan	Red	Spruce	Poplar)	
Pine	Almon	Sitka	Redwood	Pine	
Caribbean	Bagtikan	Sweetgum	Spruce	Eastern White	
Ocote	Mayapis	Tamarack	Black	Sugar	
Pine, Southern	Red Lauan	Yellow Poplar	Engelmann		
Loblolly	Tangile		White		
Longleaf	White Lauan				
Shortleaf					

special ordered. You'll most likely find it in stock at retailers who cater to the professional carpenter, at millwork and cabinet shops, and, sometimes, at lumber wholesalers and distributors.

Plywood is priced by the piece. If you buy a large quantity of the material, the retailer may give you a discount, but you must ask for it.

Many retailers stock "ready-cut" plywood. These pieces range in thickness from ¼ to ¾ inch and in size from 2×2-, 2×4-, and 4×4-feet. The pieces are individually priced; sometimes the raw edges are filled with wood putty and smoothed. Softwood-faced plywood is the most common in ready-cut plywood; birch-faced hardwood plywood sometimes is stocked. Fine hardwood veneers such as walnut, oak, and cherry are seldom stocked, and usually can't be ordered.

Some retailers who have sawing facilities will cut plywood sheets to your specifications for a fee. Most retailers with sawing facilities will not let you operate the saw yourself because of insurance restrictions. Many retailers have a public hand saw that they will loan you to cut plywood sheets so you can load the pieces in your auto.

The sizes of most plywood panels (softwood-faced and hardwood-faced) are ¼, ⅜, ½, ⅝, ¾, and ⅞ inches thick by 4 feet wide by 8 feet long. This size never varies as do the sizes of milled solid wood boards and lumber. Other lengths and thicknesses are available on a special-order basis.

Special-order plywood

Hardwood-faced plywood usually has to be special-ordered by the retailer. The only exception is a birch-faced plywood, which most retailers stock. However, the thickness of the material may be limited to two or three sizes.

Marine type plywood is a special-order item, although you may be able to find it at a retailer selling marine supplies. Decorative panels that are rough sawn, brushed, grooved, striated, or embossed on one side are stocked by many retailers; a special order for these may not be necessary if you have time to shop around.

Panels that have a hardboard face and back are available. The hardboard may be tempered, standard, smooth, or screened hardboard. The cores are C and D and the thicknesses are ½, ⅝, and ¾ inches. This panel usually is a special-order item. Exterior tempered hardboard plywood panels also are available.

Other faces that are usually special ordered include N-N Interior, N-A and N-B Interior, N-D Interior, and 2-4-1 Underlayment.

It is sometimes impractical for a retailer to order one or two pieces of special plywood paneling since he often has to purchase them in quantity. After filling the order for a couple of pieces, the retailer is stuck with 30 or 40 panels that he can't sell. If, after checking local millwork and cabinet shops for the product, you can't locate the panels you want, ask a retailer for the address of the nearest outlet of any one of the large plywood manufacturers such as Georgia-Pacific, Weyerhaeuser Co., and Boise-Cascade Corp. A letter directly to one of these firms will bring fast results.

Plywood veneers

Most retailers sell a veneer edging tape for raw plywood edges. This tape is a thin (about ¹⁄₁₆ inches by ¾ inches wide) strip of real wood.

Some hobby and craft shops stock a small selection of wood veneers for inlays. These pieces are wider than edging tape, but they are not long enough to surface a large piece of wood or a panel. For this material, contact any one of the suppliers listed below.

Constantine & Son
2050 Eastchester Rd.
Bronx N.Y. 10461

H.L. Wild
510 East 11th St.
New York, N.Y. 10009

Real Wood Veneers
107 Trumbull St.
Elizabeth, N.J. 07206

Exotic Woodshed
65 North York Rd.
Warminster, Pa. 18974

Bob Morgan Woodworking Supplies
1123 Bardstown
Louisville, Ky. 40204

Craftsman Wood Service
1735 West Cortland Ct.
Addison, Ill. 60101

The Woodworkers' Store
21801 Industrial Blvd.
Rogers, Minn. 55347

M&M Hardwood
5344 Vineland Ave.
North Hollywood, Calif. 91601

Robert M. Albrecht
18701 Barthcnia
Northridge, Calif. 91324

Veneer tape, applied with white glue, hides the raw edges of plywood cores.

Buying Hardboard

What it is

You most likely know hardboard as "Masonite" or "Pegboard." These trademark names have become synonymous with the hardboard panels manufactured by many different firms, as well as by the developer of the product, The Masonite Corporation.

Hardboard is real wood; it has some characteristics of wood plus some features that ordinary wood products don't have. Simply stated, hardboard is made from wood chips that have been mashed and whipped into a cake-like batter and pressed under extreme heat to form panels, underlayment, screening, decorative paneling, concrete forms, siding, and other building and remodeling products.

Typical panels are brownish in color. They're smooth on one side and screened, or textured, on the other. Sheets with smooth faces and backs are also available. The hardboard surfaces are extremely dense; the smooth sides are ready for finishing.

Hardboard can be machined easily, accurately, and attractively. The grooves in this ¼-inch-thick wall paneling are 2 inches apart. The panels will go over studs or existing wall and ceiling surfaces.

The material will not split, crack, or splinter. It may be easily bent or curved; it has no knots, sap or mineral streaks, or grain. You can nail, drill, route, saw, and plane it with regular woodworking tools.

Where it's used

Decorative paneling is hardboard's major role in building construction. These panel products vary from embossed, perforated and die-cut filigreed to simulated wood grain and marble patterns. They are so realistic that it almost takes an expert lumberman or mason to tell them from fine hardwoods and stone.

Prefinished hardboard with wood grain is also used extensively in the manufacture of cabinets, tables, and other furniture pieces, while panels in less-decorative, or plain finishes, are used for subfloor and countertop underlayment, fencing, screens, room dividers, ceilings, walls, soffits, siding, concrete forms, molding, trim, tileboard, and signs.

How it's sold

Unlike plywood, boards, and lumber, hardboard is not graded. It is known by *type,* and it usually is sold by the piece, although you may be able to get a quantity discount by asking the retailer for it.

Standard stocked sizes are ⅛-, ³⁄₁₆-, and ¼-inch thicknesses by 4 foot widths and 8 foot lengths (see the hardboard chart). Some retailers sell ready-cut panels in standard thicknesses and in 2×4- and 4×4-foot widths and lengths. Usually these ready-cuts cost more than uncut panels because of the labor involved in cutting. Some retailers will saw hardboard panels to your measurement requirements for a small fee or for free. But you usually have to buy the entire panel, not a piece of it after it has been cut. Most retailers with sawing facilities will not permit you to use the equipment because of insurance restrictions. However, most retailers provide a public hand saw for customers who want to cut the panels to a size they can load into a car.

TYPES OF HARDBOARD.

Standard hardboard is moisture-resistant and may be used for interior applications where wetness and high moisture is not a problem. The material is not recommended for exterior applications.

Tempered hardboard is water-resistant. It may be used where high humidity and occasional wetness are present. A special compound is mixed into the hardboard batter before it is pressed, which makes the end product harder—more dense—than standard hardboard. You can usually spot the difference between standard and tempered hardboard by the color. Tempered hardboard will appear darker. If you have any doubt about moisture problems, buy tempered hardboard. Although it usually costs more than standard hardboard, the price is not prohibitive.

Black tempered hardboard is very similar to tempered hardboard, but its surface is flat black for effect. The color is produced by a black dye that is added to the hardboard batter at the time of manufacture. This is not a stock item at many retailers.

Underlayment is designed for applications where tile, carpeting, linoleum, and other materials will cover the surface. Underlayment hardboard must be backed by a lumber, board, or plywood subfloor. It may, and usually is, specified for use over old,

Hardboard lap siding is an alternative to cedar shakes. The siding comes in 8- or 16-ft. lengths; it's 12 inches wide and ⁷⁄₁₆- or ½-inch thick. Thickness creates shadowline.

Hardboard Selection Chart

NOMINAL THICKNESS (IN.)	SIZES	NOMINAL THICKNESS (IN.)	SIZES
Standard hardboard		**Black tempered hardboard**	
1/8	4×4, 4×7, 4×8, 4×9, 4×10, 4×12, 4×16	1/8	4×4, 4×8, 4×10, 4×12
3/16	4×4, 4×7, 4×8, 4×9, 4×10, 4×12, 4×16	1/4	4×4, 4×8, 4×10, 4×12
1/4	4×4, 4×7, 4×8, 4×10, 4×12, 4×16	**Tempered, both faces smooth**	
5/16	4×4, 4×8, 4×9, 4×10, 4×12	1/8	4×4, 4×8, 4×10, 4×12
Panel hardboard		3/16	4×4, 4×8, 4×10, 4×12
3/16	4×8, 4×10, 4×12, 4×16	1/4	4×4, 4×8, 4×10, 4×12
1/4	4×8, 4×10, 4×12, 4×16	5/16	4×8, 4×10, 4×12
Underlayment		**Die-cut filigree hardboard**	
1/4	3×4, 4×4	1/8	16×6, 2×4, 2×6, 4×8
Standard, both faces smooth		**Hardboard tile panels**	
1/8	5×8, 5×16, 4×8, 4×16	1/8	4×4, 4×8, 4×10, 4×12, 4×16
3/16	5×8, 5×16, 4×7, 4×8, 4×16	**Embossed hardboard**	
Perforated hardboard (standard and tempered)		1/8	4×4, 4×6, 4×8, 4×12, 4×16
1/8	4×4, 4×8	1/4	4×7, 4×8, 4×10
1/4	4×8	**Concrete form hardboard**	
Tempered hardboard		3/16	4×8, 4×12
1/8	4×4, 4×7, 4×8, 4×9, 4×10, 4×12, 4×16	1/4	4×8, 4×12
3/16	4×4, 4×7, 4×8, 4×9, 4×10, 4×12, 4×16	**Siding (in panels)***	
1/4	4×4, 4×8, 4×10, 4×12, 4×16	7/16	4×6, 4×7, 4×8, 4×9, 4×10, 4×12, 4×16
5/16	4×8, 4×9, 4×10, 4×12	**Siding (lap)***	
		1/4, 5/16, 7/16	9", 12", 16", 24" widths; 8-, 12-, 16-ft. lengths

* Thickness and lengths and widths vary with design and manufacturer.

uneven floors to level them for a finished floor covering. However it's used, underlayment hardboard can't serve as the prime subflooring because it is not strong enough. Standard sizes are 3×4- and 4×4-ft.

Panel hardboard is a bit more dense than standard hardboard, but not as dense as tempered hardboard. It is best used where you don't need high strength and hardness, such as on walls, ceilings, and for soffits.

Concrete form hardboard is tempered so it will withstand the moisture content in concrete. This product makes excellent forms since it can be bent easily.

Siding is tempered and usually prime painted. It is best used over a sheathing material, but, in some cases, can be nailed directly to the framing members, which should be 8 inches on center. The finish coat of paint must be applied to the preprimed exposed surfaces within 10 days after the siding is installed.

Perforated panels have drilled holes on 1/2- and 1-inch centers. The holes are 1/8 or 1/4 inch in diameter. You can buy a wide variety of wire hangers to match the holes and thickness of the panel for hanging tools, utensils, pictures, and so forth.

Prefinished panels are laminated with a super-thin plastic material to simulate fine hardwood paneling. A *bathroom panel,* finished with a melamine topcoat, is made for high-moisture areas such as kitchens, laundry areas, and bathrooms. Special plastic moldings are made to match these panels (see the Moldings section).

Embossed hardboard is tempered and has a patterned surface that is produced by embossing the smooth or finished side of the panel. Many patterns are available.

Filigree hardboard is die-cut, and the panels have several patterns. The product is generally used for room dividers, screening, and other special design effects.

Special order

Most retailers stock standard, tempered, perforated, siding, prefinished, and bathroom or melamine-coated hardboard panels. The selection may not be as great at home center stores as at lumber dealers selling to the professional contractor. However, you will probably find a better decorative room panel choice at a home center store. Other panels such as embossed, filigree, underlayment, and concrete forms may have to be special ordered, although telephone calls to several building material outlets may locate the hardboard product you want.

Special sizes almost always have to be special ordered (see chart). But before special ordering, check retailers that cater to the professional.

Below is a brief listing of hardboard manufacturers in the United States. If you can't find the hardboard product you want in your area or a retailer can't get the product, write directly to the Consumer Information Director of the firm.

Masonite Corporation
20 North Wacker Drive
Chicago, Ill. 60606

Georgia-Pacific Corp.
Box 311
Portland, Ore. 97204

Weyerhaeuser Co.
Wood Products Div.
Tacoma Building
Tacoma, Wash. 98401

Celotex Corp.
1500 North Dale Mabry
Tampa, Fla. 33607

Special considerations

Since hardboard is grainless, it must be fastened—nailed or screwed—to a material that will hold the fastener, such as framing lumber, concrete block, sheathing, or subflooring. Hardboard can not be toenailed or edge-nailed.

Hardboard Fasteners and Finishes

TYPE	FINISH	FASTENERS
Standard and Tempered	Smooth face; matte or screen back. Or both sides smooth.	Adhesive, nails, power nails, staples, bolts, clips, frames, tracks.
Tempered (black)	Same as Standard with a flat black color.	Same as Standard.
Perforated	Same as Standard.	Adhesive, nails, screws, frames, tracks.
Embossed	Varies with brushing, striations, cuts.	Same as Standard.
Filigreed	Smooth on both sides.	Same as Standard.
Concrete forms	Smooth; specially tempered for moisture.	Double-headed nails, stakes, wire, braces.
Panel siding and Lap siding	Unpainted; primed. Smooth or textured surface treatment.	Nails.

As a rule of thumb, the center of the panel must be nailed first; then nail around the edges on the face. Keep about ¼ inch from the edges—more if possible—with nails and other mechanical fasteners such as screws, toggles, and clips. Underlayment is special: It should be fastened with ringed nails driven 4 inches apart across the panel face. The edge joints of underlayment should be spaced about ¹⁄₃₂ inch apart; the joints should be staggered across the area, that is, the fewer common joints, the better.

Underlayment should be installed so its joints don't coincide with the joints in the subflooring material.

Hardboard may be worked with regular woodworking tools that have super-sharp cutting edges. Regular circular saw blades (fine tooth) may be used, although carbide-tipped blades work better and longer, if a great deal of hardboard is being cut. The panels may be installed over furring, framing, concrete, concrete blocks, brick, plaster, gypsumboard, and similar materials. It may be finished with any product suitable for wood, such as paint, shellac, stain, texture paint, varnish, and sealer. The surface should be sealed with a primer and sanded lightly before any type of finish coat is applied.

Hardboad panels should not be butted tightly together to allow for expansion and contraction caused by humidity (moisture vapor). About ¹⁄₃₂-inch space should be left between adjoining panels. Leave the panels in the room in which they will be installed for at least 30 hours so they can adjust to the humidity in the room. Always stack the panels flat on the floor.

Edges may be finished with moldings and special trim pieces (cap, cove, and joint strip) made especially for hardboard. Prefinished trim is available. Exposed joints can be V-grooved with a block plane, rounded, or covered with a batten molding or strip. Inside corners may be trimmed with cove moldings or special inside corner trim; outside corners may be treated with wooden outside corner trim or metal molding made for hardboard products.

Minimum Bending Radii for Hardboard

THICKNESS OF PANEL	COLD DRY BENDS		COLD MOIST BENDS	
	Smooth Side Out	Smooth Side In	Smooth Side Out	Smooth Side In
Standard hardboard				
⅛	12	10	7	5
³⁄₁₆	18	16	10	8
¼	27	24	15	12
⁵⁄₁₆	35	30	22	18
Panel hardboard				
³⁄₁₆	20	18	12	10
¼	30	27	18	15
Both faces smooth				
⅛	10		7	
³⁄₁₆	16		12	
Tempered hardboard				
⅛	9	7	6	4
³⁄₁₆	16	14	9	6
¼	25	22	14	10
⁵⁄₁₆	35	30	20	16
Tempered, both faces smooth				
⅛	10		7	
³⁄₁₆	16		12	
Embossed finishes				
⅛	10		7	

Hardboard and Adhesives

Standard panel or subflooring adhesive that is available in a caulking tube may be used for installing hardboard over wall and floor surfaces and in some countertop underlayment installations. You should read the manufacturer's instructions on the cartridge or container before you make a buying decision.

One tube of adhesive usually is enough to fasten three panels. If the surface over which the panels will be installed is especially porous, allow one tube of adhesive to two panels. One quart of adhesive will fasten two to three panels, depending on the porous surface.

In addition to adhesive for installing decorative wall paneling, colored matching paneling nails also should be used for support. One standard box of paneling nails is usually adequate for two to three panels.

The adhesive forms a better bond if you apply it to the back of the panel, press the panel firmly in place, and then pull the panel off the surface. Replace the panel in position immediately and nail it down. The pressing procedure helps distribute the adhesive on the panel and the surface, and provides a larger bonding area.

Moldings and Trim: The Finishing Touch

Moldings and trim pieces serve two purposes: They hide mistakes, and they give a carpentry job a professional look.

What it is

Molding and trim are strips of wood or plastic that have been milled or extruded into special shapes called coves, corners, caps, rounds, half-rounds, stops, and bases.

Wood moldings and trim are usually manufactured from clear pine stock, although hardwoods may be used. Plastic molding and trim may be in a solid color such as white, brown, and black, or it may have a simulated wood grain film laminated to its surface. The grain simulations are nearly perfect; it's difficult to tell the plastic from real wood. Some plastic trim is embossed with wood grain designs; this gives the material a textured appearance similar to rough or unsanded wood.

Moldings and trim also can be manufactured from metal—usually aluminum or stainless steel. You can buy molding and trim that has been covered with a fabric to match carpeting and draperies.

Molding and trim often are designated by the term *millwork*. Millwork in the lumber industry simply means a piece of wood that has been cut according to a special pattern. The term is all-inclusive, including the simplest lattice molding that completes stairways and window and door systems. For the do-it-yourselfer, molding and trim are usually sold under these specific names. The "millwork" label still continues at lumberyards and cabinet shops that sell to the professional carpenter and builder.

Although moldings and trim are synonymous to the nonprofessional, the terms refer to different materials. *Molding* is patterned material such as crowns, chair rail, and cove. *Trim* is base shoe, quarter-round, and window and door casings. You may find molding and trim intermixed in some stores and separated in others.

There are hundreds of different molding patterns and new ones are introduced annually. These patterns have been standardized and grouped into classifications. Because of this organization, you can go into almost any home center or building materials outlet and replace a piece of molding by shape or number (if you know the number; see pattern illustrations). If you can't find the molding you want, a cabinet or millwork shop probably can duplicate the pattern; you may even be able to cut the pattern yourself with a router.

Where it's used

Molding can be used as a finishing material almost anyplace—at inside and outside corners, where walls meet ceilings, chair rails, as batten strips over butt-joined materials, edging strips, to fasten screen wire to frames, picture frames, and as decorative screens and lattice. Molding can pro-

A molding combination can be used to create a special effect—here an "old-fashioned" baseboard. The base is 1×6 Select pine, topped by a cap molding and finished at the floor with quarter round molding.

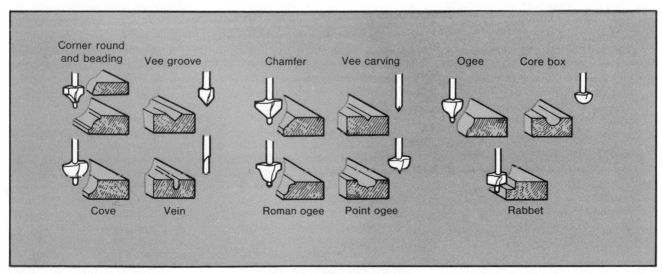

Using a router and special bits, you can make your own molding pattern designs and edge treatments. The more popular patterns are illustrated.

  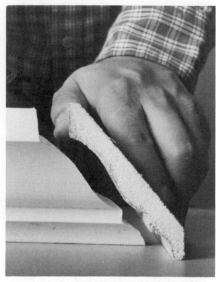

Left: Moldings are mitered or cut at 45° and 90°. A miter box is used so the cuts are true angles. To allow for mitering and straight cuts, you should buy 1 foot more molding than the measurement calls for. To miter crown molding, cut the miter through the face of the molding, as shown here. *Middle:* Follow the

contour of the crown pattern with a coping saw so the cut is about 45° along the back side of the molding. Back-miter it. This removes the excess wood and leaves a sharp edge along the pattern. *Right:* Butt the coped edge against the face of the adjoining molding and tap it lightly (at the opposite end) with a

hammer handle. The procedure to install molding is this: First, cut the molding to fit the two longest spans in the room. Trim the ends square so the ends butt against the walls. Nail this molding in place. Then, miter and cope the shorter pieces to fit against the longer pieces of moldings.

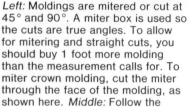

vide decorative trim, accents, and special shadow lines for architectural beauty. You can even make kite sticks from it.

Trim can be used as a finishing material to finish walls and jambs and headers around doors and windows, for baseboards at floor level, ceiling beam coverings, to hold up shelving, and for special accents.

As a do-it-yourselfer, you probably will use the molding and trim *standards.* Here is a list of these patterns and where they are applied:

Stop. Around door jambs for doors to shut (stop) against. Also, around window jambs to form channels for window frames.
Cove. For vertical and horizontal surfaces that butt at a 90-degree angle, such as inside corners of walls.
Chair rail. Horizontally around walls, about 3 feet from the floor, forms a wainscotting division on the wall.
Crown. At the ceiling where the walls meet the ceiling. It also may be used to frame murals and at fireplace mantels.
Base. Around walls at the floor level. It is generally used with shoe or

quarter-round molding, and, sometimes, with cap.
Shoe. Along the bottom edge of base moldings, to hide edges of carpeting and other floor coverings.
Quarter-round. Same as shoe; often is used to simulate raised panel doors and as a decorative trim around wall and ceiling accents.
Stool. Milled especially for use between the frame of a window and its apron.
Corner bead. For inside and outside corners where walls meet at 90° angles.
Lattice/seam. To cover joints where materials butt, e.g., with paneling and sidings.
Cap. Above doors and windows to drain water. *Ply cap* is used to trim raw edges of plywood and as a molding for wide baseboard installations, as found in older houses.
Half-round. Same as lattice/seam. Rabbeted (grooved) stock is available.
Screen bead. For edging treatments over raw plywood and solid wood (shelving). Also used to cover staples and tacks that hold screening to frames.

Bullnose. Between horizontal and vertical joints—usually in paneling applications. The paneling butts against the faces of the bullnose molding.
Casing. Trim that goes around windows and doors against the jambs and walls.
Paneling strips. Also called *clear strip.* May be used as a baseboard, door and window trim, batten strips, framing strips, and decorative accent molding.
Picture. For framing murals and pictures, or as an accent molding.

How it's graded

Molding and trim are not graded like dimension lumber and boards, according to "Select," "No. 1 Common," or other categories. The wood used for moldings and trim is usually select softwood such as western pine. It is ideal for either a clear or natural finish, or a paint finish.

Hardwood moldings vary in quality as to wood species. As a rule, you pick the quality you want. If ordered, you probably will get a mixed quality and random lengths. Hardwood moldings are not graded.

How it's sold

Molding and trim pieces are sold by the linear foot or bundle—never by the board foot. Standard piece and bundle lengths are 6, 8, 10, and 12 feet.

The material also is priced by the pattern: Complex patterns such as panel moldings cost more than simpler bases and casings. Size often is used as a pricing base. For example, cove molding is made in several different widths; the small sizes are less costly than the larger sizes of the same pattern.

Prefinished wood and plastic moldings and trim are sold by the piece. In some rare cases, they may be sold by the linear foot and bundle. They are not graded. Pattern configurations and sizes (widths and lengths) can be a pricing factor; the simple patterns are less costly than the complicated patterns. Standard stock sizes are 8 and 10 feet.

Most retailers will not cut molding or trim to your size (length) requirements. If you want a piece of molding 2 feet long, you probably will have to

purchase the shortest piece sold (6 feet) and cut it yourself to the 2-foot length. The only exception to this is broken molding or trim that the retailer may have culled from a manufacturer's shipment. Many retailers will give you a price on this broken or damaged material, but you must inquire.

When you buy molding and trim, always purchase one linear foot more than your measurements call for. The extra length is used for squaring and mitering purposes during assembly.

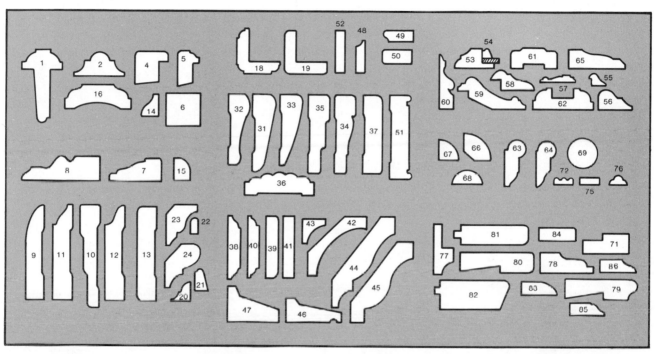

No.	Molding Pattern	No.	Molding Pattern	No.	Molding Pattern	No.	Molding Pattern
1	T-astragal	21	Glass bead	46	Drip cap	65	Rake molding
2	Flat astragal	22	Glass bead	47	Drip cap	66	Quarter-round
4	Backband	23	Bed molding	48	Fillet	67	Quarter-round
5	Backband	24	Bed molding	49	Fillet	68	Half-round
6	Baluster	31	Casing	50	Fillet	69	Full round
7	Band	32	Casing	51	Hook strip	71	Comb. screen stock
8	Band	33	Casing	52	Lattice	72	Screen molding
9	Base	34	Casing	53	Mirror molding	75	Screen molding
10	Base	35	Casing	54	Mirror molding	76	Screen molding
11	Base	36	Casing	55	Mirror molding	77	Shelf cleat
12	Base	37	Casing	56	Nose and cove	78	Shingle molding
13	Base	38	Casing (mullion)	57	Panel molding	79	Stool
14	Base molding	39	Casing (mullion)	58	Panel molding	80	Stool
15	Base shoe	40	Casing (mullion)	59	Panel molding	81	Stool
16	Batten	41	Casing (mullion)	60	Panel molding	82	Stool
18	Corner guard	42	Cove	61	Partition cap	83	Stop
18	Corner guard	43	Cove	62	Partition shoe	84	Stop
19	Corner guard	44	Crown	63	Picture molding		
20	Glass bead	45	Crown	64	Picture molding		

Many of these molding patterns are stocked by lumberyards catering to the professional. Some of the patterns—the most popular ones—are stocked by home centers. You can buy different sizes of similar patterns.

The numbered patterns shown here are in similar classifications, i.e., the casing patterns Nos. 31 through 41.

Special order

Most home centers will not special-order molding and trim for you unless the order is large. Building material stores that cater to the professional often will order small amounts of special molding and trim, but as a rule, a well-stocked supplier will have the pattern you want.

If these retailers can't fill your order, try a wholesale building material distributor, a cabinetmaker, or a millwork company. You'll find these businesses listed in the telephone book advertising pages. Also, don't overlook lumber salvage yards and house wrecking sites.

Still another source for moldings and trim is to make the pattern yourself with clear strip and a portable electric router with special molding bits. You can buy bit assortments at many hardware stores and home centers; you can also find them at many tool rental stores.

2

FASTENERS

Twenty-penny spikes are not the best fastener to use when hanging wallpaper. Wallpaper paste is not the best fastener to hold together a cantilevered deck. These examples are ridiculous, of course, but they make a key point: Fasteners must match the requirements of the job. They should be selected for strength, ease of application, and to give a professional finished look to the completed job.

Nails, screws, and bolts are The Big Three of building construction fasteners. They play major roles in holding materials together. However, many innovations have come along that can handle fastening jobs better, easier, and at lower cost. But instead of giving an endless list of names, we've classified fasteners into practical groups—those you'll most likely use in routine home maintenance and improvements. And we're including those that are most readily available.

Nail Fasteners

Nails are the most common mechanical fasteners used in joining pieces of wood or other materials together. Most nails are manufactured from wire; cut nails are punched out of steel plate in nail shapes.

In most applications, nails with smooth shanks don't hold as well as nails with square and triangular shanks. Barbed nails hold better than smooth-, square-, and triangular-shanked nails, but not as well as nails with threaded shanks.

Nails hold through a wedging action. As a nail is driven into wood, the wood fibers are separated by the shank. The fibers of the wood then grip the shank and act as tiny wedges. If the fibers are bypassed by the nail shank, the fibers then act on the shank like a rope looped around a broom handle. The more wedges, the better the holding power. That's why barbed- and threaded-shank nails get the best rating: they add their own wedges to those formed by the material.

Nail points are an important consideration in nail selection. As a rule of thumb, blunt pointed nails tend to split softwoods less than sharp pointed nails. Hardwoods split easier than softwoods. For hardwoods, chisel-pointed nails are best. They not only reduce splitting, but add strength through deep penetration into the wood. Other buying considerations include these:

- Smooth-shanked nails driven into green and wet wood lose their holding power when the wood dries and shrinks. If you must use green or wet wood, join it with barbed or threaded-shanked nails.
- When possible, nails should be driven at a slight angle.
- When possible, nails should be driven across the grain, not with it. Driving across the grain produces wedges.
- Stagger nails. Nails in a row in the same grain pattern have less holding power. The wood also tends to split.
- Stay away from edge nailing. Edges split very easily. Move the nail back from the edge at least ¼ inch.
- When possible, pilot holes should be drilled for nails; this prevents splitting. The pilot holes should be slightly smaller than the diameter of the nail shank. Putting soap on

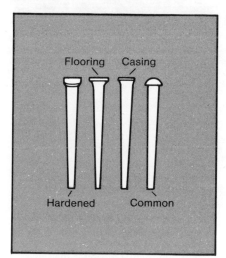

Cut nails are stamped from plate steel, while common, finishing, and casing nails are made from steel wire. Blunt points of cut nails help prevent splitting.

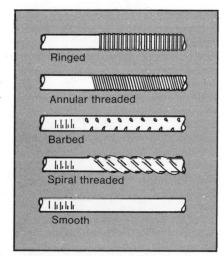

Body or shank of nails provides the holding power or grip in materials. The progression is: smooth, barbed, ringed, annular threaded, and spiral threaded. Therefore, a spiral-threaded nail has more holding power than a smooth-shank nail.

Clinched nails provide an exceptionally strong joint if at least 1 inch of the nail protrudes through the stock in order to clinch it. To strengthen the joint even more, use adhesive and bend the nail points down with pliers to embed the points in the wood.

nail shanks also helps prevent splitting; so does blunting the points of nails with a hammer before driving the nails. Too much blunting, however, can weaken the holding power of the nail, causing pop-outs.

Types of nails and their use

The names used here are the ones most often found where nails are sold. *Common wire nails* are for general construction use. The nail heads

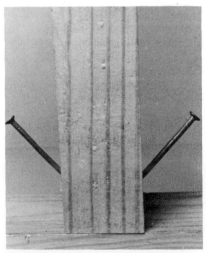

Toenailed joints are difficult to make because the nails have to be driven at a 30° angle. Use three nails, driving the first one (left) in the center of the wood; then the other two straddling the first on the opposite side. Keep the work aligned.

are flat and the points have a diamond pattern. In larger sizes, the points may be flattened slightly.

Box nails are similar to common nails except the shanks of box nails are slightly smaller. The penny (d) size or length is the same for common and box nails. Example: a 6d common nail is 2 inches long; so is a 6d box nail. Smaller shanks prevent splits. Box nails are best used for light fabrication, although they may be used for general construction work.

Finishing nails have small heads with a slight cup in the center of the head. The smaller heads distinguish them from common nails. The cup in the head is made to accept the tip of a nail set, which is used to countersink, or drive, the finishing nails below the surface of the material being nailed. The hole left by the nail and the set generally is filled with wood putty, wood plastic, or similar filler.

If a finishing nail is less than 1½ inches long, it is called a *brad*. If the brad has a flat head, it is called a *wire nail*. Both brads and wire nails are in the same classification as common and finishing nails.

Finishing nails are used for finish work such as applying moldings and trim. The nails may be used indoors or out and for fine jobs such as cabinets.

Before driving a finishing nail—especially a smaller sized one—check the head for defects. Sometimes the heads are slightly bent or missing altogether. Mass production is to be blamed; misforming can't be 100% controlled by manufacturers.

Casing nails are similar to finishing nails, except the heads of the nails are flat on top and slightly tapered along the shank so they may be driven flush against the surface of the material without countersinking them with a nail set.

Casing nails may be used for general construction work and almost anywhere a finishing nail is used. The shanks of casing nails are slightly larger than finishing nails and thus have more holding power.

Gypsumboard nails have ringed shanks and are especially designed for holding gypsum wallboard (Sheetrock) to framing members. In stores, these nails may be labeled "drywall nails," "gypsumboard nails," or "drywall screws." The head of the fastener is slightly concave and has a

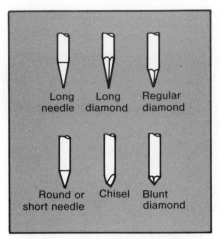

Nail points vary. As a rule, the sharp points are for soft woods and the blunt points for hardwoods. Most common in stores are regular and blunt diamond.

dimple in the center of it. This design helps hold joint compound around the head of the nail after the compound dries.

Plasterboard nails are also made for gypsumboard installation. They are blue and have flat heads with elongated diamond points. A *coated* gypsumboard nail also is available. The coating on the nail shank provides extra holding power to prevent popouts after application.

You should use two plasterboard or coated gypsumboard nails—slightly

Always stagger nails and drive them at an angle when possible. This "direct" nailed butt joint is stronger than a toenailed joint, provided the end of the joining piece is cut square. Coated nails, shown here, also provide a stronger joint mechanically.

staggered—at each nailing point; this helps prevent pop-outs. These nails should be slightly countersunk below the surface of the gypsumboard. Do this by driving the nails flush with the material and then hitting the heads one more time with the hammer to drive them below the surface. The indentation in the board made by the hammer provides a holding surface for the joint compound when it is applied.

For tongue-and-groove flooring, two nail types may be used: cut flooring and spiral-shanked flooring nails. The cut nail has a flat, broad shank with a blunt tip; the spiral-shanked nail has a casing head or a countersinking head. The cut nail is excellent for blind nailing through the tongues of flooring; the spiral-shank nail goes into the flooring material much like a threaded screw does.

Flooring nails come in 2-, 2¼-, and 2½-inch sizes (6d, 7d, and 8d). The nails are labeled "cut" and "flooring" in stores; lengths usually are specified.

Spikes measure from 6 to 12 inches and go by penny sizes, for example, 20d, 60d. The larger the penny size (d), the bigger the spike. In stores, they are usually sold per spike and not by the pound, as other nails are.

Underlayment nails have flat or countersunk heads and ringed shanks; they are used for fastening down sheathing and floor underlayment.

Roofing nails can have smooth, ringed, or spiral shanks. The tips are diamond-pointed and the entire nail usually is coated with a galvanizing material. Roofing nails have large heads, and the size of the head depends on the length of the nail. Roofing nails are designed basically to fasten down composition roofing; they may also be used to install asphalt building paper.

You will need about 2½ pounds of roofing nails per square (100 sq. ft.) of roofing material. Be sure to buy nails long enough to go through the new roofing, and old roofing and asphalt paper, and into the roof sheathing.

Sealing roofing nails are for fastening metal roofs to framing members. A lead or plastic-like washer is fixed just under the head of the nail. When driven tight, the washer compresses against the metal to seal out the weather.

The heads are large, similar to a standard roofing nail, and the shanks may be spiral or ringed. In the store, these nails are labeled "gasket roofing" or "sealing roofing" nails.

Shingle nails look like small, short versions of box nails. They measure from 1¼ to 1¾ inches in length. *Red cedar shingle* nails are similar to standard shingle nails; lengths are from 1¼ to 2 inches. Be sure to buy nails long enough to go through new and

old shingles and the roof sheathing. A 2-inch nail works best.

Gutter spikes are aluminum spikes in 40- and 60-penny (d) lengths. They may be sold with a tubular ferrule. The ferrule goes between the sides of the gutter and the nail is driven through the ferrule to provide strength and protection.

These spikes may be used for exterior projects such as retaining walls and decks. Since the metal is aluminum, you must drill pilot holes for the spikes or they will bend when driven.

Siding nails are used for attaching wooden lap siding to sheathing. Also ideal for siding applications are ringed nails and barbed shingle nails.

Concrete nails and *masonry nails* are extremely hard and have flat, countersunk heads and sharp diamond points. One type has a round shank; others have a square or fluted configuration. Helix concrete nails are longer than the standard types; they usually have a screw-type shank.

These nails may be used for fastening or hanging objects to placed concrete, concrete block, cinder block, and in mortar lines between courses of bricks.

A fairly recent newcomer to the family of concrete nails is the concrete *stud* nail, which is driven with a special holding tool and sledge hammer to prevent the nail from bending.

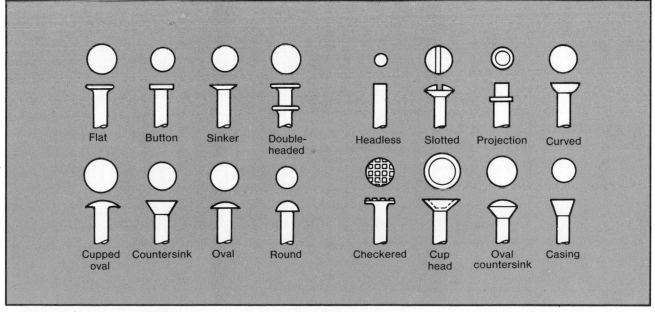

| Flat | Button | Sinker | Double-headed | Headless | Slotted | Projection | Curved |

| Cupped oval | Countersink | Oval | Round | Checkered | Cup head | Oval countersink | Casing |

Nail head types are shown in this selection. "Decorative" heads include: projection, cupped oval, oval countersink, and slotted. Double-headed nails are used for concrete forms and scaffolds which are disassembled after use; hence the double heads.

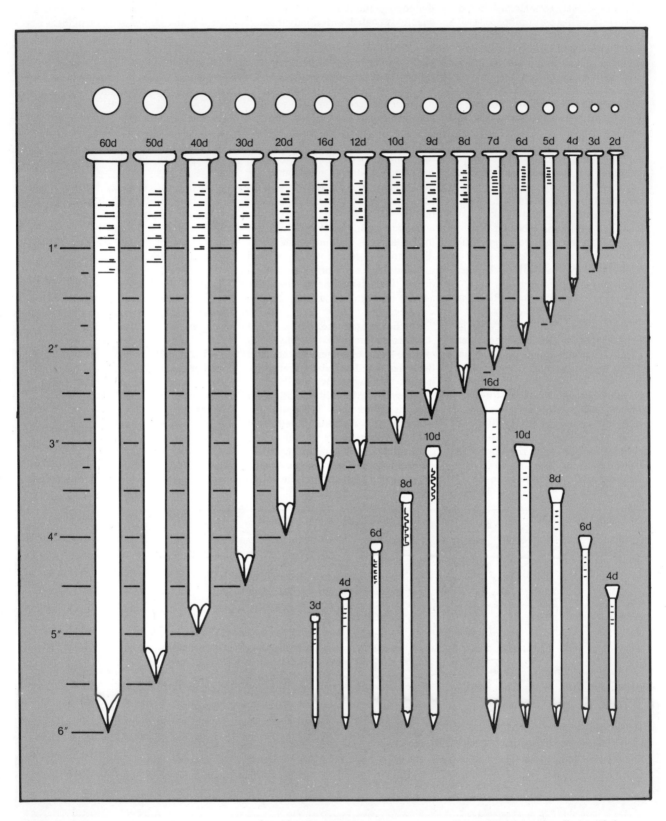

Nail size selector for common, finishing, and casing nails. The actual lengths of nails are shown for matching purposes. The diameter of the nail increases as its length increases.

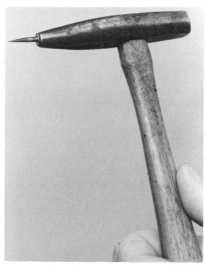

Tacks have very sharp points and are best started in materials with a magnetic tack hammer. Once started, the head of the hammer is used to drive the tack.

Standard studs are smooth-shanked; you can also buy threaded studs.

If you have a lot of nails to drive into masonry or concrete, you may be able to rent a cartridge-type nail driver. This tool is like a pistol, but it shoots concrete nails instead of bullets. A .22 calibre rim-fire cartridge drives the nails into the material when the trigger is pulled. A safety device prevents accidental firing when the tool is not held against the material to be nailed.

Caution: Concrete and masonry nails are extremely hard and should be driven with a baby sledgehammer, not a regular claw or ripping hammer. You should always wear safety glasses when driving these nails. For greater holding power, drive the head of the nail just flush with the work. Don't continue to hit the head of the nail once it is flush. Further pounding only loosens the nail in the hole.

Tacks are manufactured in many different sizes; the shanks may be round or cut. These fasteners are basically used to fasten carpeting and fabric to flooring and stairs. The large heads pull out easily; usually the carpet or fabric is pulled to release the tacks.

Hammer-driven staples
There are many different types available for fastening fencing, electrical wire, screening, etc. Some staples are insulated with a collar for electrical wiring installations. In stores, the fas-

teners may be labeled "electrical staples," "fencing staples," or just "staples." They are usually not found alongside staple gun staples, which are sold in specific departments such as carpeting, ceiling tile, and lumber and millwork.

Upholstery tacks or nails have large decorative heads and smooth, round shanks. They are used to fasten fabrics where the heads will show. If the heads won't show, use regular tacks. Upholstery fasteners are usually sold in packages.

Corrugated fasteners are also known as "wiggly nails" and "Scotch fasteners." They are used to fasten butt and miter joints in light framing, such as picture frames, drawer guides, and screen frames. The fasteners are usually sold in packages.

How nails are sized and sold
Long ago, nails were priced by the hundred. The penny, or price, was translated into numbers—so many nails per penny. The larger the nail, the higher the price, and the smaller the number of nails per penny. Nails still have a penny rating, indicated by the letter d; this is an abbreviation for the Latin word *denarius* (which means penny) that we have inherited from the English. The higher the penny number, the larger the nail. Nails also are ranked by inches. Both inches and d size are interchangeable, however. If you buy a 6d nail, for example, the length is 2 inches. Or, if you buy a 2-inch nail, the penny size is 6d.

As the length of a nail increases, so does the diameter of the nail shank.

Some special types of nails come in only one size, e.g., flooring brads. Some nails, such as roofing nails, come in only one shank diameter size.

In home center and hardware stores, nails are usually packaged, labeled, and sold in 1- and 5-pound boxes. However, some stores still sell nails in bulk by the pound. Most stores carry nails made of different metals such as copper, brass, steel, galvanized, monel, stainless steel, and bronze.

It is important that you don't mix metals when fastening metals. For example: you should use aluminum nails when fastening aluminum sheet and copper nails when fastening copper sheet. Mixed metals create corrosion, causing the nails to break or ruin the appearance of the materials

Corrugated nails or wiggly nails are for light framing. You can buy a special punch to drive these fasteners. Work on a solid surface to prevent splitting.

they hold. Use galvanized or aluminum nails where the nailheads will be exposed to weather. Weathering can cause rust, damaging the nails and streaking materials.

If you have lots of nailing to do—as when you frame in a room addition—you may be able to buy nails by the *keg* at some reduction in price. A keg of nails may weigh 50 or 100 pounds. The keg usually is a cardboard box—not the wooden tub used in years past.

Special-order nails
If you can't find the type of nail you need for a specific job, you may be able to special-order it through a hardware store, lumberyard catering to the professional builder, or a cabinet or millwork shop. Or, you may be able to order the fastener directly from a manufacturer of nails and fasteners. Below are the names and addresses of three fastener manufacturers who may be able to fill special needs. Address your request to the Director of Consumer Information.

Steel and Wire Products Co. Inc.
Box 207
Baltimore, Md. 21203

Hillwood Manufacturing Co.
21700 St. Clair Ave.
Cleveland, Ohio 44117

W.H. Maze Co.
Peru, Ill. 61641

Screw Fasteners

Threaded screws have more holding power than nails, with the possible exception of threaded and barbed nails. The big advantage with screws, however, is that they may be removed easily to disassemble the work without damaging or weakening the material in which the screw was driven. The only exception would be a rusted screw that can't be removed.

Screws have the same wedging action against wood fibers as nails. Screws also form ridges in materials and these ridges interlock with the screw threads forming an integral unit. Common screws are manufactured from steel. Other metals used include stainless steel, brass, and aluminum. Steel screws may be plated with brass, copper, bronze, zinc, cadmium, or chromium for rust resistance.

Standard wood screws include flathead, oval head, and roundhead. The slots for driving the screws are slotted (straight) and cross-slotted (Phillips or Reed & Prince). The slots can vary in size and this usually is determined by the size (length and diameter) of the screw. To drive screws properly, the tip of the screwdriver should fill the slot perfectly. If the tip is too small

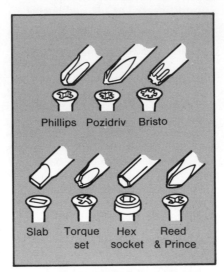

Screw-head slots vary considerably. The fancy ones are not usually stocked by home centers and hardware outlets, but Phillips and Reed & Prince are standard. The specialized heads require matching screwdrivers. The tips of these drivers are shown directly above the screw heads.

for the slot, the screwdriver will twist out of the slot. If the screwdriver is too wide, the edges of the tip will hang over the slot and damage the material surrounding the screw head as it is driven flush with the material. If the tip is too large, the slot will be damaged through turning pressure on the screwdriver handle.

Screw length is the most important factor when selecting the right screw for a job. About two-thirds of the length of the screw should be in the base material; the rest of the length should be in the material being screwed to the base.

Screws are measured by length and diameter, or gauge. The length is always in inches; the gauge is specified by number: from 2 to 16. The larger the number, the larger the diameter or screw shank.

It is usually advisable to drill pilot holes for screws in both soft and hardwoods. Although screws are fairly easy to drive and draw in softwoods without splitting the wood, pilot holes are insurance against wood damage and make the job go easier.

For pilot holes, you can buy drill bits shaped to match the threads, shank, and heads of flathead screws.

These bits are normally used in a power drill; you can also drill the pilot holes by hand and countersink the material with a countersink bit for flathead screws. Oval-head screws also may be countersunk; roundhead, dome-head, and pan-head screws are not countersunk. Therefore, the screws must be matched to the project: use fancy heads if the fasteners will show; use standard screws if the fasteners will not show or be objectionable.

When drilling pilot holes in hardwood, two holes are needed: one for the threads and one for the shank of the screw. The hole for the threads should be about one-third the total length of the screw and about 70 percent of its diameter, or gauge. The hole for the shank should be the same length as the shank and the same diameter.

Driving screws in hardwoods is easier if the screw has been lightly lubricated with soap or paste wax.

Screw washers do two jobs: they help distribute pressure from the screw head to the work, thus adding strength to the joint; they also decorate.

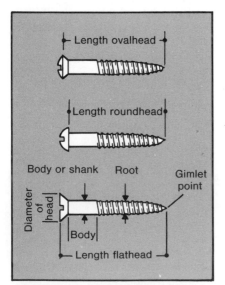

Anatomy of a screw. These drawings name the parts, and show how screws are numbered as to length size: flathead from the tip to the top; roundhead to the bottom of the head; oval to the center of the head.

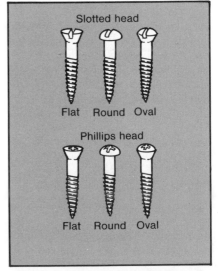

Screw types are classified by the head of the screw. Common types with slotted heads are flat, round, and oval, and with Phillips heads flat, round, and oval. Phillips-head screws provide more driving/drawing surface for screwdriver tips. They are more decorative in place.

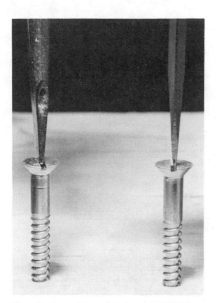

Tip of screwdriver blade must fill the screw slot. Otherwise, the torque on the screwdriver will damage the head or slot of the screw so it can't be drawn—or even driven. Both examples above show wrong-size screwdrivers.

Three types of washers are available, and they are flat, countersunk, and flush. The washers are made in different metals: steel, brass, copper, bronze, etc., and they should be matched to the metal of the screw. Don't mix metals.

Metal fasteners

For assembling sheet metals and some bar and round metal stock, you can buy pan-head screws that either form or cut their own threads. All four basic types listed below are set flush with the surface of the metal; they usually are not countersunk, but they may be counterbored if the material is thick enough.

Pointed pan-head screws may be used for wood, as well as metal. A pilot hole is required for best results.

Blunt pan-head screws are for metal assembly only. Pilot holes are needed.

Partial-tapping pan-head screws cut their own threads, similar to a tap drill. This screw may be used for thicker metals. Pilot holes are necessary.

Self-tapping pan-head screws are similar to partial-tapping fasteners, but they are generally used for thicker metals. A pilot hole the exact size of the diameter of the screws is necessary.

OTHER SCREW TYPES. Other screw types you'll find for sale include these important fasteners:

One-way screws are designed for lock-sets; they have slip-out screwdriver slots. If a burglar tries to remove the screws to remove the lock, the tip of the screwdriver blade will not engage the slot, so the screw can't be turned.

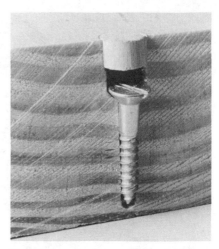

Counterbored screws require two predrilled holes: one for the screw and one to accept the dowel plug that hides the screw head. The grain of the plug should match the grain of the wood and should be the same wood species if possible. You can buy plug-cutters for this. Bolts also can be counterbored so the heads don't show.

Hanger bolts are really screws, but they may be labeled "bolts" in stores. One end of the fastener has threads similar to a wood screw. The other end has machine threads to accept a hex or square nut. After the bolt is driven, the object to be hanged is secured to the shank of the bolt and

Pilot Hole Drill and Bit Gauge Numbers

SCREW NUMBER	DECIMAL DIAMETER	SHANK HOLE		PILOT HOLE								AUGER BIT NUMBER	SCREW THREADS PER INCH
				Hardwood				Softwood					
		Twist Bit	Drill Gauge	Twist Bit		Drill Gauge		Twist Bit		Drill Gauge			
				s	p	s	p	s	p	s	p		
0	.060	1/16	52	1/32	—	70	—	1/64	—	75	—	—	32
1	.073	5/64	47	1/32	—	66	—	1/32	—	71	—	—	28
2	.086	3/32	42	3/64	1/32	56	70	1/32	1/64	65	75	3	26
3	.099	7/64	37	1/16	1/32	54	66	3/64	1/32	58	71	4	24
4	.112	7/64	32	1/16	3/64	52	56	3/64	1/32	55	65	4	22
5	.125	1/8	30	5/64	1/16	49	54	1/16	3/64	53	58	4	20
6	.138	9/64	27	5/64	1/16	47	52	1/16	3/64	52	55	5	18
7	.151	5/32	22	3/32	5/64	44	49	1/16	3/64	51	53	5	16
8	.164	11/64	18	3/32	5/64	40	47	5/64	1/16	48	52	6	15
9	.177	3/16	14	7/64	3/32	37	44	5/64	1/16	45	51	6	14
10	.190	3/16	10	7/64	3/32	33	40	3/32	5/64	43	48	6	13
11	.203	13/64	4	1/8	7/64	31	37	3/32	5/64	40	45	7	12
12	.216	7/32	2	1/8	7/64	30	33	7/64	3/32	38	43	7	11
14	.242	1/4	D	9/64	1/8	25	31	7/64	3/32	32	40	8	10
16	.268	17/64	I	5/32	1/8	18	30	9/64	7/64	29	38	9	9
18	.294	19/64	N	3/16	9/64	13	25	9/64	7/64	26	32	10	8
20	.320	21/64	P	13/64	5/32	4	18	11/64	9/64	19	29	11	8
24	.372	3/8	V	7/32	3/16	1	13	3/16	9/64	15	26	12	7

s: Slotted head   p: Phillips head

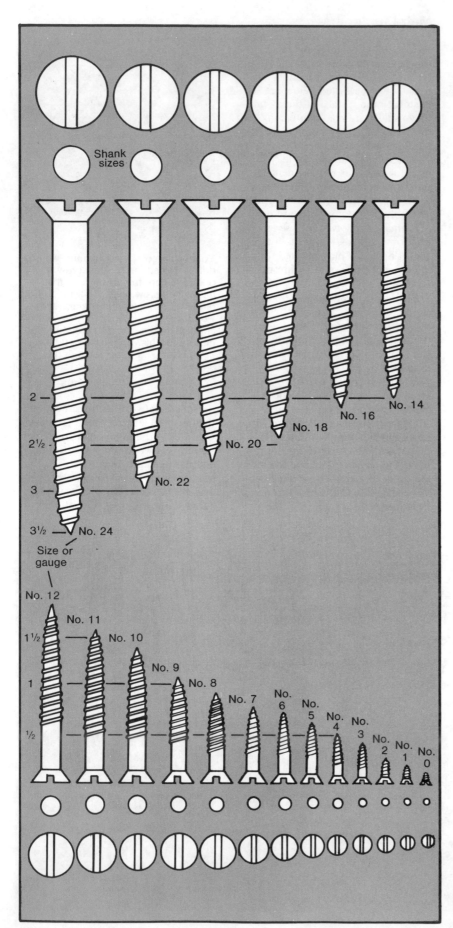

Shank sizes

2

2½

3

3½ — No. 24

Size or gauge

No. 22

No. 20

No. 18

No. 16

No. 14

No. 12

No. 11

1½ — No. 10

No. 9

1 — No. 8

No. 7

No. 6

No. 5

No. 4

No. 3

½

No. 2

No. 1

No. 0

Screw size selector for flathead wood screws shows actual sizes. Screw sizes go by numbers: the larger the number, the larger the gauge or diameter of the screw. Lengths can vary within a number classification.

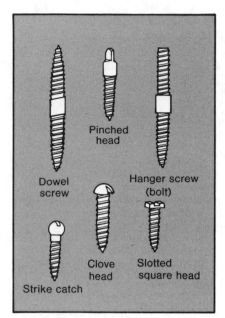

Specialty screws are basically for decorative purposes. Most are stocked by hardware stores. Dowel screws are for joining stock at edges and faces.

Pinched head

Dowel screw

Hanger screw (bolt)

Strike catch

Clove head

Slotted square head

fastened with the hex or square nut.

Lag bolts, which are labeled "bolts" or "screws," are often used with lead anchors in concrete and masonry materials. The bolts are driven or drawn with an adjustable wrench or an open-end wrench. Because of their strength, lag bolts often are used to assemble dimension lumber and timbers.

Screw hooks are hooks, rings, eyes, and hangers, with one end of the hook threaded and the other end bent into a hook or eye, or closed to make a solid ring. Screw hooks are generally used to hang utensils, tools, and lightweight equipment, although some types are strong enough for gate latches and to hang swings. Square bend hooks are designed for hanging curtain rods.

How screws are sold

In most stores, screws are sold in packages and identified by number and length. Many hardware stores and some home centers still sell single screws; you'll find them in small marked boxes or metal bins.

Screws seldom are sold in bulk like nails, but you may be able to get a "price" on quantity if you ask for it.

Specialty screws almost always are sold by the package and types are identified on the package.

Washers may be sold individually, but usually by the package. They are identified by number. For example, a No. 2 washer has an outside diameter of 5½ inches; a hole size of 3⅛, and takes a 3-inch bolt.

Washers also are sold by type. The standard types include spring-lock, flat, external tooth, and internal tooth.

Washers must always be matched to the screw, nut, or bolt heads that will top them. For example, a countersink washer can't be used under a roundhead screw.

Special-order screws

Home centers may offer only a limited variety of screws. Hardware stores and lumberyards catering to professional carpenters and cabinetmakers generally have a wider selection.

Because of volume buying, home centers may not be able to special order screws for you. However, hardware stores and lumberyards often will.

If you can't find the screw fastener you want, try writing to the Consumer Information Director of these screw manufacturers:

Elco Industries Inc.
1111 Samuelson Rd.
Rockford, Ill. 61101

ITT Harper
8200 Lehigh Ave.
Morton Grove, Ill. 60053

American Screw Co.
Third & Marshall Sts.
Wytheville, Va. 24382

Bolt Fasteners

Bolts are stronger fasteners than either screws or nails. They also have the advantage of being easy to take apart without damaging any materials.

Bolts can be broadly classified into three types: machine, carriage, and stove. But there are other bolt-like fasteners available that fall into the bolt classification. These include toggle bolts, Molly bolts, masonry fasteners, and threaded rods.

Bolts are usually manufactured from steel. They may have round, square, hex, flat, oval, oven, and slotted heads; they may be set flush or countersunk; and they may be used with or without washers. The body of the bolt may be threaded from its tip to the head of the bolt, or it may be partly threaded with a smooth body between the top of the threads and the bottom of the head.

The threads are the key to bolt selection: The number of threads per inch determines the thread size. This is indicated by a number that appears next to the diameter of the bolt. For example: the numbers ¼" × 20" means that the bolt is ¼ inch in diameter and has 20 threads to the inch.

Most stores carry bolts in sizes from ⅛ × 40 to ½ × 13. Lengths stocked are from ⅜-inch to 6 inches.

Machine bolts range from ¼ to 2 inches in diameter and up to 30 inches in length.

Carriage bolts are stocked from 3/16 to ¼ inch in diameter and from ½ inch to 10 inches in length.

Machine bolts are made with fine or coarse threads. Most store inventories would show more coarse threads than fine ones. Also, large-sized bolts often are considered specialties.

Nuts for bolts (the part that twists on the threads) are specialized, too. Types include square, hex, jam, wing, castle, lock, flat square, and knurled. Nuts often are packaged with the bolts; if you want a different type, you will have to buy it separately.

Jam nuts and stop nuts are types of locking nuts. They may have a fiber-like lining next to the threads which prevents the nut from loosening under stress and vibration.

Castle, or castellated, nuts are designed for use with cotter keys; the

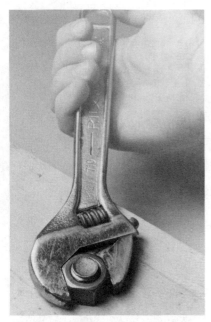

Always pull against the fixed jaw of an adjustable wrench when loosening or tightening fasteners. Make absolutely sure that the jaws fit the fastener to be turned. If they don't, the wrench can damage the fastener so badly it can't be turned.

key is slipped through a slot in the nut, through a hole in the bolt and out the other side.

Cap nuts are decorative nuts that cap off the threads of the bolt so they don't show. Wing nuts are used where the nut will be removed often. You can drive or draw a wing nut with your fingers.

Washers for nuts and bolts come in three types: flat, split-lock, and shakerproof, which includes internal and

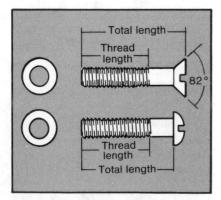

Stove bolts are available in two types: roundheads and flatheads for countersinking. Length is measured from tip to bottom of head on roundhead types; from tip to top of head on flathead types. Treads also may extend the full length of the body of the bolt.

external teeth. Flat washers provide a bearing surface for the bolt/nut; the lock washers prevent the nuts from loosening under vibration.

Cotter keys sometimes are used with bolts and nuts to prevent the nut from turning off the threads, as described above. The keys are manufactured from soft steel or stainless steel, which resists rust. Cotter keys are measured from the short leg to the head of the key or pin. A large variety of diameter sizes and lengths are manufactured; Smaller sizes from ½ to 3 inches are usually stocked in home centers and hardware outlets.

Types of bolts

STOVE BOLTS. Stove bolts are so named because they were once used in the assembly of wood and coal stoves. They now have become a general utility fastener and may be used in light- to medium-weight construction.

Stove bolts have flat, oval, and round heads that are slotted to accept a standard-blade screwdriver. The flat- and oval-head bolts are also countersunk like regular flat- and oval-head screws. The threads run from the end of the bolt to the bottom side of the head, and are usually coarse cut.

Lengths of stove bolts range from ⅜ to 6 inches, and the length depends on the diameter of the bolt. Diameters include ⁵⁄₃₂, ³⁄₁₆, ¼, ⁵⁄₁₆, ⅜, and ½ inch. You'll find these lengths and diameters in most home centers and hardware outlets. In assembly, stove bolts almost always are used with flat or locking washers under the nuts. Without washers, the nuts tend to work loose under even the slightest vibration.

Stove bolts with flat and oval heads may be countersunk with a rose countersink in a hand drill; pilot holes the diameter of the bolt always have to be drilled in the material to be assembled with the bolts.

MACHINE BOLTS. These fasteners have more strength than stove bolts. You will know them by their heads: square or hex. The nuts are either square or hex, too, although you can buy special nut types to fit the standard—usually coarse—threads.

Heads of machine bolts may be set below the surface of materials if the material is counterbored to accept the head of the bolt and the socket to drive it. Flat washers almost always

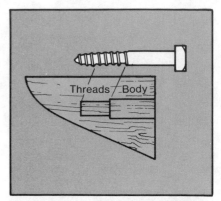

Lag bolts in wood sometimes require predrilled pilot holes to prevent the fastener from splitting the wood. Two different-sized holes are necessary: one for the threads and one for the body or shank of the bolt. Drill the shank hole first.

are used under the bolt heads to distribute pressure; lock nuts or lock washers may be used under the nuts to prevent the nuts from loosening.

Machine bolts range in length from ¾ inch to 30 inches. They range in diameter from ³⁄₁₆ to 1¼ inches, and the diameter is always related to the length: the longer the bolt, the larger the diameter. Typical diameters in stores include ³⁄₁₆, ¼, ⁵⁄₁₆, ⅜, ½, ⁹⁄₁₆, ⅝, ¾, ⅞, 1, 1⅛, and 1¼ inches.

For assembly, two wrenches are needed; the type of wrench (box, open, or adjustable) depends on the work being done.

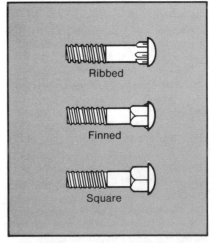

Carriage bolts have rounded heads and different neck designs. The neck secures the bolt in the material. Three basic types include square, finned, and ribbed neck. Nuts usually require washers between the nut and the material.

Anchor shields are slipped into pre-drilled holes in masonry and concrete. The bolt is driven into the shield which expands to grip the sides of the pre-drilled hole. For heavy-duty, metal anchors are used. For light-duty, use plastic or fiber anchors.

CARRIAGE BOLTS. These fasteners are used in medium to heavy assembly. They have smooth, round heads with a square collar directly underneath the head; the collar slips into the material to prevent the bolt from turning when the nut is tightened on the threads.

Threads are coarse, and the body of the bolt usually is threaded approximately one-third of its length.

Carriage bolts are manufactured from steel. They are available in a variety of lengths and diameters (see the bolt chart). When buying carriage bolts remember that the unthreaded body of the bolt should be approximately the same thickness as the material being assembled. The last thread toward the head of the bolt should lie outside the material. When the nut is turned down tight, the threads are flush with the bottom of the nut, with no threads showing. Flat washers may be used to decrease the thread length, if necessary.

THREADED ROD. This is exactly what its name implies: a length of steel rod—usually 3 feet long—that is threaded from one end to the other end. There are many diameters of threaded rod manufactured; stores stock a standard variety, usually ⅛, ¼, ⅜, and ½ inches. The threads may be fine or coarse, and you can buy a variety of nuts to fit the threads.

MASONRY BOLTS AND ANCHORS. These bolts, similar to machine bolts, have square or hex heads, a smooth body, and threads about one-third the length of the body. An-

chors may be called either *shields* or *anchors*. Shields, made of iron, usually use lag screws, while anchors, made of lead, use screws or bolts. The action of both devices is about the same: a shield is hinged and expands in the hole drilled for it in masonry as the screw is tightened; an anchor is solid and is expanded by the bolt as it is driven in.

Both anchors and shields are forced against the sides of the hole as they expand, producing a wedge-type grip. The more the bolt is tightened, the more gripping power the anchor has—but there is a limit. You can strip an anchor or shield so that the threads of the bolt won't hold securely.

Bolt size is important when buying anchors. The bolt (or screw if a plastic or fiber anchor is used) can be no longer than the depth of the hole, and must include the thickness of the material to be fastened. A minimum size would be a bolt as long as the thickness of the material, plus the diameter of the screw or bolt. The shields are approximately half again as long as anchors. Shields may be considered stronger than anchors, although strength is really determined by the material you are using.

Most stores stock the ¼-20 size shield. The numbers indicate that the shield will take a bolt ¼ inch in diameter with 20 threads per inch. This size is recommended for attaching furring strips and light framing to masonry surfaces. Other sizes are listed in the bolt chart, along with bolt/screw recommendations. You also can buy fiber and plastic anchors that are used with regular wood screws. The fiber anchors may be lined with lead to accept the screw threads or they may be solid fiber.

Both plastic and fiber anchors work the same way as their stronger cousins, anchors and shields. However, they should be used for light work only.

Caution: Drilling holes in concrete and masonry for anchor installation creates chips, dust, and other harmful residue. Always wear safety glasses when drilling into this hard material. If you use a star drill and baby sledge hammer, you should also wear gloves.

TOGGLE BOLTS. These are used in hollow wall construction such as gypsum wallboard over stud framing members. The bolts have round and flat slotted heads, and the body of the bolt is threaded from the end to the bottom of the head. The nut is a spring-loaded wing-shaped device. The wings collapse against the threads of the bolt, and then spring out to grip the back of the wall when the bolt is turned down tightly.

Toggle bolts will support lots of weight—up to 1,800 pounds. These fasteners are ideal for any construction that is hollow, including gypsumboard, concrete and cinder block, and plaster over wooden lath.

To hang an object with a toggle bolt, a hole for the folding wings

Load Capacity on Plastic Anchors		
SCREW NO.	ANCHOR NO. AND LENGTH	LOAD (lbs.)
4-6-8	No. 1 (⅞ in.)	650
10-12	No. 2 (1 in.)	850
14-16	No. 3 (1 ½ in.)	1075

Sizes and Loads for Machine Bolt Anchors			
SIZE (in.)	HOLE DIAMETER FOR ANCHOR (in.)	ANCHOR LENGTH (in.)	LOAD (lbs.)
¼	½	1½	500
5/16	⅝	1½-2	800
⅝	¾	1½-2⅜	1,000
7/16	⅞	2-2½	1,000
½	⅞	2-2⅞	1,500
⅝	1-1⅛	2½-3¼	2,000
¾	1¼-1⅜	3½-4	2,000
⅞	1⅜-1½	4-4¼	2,300
1	1⅜-1¾	4¼-4½	2,400
1¼	2⅛	5½-6	2,500

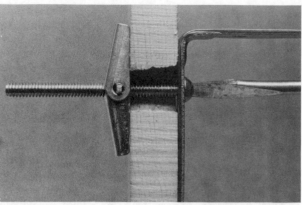

Left: Toggle bolts require a predrilled hole that matches the size of the folding wings of the bolt. The object to be hung must be inserted on the bolt before the bolt and wings are inserted into the hole. *Right:* Once behind the surface material (wall, ceiling, tile, block) the wings of the toggle flip open and grip the back of the material as the bolt is tightened. When the object is removed, the wings of the toggle will drop behind the surface material.

must first be drilled in the wall or block. The wings are then removed from the bolt, and the bolt is inserted through the object to be fastened. Then the wings are threaded back on the bolt. The wings are then folded back and inserted in the hole. The bolt is then tightened and the wings grip the back of the surface.

The only disadvantage to toggle bolts is that when the object fastened has to be removed, the wings drop down behind the surface and can't be used again.

Standard sizes of bolts and the loads they will carry are listed below. You will find most of these sizes stocked in home centers and hardware stores, as well as in some drug, grocery, and variety outlets.

Length (in.)	Diameter (in.)	Load (lbs.)
2-3-4	⅛	200
2-3-4-5-6	⅜	450
3-4-5-6	¼	925
3-4-5-6	⁵⁄₁₆	1,150
3-4-5-6	⅜	1,500
4-6-8	½	1,800

MOLLY BOLTS. *Molly bolts* are sometimes called "expansion fasteners." The name Molly is a trademark that has become almost generic with the fastener. Molly bolts are designed for hollow wall construction and are like toggles—with a difference: Molly bolts have a sleeve that stays in the wall after the expansion strips have been activated to grip the back of the wall. This way, the object fastened may be removed without the bolt disappearing behind the wall. If the fastener has to be removed, it is tapped through the wall with a punch and the hole in the wall is patched over.

To hang an object with a Molly bolt, you drill a hole in the wall to accept the diameter of the fastener (see chart below). The Molly is then inserted in the hole and the screw or bolt in the center of the Molly is turned to swell the expansion strips behind the wall. The bolt is then removed, slipped through the object to be hanged, and reinserted and tightened in the fastener in the hole in the wall.

Molly bolts will support about 50 to 500 pounds of load, depending on the size of the fastener; the larger the Molly, the more load it will carry.

Size	Length (in.)	Wall Thickness (in.)
XS	¾–⅞	To ¼
MS	1¹⁄₁₂	¹⁄₁₆–½
S	1½–2¼	⅛–¾
L	2–2¾	⅝–1¼
XL	2½–3½	1¼–1¾

Special toggles and anchors

Some stores stock special toggles for mounting electrical junction boxes and wire, and metal rods. These products work the same as a regular toggle bolt; the difference is in the head of the bolt, which may be threaded to accept a nut or designed as a hanger for wire and rod. Other bolt fixtures include L and J clips, and a surface or screw plate device that can be slipped over the protruding bolt and held with a nut.

New fasteners include the strap toggle and the nylon sleeve. The strap toggle has two plastic strips attached to the toggle, which fits behind the wall. As the straps are pulled, a washer is pushed toward the wall until the washer is seated against the front of the wall. A mounting screw is then inserted into the object to be hung, through the washer, into the toggle and then tightened.

The nylon fasteners can be used in both hollow and solid wall construction. A hole is drilled in the material and the nylon sleeve inserted. Then the object to be hung is threaded onto the screw and the screw is turned into the sleeve. The sleeve expands and grips the hole in the material. Any

Molly bolt has expansion strips that unfold in back of the surface material to grip the material when the bolt is turned. This fastener is activated before the object is hung; the object may be removed.

type of screw may be used; the sleeve may be pulled out of the hole and used again, if necessary.

I, J, AND U BOLTS. These are so named for their shapes. An I, or eye, bolt has an enclosed end forming a ring. The other end is threaded to accept a nut. J bolts have the shape of a letter J, also with the opposite end threaded for a nut. U bolts have a U shape; both ends are threaded to accept nuts. These steel fasteners are basically used for hanging and strapping objects; there are a variety of sizes and bolt diameters available at most stores.

You can make these different shapes from threaded rod. The nuts may be purchased separately, along with hasps and snaps for use with the various shapes.

TURNBUCKLES. Turnbuckles have two bolts that screw into a metal sleeve. Manufactured from steel, turnbuckles are used to tension wire, rope, and cable; the ends of the bolts are shaped into a ring or eye for fastening purposes. One bolt has right-handed threads; the other has left-handed threads. When the sleeve is turned, the bolts tighten or loosen, depending on the direction the sleeve is turned.

Turnbuckles are sold in a wide range of sizes (the largest are used for suspension bridge cables); do-it-yourself outlets usually stock small to medium sizes for supporting gates, gateposts, fencing, retaining walls, and screen-door framing.

How nuts and bolts are sold

Most of these fasteners for home maintenance and improvement are sold in packages and labeled as to size. Some manufacturers even include do-it-yourself instructions on the back or in the package.

In stores that cater to the professional—lumberyards and hardware outlets—nuts, bolts, and accessories

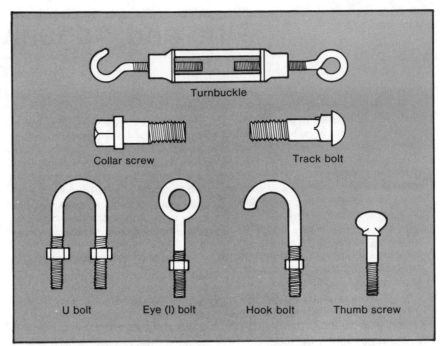

Specialty bolt types are shown above. You can make your own hook, eye (I), and U bolts by bending threaded rod.

Turnbuckles are used to tighten sagging gates, fencing, and screen frames.

often can be purchased as single items. Here, the merchandise is in bins or boxes. The advantage to this is that you can select nuts and accessories for the bolts and make sure they fit before buying them. Prices, however, are usually slightly higher than for packaged fasteners.

Special order

Unless you are buying a huge quantity of nuts and bolts, special order by a home center for one or two special bolts or nuts is not available. Some lumberyards and hardware outlets will special-order, but you will pay extra for this service—usually for transportation costs. Don't overlook cabinet shops in your search for a special fastener; general catalog outlets, such as Sears and Wards, also are good places to search.

For fasteners that are used in machinery autos, appliances, motors, bikes, etc.—your best sources are retailers who deal in these specific products. It's unlikely that you'll find them in a home center or lumberyard.

If you can't find the fastener you want, try writing to the Consumer Information Director of the following manufacturers:

Geauga Bold & Screw Co.
Industrial Parkway
Chardon, Ohio 44024

Lamson & Sessions Co.
2000 Bond Ct.
Cleveland, Ohio 44114

American Screw Co.
Third & Marshall Sts.
Wytheville, Va. 24382

Glue and Adhesives

Time was when a glued joint was considered a weak joint. Not so today. Aircraft parts are often held together with adhesives, not to mention the unbreakable bonds that can be made with modern construction adhesives. Fastening with glues and adhesives often is the best and easiest way. For example, construction adhesive may be used to fasten partition wall sill plates to concrete floors, eliminating bolts and anchors that take time and muscle to install.

The adhesive selection in most stores is usually a confusing maze of cans, tubes, bottles, and plastic containers. The tough job is to determine which adhesive will do the job. Find the answer by asking questions:

Is the material to be joined porous or non-porous; will the adhesive be subjected to the weather, heat, cold, moisture? Knowing these answers automatically eliminates about 50 percent of the adhesives on sale.

An adhesive selection chart may be found in this chapter.

Below are the most common adhesives and glues available, along with a brief description of what each will or will not do.

POLYVINYL ACETATE (PVA). This is standard white glue and goes under the trade name "Elmer's," which has almost become generic for all white glue products. It is strong stuff and may be used for porous materials such as wood, fabric, and paper stock. It is waterproof, but should be used indoors for best results.

POLYVINYL CHLORIDE (PVC). This adhesive is white, and is very similar to polyvinyl acetate glue. It is for non-porous materials (glass, metal, plastic); acetone is used as a clean-up solvent. PVC is moisture-resistant; it dries fast and clear.

EPOXY. Made basically for non-porous materials, this two-part adhesive usually is sold in tubes. Follow the mixing instructions on the container to the letter for best results. The adhesive has a super-strong bond, but the bond is not flexible. Acetone is needed for clean-up; epoxy is both waterproof and heat-resistant.

CYANOACRYLATE. This is the wonder-glue seen on television. The workman glues his hardhat to the steel girder with cyanoacrylate and then hangs from the hat. This adhesive is for non-porous materials. It sets in 30 to 90 seconds and requires no clamping; it is water- and chemical-resistant and requires acetone as a clean-up solvent.

CONTACT. It looks and smells like rubber cement, and is basically used for sticking together dissimilar materials that are either porous or non-porous. The adhesive is spread on two surfaces to be joined. When the adhesive dries to a sheen, the surfaces are pressed together; it bonds instantly on contact. Manufacturers often use this adhesive for joining countertop laminates—such as Formica—and large sheets of plywood and hardboard to a substratum under high pressure. It is a heavy-duty construction glue.

PANEL ADHESIVE. This is popular in caulking gun cartridges, although you can buy it in quart and gallon containers and apply it with a notched applicator. The adhesive is used basically to install paneling and subflooring. It is tough enough to laminate boards and dimension lumber, as the illustration below, at left, shows. Coverage is about three 4×8-foot panels per tube. Panel adhesive works best on porous materials; clean-up requires mineral spirits.

RESORCINOL. This water-proof adhesive is for porous materials and is mixed from a two-part can (one can usually is taped to the bottom of another). One can holds a liquid resin while the other has the hardener. You must work fast with this adhesive; pot life is about three hours or less. Use water for clean-up while the adhesive is still soft. Once dry, the adhesive can't be removed. Application temperature must be at least 70°F; clamps are needed.

PLASTIC RESIN. This adhesive is also called urea-formaldehyde. It is for porous materials; the joints to be glued must be perfectly straight and clean. It is ideal for gluing veneers. Working temperature is 70°F and clamps are required.

Adhesives sometimes work better than nails, screws, or bolts to fasten or join surfaces together. Adhesives may be used to strengthen joints held mainly by nails, screws, or bolts. Here, paneling adhesive in a caulking gun tube is being applied to the back of wall paneling. Paneling nails also will be used; they are driven into studs.

Dowels often are used to edge-join wood. Dowel centers are being used here to locate drilling points in the wood. The grooves in the dowels spread the adhesive as the dowels are inserted, providing better holding power. Dowel rods come in various sizes up to 3 feet long. Precut, grooved dowels for fastening also are available in packages.

Adhesive Selector

ADHESIVE TYPE	USE	MOISTURE RESISTANCE	SET TIME	CURE TIME
Epoxy	For most materials; mixing necessary	Good	1–10 mins.	1–12 hrs.
Contact	High-pressure laminate; wood veneer; hardboard; plywood	Good	On contact	30–50 hrs.
Mastic	Ceiling tile; floor tile; plastics; paneling; woods; cork	Good	On contact to 3 hrs.	3 days
Polyvinyl (white glue)	Paper; wood; hardboard; plywood; boards; dowels	Poor	5 hrs.	30 hrs.
Resorcinol	Wood; plywood; particleboard; chipboard; hardboard; fiberboard	Good	10 hrs.	27 hrs.
Cyanoacrylates	Hardwood; plastic; glass; ceramics; metal; rubber	Fair	On contact	12–24 hrs.
Latex	Fabrics; paper	Fair	On contact; 8 hrs.	8–60 hrs.
Paste	Wallpaper	Poor	30 mins.	10–24 hrs.
Rubber-base	Wood; wood to concrete; paper	Good	On contact to 6 hrs.	30–60 hrs.

PLASTIC CEMENT. Fast setting, this adhesive works on both porous and non-porous materials. Glue bonds are fairly water-resistant and mildly heat-resistant. Work with ventilation; the fumes from the adhesive are toxic.

ALIPHATIC RESIN. This is similar to white glue, but it is cream-colored in appearance and is touted as carpenter's glue. It sets in about 30 minutes, but needs clamping. Aliphatic works best on porous surfaces; it is water-resistant.

MASTICS. These are formulated for setting floor and ceiling tiles; use them for only this purpose.

SET AND CURE TIMES. When you buy adhesive, make sure you check the label for the set and cure times of the adhesive. They are different and you can be misled by advertising claims unless you understand what they mean. Set time is usually the fast time: "bonds in 30 seconds." The cure time is the time it takes for the adhesive to reach its maximum strength. The cure time can be 30 hours or more.

Also note the adhesive's water resistance. Some adhesives have fast set and cure times, but very poor resistance to water and moisture conditions. Match the adhesive's characteristics to the job requirements.

GLUE GUNS. These look similar to a soldering gun, but they eject a hot melted glue that is ideal for porous materials. It is waterproof and provides a fairly strong bond or joint. The guns and sticks are sold as a package; glue sticks for the gun may be purchased separately. The gun operates on house power.

How they're sold

Adhesives are almost always packaged in some sort of container: metal, plastic, cardboard. If you don't see the adhesive you want on the shelf, ask for it. Sometimes adhesives are separated into different store departments, for example, the mastics may be in the floor and ceiling tile area.

You should always read the manufacturer's small print description of the adhesive product before you buy it. A few minutes' study at the store can save you grief when you get the adhesive home and start using it. Look especially for restrictions such as temperature and water-resistance.

Special order

Home centers usually won't special-order adhesive for you—unless you buy a large quantity of, say, panel adhesive. Lumberyards and hardware stores may special-order, but you will pay for transportation costs. If you can't find the adhesive you want, try contacting the Consumer Information Directors at:

Borden Chemical Division
Borden Inc.
180 East Broad
Columbus, Ohio 43215

Magic-American Chemical Corp.
23700 Mercantile Ave.
Cleveland, Ohio 44122

W.J. Ruscoe Co.
483 Kenmore Blvd.
Akron, Ohio 44301

Leech Products Inc.
West 4th & Hendricks Sts.
Hutchinson, Kan. 67501

Hangers and Plates

Designed basically for use by the pre-fabricated housing industry, structural wood connectors, called hangers and plates, are now available at many building materials outlets catering to the do-it-yourselfer. The connectors do two jobs: fasten and support. They also are great time-savers and produce professional-looking results.

The hangers are strictly for wood joints used in framing. They are manufactured from steel plate or aluminum sheet in the types briefly described below.

JOIST HANGERS OR CLIPS. For dimension lumber in five sizes: 2×4- to 2×14-inch for individual joints; 2×6- and 2×14-inch for double joints. Holes for nails are prepunched; the hanger slips over the end of the joist and is fastened to the joist and header members.

FRAMING CLIPS. For two- and three-way ties between wall, roof, and floor framing. Nail and lag bolt holes are prepunched; you may have to specify left- or right-handed clips, although universal clips are made.

BEAM CLIPS. For post-and-beam construction (framing). The clip straddles the post and flush-mounts to the beam. The nail holes are prepunched and staggered.

TRUSS CLIPS. Teeth for gripping the wood are prepunched in these flat clips that are used for butt-joining lengths of dimension lumber—usually 2×4s. To use this clip, position it over the joint and drive in the teeth with a hammer. Each tooth will support about 50 pounds load.

Bridge clips go between joists and replace the old wooden 1×4 bridging that had to be mitered and toenailed. They are made in 2×8 and 2×10 sizes.

BASE CLIPS. For anchoring 4×4 posts to concrete, these clips or anchors are attached to a sill bolt in the concrete. An insert keeps the post off the concrete to prevent rot. Nail holes are prepunched in the clip for attaching the post.

Anchor clips are used for attaching wood to masonry and concrete surfaces. The clips may be bent to accommodate different angles and sizes of materials.

Storm clips. These are for fastening trusses or rafters to top plates and stud framing members. Available in three sizes, the clips are prepunched for nails.

Drywall clips. See Specialty Material chapter.

Fence post caps. Made to fit 4×4 posts, these are covers that fit over post tops to seal out the weather. You can buy aluminum caps that won't rust. Holes are prepunched for nails.

Fence brackets are nailed to posts and help support fence rails. The brackets come in many different sizes. The metal usually is aluminum; nail holes are prepunched and staggered.

MENDING PLATES. These are flat steel plates with holes drilled into them for screws. There are several shapes, sizes, and angles available such as Ts, Ls, and angled Ls. The products are best used where they won't show, although they may be mortised into the wood and then covered with wood plastic or water putty. They also may be bent in a vise to fit most any angle or offset to be reinforced.

Framing clips are used to support rafters and joists that are edge joined. There are many types of these steel or aluminum hangers available for framing and fencing.

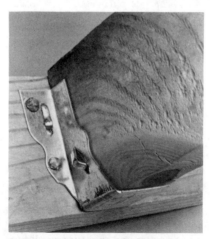

Special metal framing hangers are available to strengthen joints. Shown above is a joist hanger that is attached to a header member. A typical use would be for a deck attached to the house. Holes for nails are prepunched and staggered; note nailing prongs that are driven into the wood to help strengthen the metal joint hanger.

Metal mending plates add reinforcement to ordinary weak miter and butt joints. Many different designs are available for 45° and 90° angles. Holes for screws are prepunched and the screws often are included in the package with the plate.

Prime uses for mending plates are across butt-joined boards and dimension lumber, at corners (picture frames and screen framing), under stepladder rungs, on chair legs and backs, and at tops and legs of tables, benches, and cabinets.

How they're sold

Most hangers, clips, and plates are sold by the piece. In some cases, the products are packaged—usually two or four pieces to the package.

Selection of framing clips may be limited at home centers, but lumberyards generally stock a full line.

Mending plates are readily available at home centers, hardware stores, variety stores, furniture retailers, even drug stores.

Fence fasteners are available at home centers selling fencing and garden supplies. Most hardware stores carry them.

Special order

Lumberyards and hardware stores will order framing clips in quantity for you, although you will have to pay for transportation. Home centers usually won't place a special order. However, if the store stocks some of the fasteners, they may order for you. Expect a four-to-six-week wait—or longer.

If you can't find the fastener you want—and there are many varieties from which to choose—try writing the Consumer Information Director of

the following manufacturers of these products:

Steel and Wire Products Co., Inc.
Box 207
Baltimore, Md. 21203

Panel-Clip Co.
2700 Oak Industrial Dr., NE
Grand Rapids, Mich. 49505

Wood Connector Products
Division of Ray Laboratories Inc.
340 West Colfax
Palatine, Ill. 60067

Stanley Hardware
195 Lake St.
New Britain, Conn. 06050

Staples and Rivets

As fasteners, staples and rivets have more holding power than you might guess. Properly installed, staples will fasten a wide variety of materials faster, easier, and better than some nails, screws, or glues. Rivets are tough fasteners, too. They're even used to make aircraft, bridges, skyscrapers, automobiles, and the hip pockets on blue jeans.

Staple applications in home maintenance and improvement include ceiling tile, insulation, weatherstripping, carpeting, upholstery, and screening. For the most part, staples are for light fabrication; they may be hand- or machine-driven.

There are three basic types of machine or mechanical staplers that are suitable for most home maintenance/improvements: staple guns, plier staplers, and hammer staplers. The first two are easier to use because you can position them on the work and pull the trigger. Since the hammer stapler is swung like a hammer, you have to be a natural-born crack shot to be able to hit the tongue of a ceiling tile with it. The plier stapler works like a paper stapler: both sides of the material to be joined have to be thin enough to slip the jaws of the tool around it.

If you are buying a staple gun, shop for one that can be adjusted for

Staple Sizes for Tackers, Hammers, and Pliers			
STAPLE NO.	SIMILAR TO NO. OF MANUFACTURER'S GUN	MANUFACTURER'S NAME	WILL FIT
SC-D ¼"	508D ¼"	Duofast	CT-850
SC-D ⅜"	5012D ⅜"		CT-851
SC-D ½"	5016D ½"		CT-859
SC-D ⁹⁄₁₆"	5018D ⁹⁄₁₆"		HT-550
SC-B ¼"	STCR 5019 ¼"	Bostitch	T5-8
SC-B ⅜"	STCR 5019 ⅜"		T5-8 OC
SC-B ½"	STCR 5019 ½"		P4-8
SC-B ⁹⁄₁₆"	STCR 5019 ⁹⁄₁₆"		P4-8P
SC-C ¼"	.050 ¼"	Craftsman	9-68642
SC-C ⅜"	.050 ⅜"		9-68643
SC-C ½"	.050 ½"		9-6844
SC-C ⁹⁄₁₆"	.050 ⁹⁄₁₆"		—
SC-S ¼"	904 ¼"	Swingline	—
SC-S ⅜"	906 ⅜"		800
SC-S ½"	908 ½"		900
SC-S ⁹⁄₁₆"	909 ⁹⁄₁₆"		1000
SC-M ¼"	L3A ¼"	Markwell	—
SC-M ⅜"	L3C ⅜"		L-3
SC-M ½"	L3D ½"		P-3
SC-M ⁹⁄₁₆"	L3D ⁹⁄₁₆"		—
SC-A ¼"	T50 ¼"	Arrow	T-55
SC-A ⅜"	T50 ⅜"		T50
SC-A ½"	T50 ½"		HT50
SC-A ⁹⁄₁₆"	T50 ⁹⁄₁₆"		—
SC-SS ¼"	101-4	Swingline	101
SC-SS ⁵⁄₁₆"	101-5		200
SC-AS ¼"	JT21 ¼"	Arrow	JT21
SC-AS ⁵⁄₁₆"	JT21 ⁵⁄₁₆"		JT21

soft and hard materials. You may want to consider a gun that has different attachments, such as one for round and one for flat surfaces. And don't overlook the electric-powered guns; these units are fairly inexpensive and are excellent for stapling into soft to medium-hard materials.

Staples have two classifications: hammer-driven and machine-driven.

Hammer-driven staples include: hardwood and softwood fence staples, a heavy-duty drive staple; hook-head staple, flat wire or U-staple, flat cable staple, insulated wire staple, and poultry-netting staple. These names will appear on packages in stores. U staples are sold by sizes, and these are numbered:

No.	Inside Width (in.)	Leg Length (in.)
8	3/16	13/32
9	7/32	7/16
10	1/4	15/32
11	9/32	1/2
12	5/16	5/8
14	5/16	11/16
16	3/8	3/4

Machine-driven staples are sold in six classifications: blunt point, divergent point, chisel point, round crown cable staple, tack point single leg, and a high crown. This last type of staple mashes flat at the crown when it is driven flush with the material.

Unlike hammer-driven staples, machine staples are sold by size only. Five sizes are standard; brand names may not fit all makes of staplers, although the sizes are the same. Check the package as to the proper gun.

¼-inch staples: For screen wire, window shades, light upholstery fabrics, paper, thin leather, plastic sheeting.

⁵⁄₁₆-inch staples: For thin rigid-panel insulation, heavy fabrics, medium to heavy plastics, hardware cloth.

⅜-inch staples: For asphalt building paper, rigid-panel insulation, electric wires, hardware cloth, poultry netting, weatherstripping, light wood fabrication.

½-inch staples: For carpeting, glass fiber panels, heavy plastic, canvas, felt, heavy wire mesh, light wood fabrication.

⁹⁄₁₆-inch staples: For insulation board sheathing, heavy wire mesh, roofing, heavy fabrics, carpeting, ceiling tile. (Note: you can buy a ⁹⁄₁₆-inch ceiling tile staple with legs that splay for better holding. However, make sure the staple can be used in the brand of staple gun that you own.)

Electric nail guns drive small nails to attach paneling to framing and for other light jobs such as furniture assembly. The nails, which may be purchased in colors, are 1¹⁄₃₂ inches long and are stuck together in strips similar to staples for desk (paper) staplers. Electric guns are production-type tools and can save you a great deal of time if you have many nails to drive. The cost may be prohibitive, however, for routine household chores.

How staples are sold

Hammer-driven staples are sold prepackaged in home centers, usually by the pound box. Lumberyards and hardware stores may have these fasteners in bulk, but they will be also sold by weight. If you need just a couple of staples, the retailer may give you a price, if they're sold in bulk.

Machine-driven staples are sold in boxes that are labeled as to type, size, and the staple guns they are designed to fit. In home centers, machine-driven staples may be located in the ceiling tile department, rather than in the hardware area.

Special order

Staple sizes and types are plentiful and, therefore, you probably won't find it difficult to buy the ones you need.

Most home centers and other outlets that sell staples will special-order them for you, but expect a four-to-six-week delivery period. The cost may be slightly higher than store prices due to transportation charges.

If you can't locate the staples you want, write to the Consumer Information Director of these companies:

Arrow Fastener Co. Inc.
271 Mayhill St.
Saddle Brook, N.J. 07662

Bostitch Consumer Division
USM Corp.
Muhlenberg Industrial Mall
4408 Pottsville Pike
Reading, Pa. 19605

Swingline Inc.
32-00 Skillman Ave.
Long Island City, N.Y. 11101

Rivets and Pop Rivets

Hand-assembled rivets are wonderful fasteners: They are extremely inexpensive, take no skill to use, and grip like a bulldog.

There are four basic rivet types: two-piece hollow, solid, split, and tubular. These are manufactured from aluminum, steel, copper, brass, and bronze.

Sizes vary. As a guide, hollow and solid rivets should project no more than their diameter through the thickness of the material they will fasten.

For joining metal, use the following selection chart for sizes and weights:

Metal Gauge	Size/Weight Per K
	4 16
18	3½
20	3
22	2½
24	2
26	1

DON'T MIX METALS. A rivet must not be used to join a metal different from the metal it's made of. If it is, a chemical reaction between the metals causes corrosion and rust. If the metals to be joined are aluminum, use aluminum rivets; if copper, use copper; if iron, use iron; and so forth.

Usage

Hollow and tubular rivets are best used for soft materials such as leather, fabrics, and heavy canvas. Soft, solid rivets (aluminum and copper) also may be used for soft materials, including soft metals such as aluminum and copper. Solid and split rivets are used for heavy metals.

Pop rivets are used in a rivet gun to join metal parts up to ½-inch thick. The biggest advantage to Pop rivets is that they may be used for blind riveting where a bucking block can't be used to peen the other side of the rivet. A typical example would be fastening a downspout to a gutter or a register to a metal duct.

Pop rivets have two parts: a mandrel and the body of the rivet. The size of the rivet you use depends on the size of the hole which the body of the rivet should match. Diameters range from ⅛ to ¼ inch; metals are aluminum and steel; copper and aluminum metals are available, but they may be hard to locate in some areas.

There are two types of pop rivets: closed- and open-end. The closed-end type may be used with pipes and containers holding liquids or gas. The open-end type is made for general purpose work; it is not liquid- or gas-tight. Other special types of rivets include countersunk, threaded (for greater strength), and back-up plate, which has a washer under the head.

How rivets are sold

Rivets for hand assembly are usually packaged in boxes, although some hardware stores offer them in bulk.

Pop rivets are sold in packages that are labeled as to size, metal, and type. Be sure you know the brand name of the Pop rivet gun before buying rivets for it; all rivets may not fit your gun.

Special order

Stores that sell rivets usually will special-order them for you, although the retailers may be reluctant to do so if the order is a small one.

If you run into trouble finding a specific type of rivet, contact the Consumer Information Director at the following rivet manufacturers:

Townsend/Richline
Townsend Division, Textron Inc.
Box 43518
2515 Pilot Knob Rd.
St. Paul, Minn. 55164

Reed & Prince Manufacturing Co.
One Duncan Ave.
Worcester, Mass. 01613

Parker Manufacturing Co.
149 Washington St.
Worcester, Mass. 01613

Solder and Connections

There are five basic types of solder: bar, wire, paste, powder, and ingot. Bar and wire solder are stocked most commonly in home centers; hardware stores may have a wider variety of types. Wire and bar solder—and the necessary flux—will handle most home repair and improvement jobs.

The soft solders have a melting point under 800°F, while solders used for electrical projects contain different percentages of tin and lead to give melting points of about 400°F. Soft solders may be used on copper, tin, brass, and lead.

For galvanized steel, aluminum, and stainless steel, a brazing technique is used and special solders are required. These include aluminum, steel, nickel/silver, and bronze rods that are melted with propane torch-type or welding-brazing outfits. At least 800°F heat is required for the metals listed above; a soldering gun or iron doesn't concentrate the heat enough to melt the hard solder.

Acid core solder is used for projects such as sweating copper plumbing pipes for assembly. You can buy acid flux, if you use solid or bar solder for the job. Acid core solder already has the acid flux contained within the solder.

Rosin core solder must be used for any electrical project, since the acid flux will damage insulation around the wires. Rosin core has the flux built into the product, although you can buy a rosin core flux separately.

Alloy percentages are usually marked on rosin and acid core solder. The first number is tin; the second number is lead. A good mix for most plumbing jobs is 60/40 (60 percent tin and 40 percent lead) solder, although 95/5 is ideal if you have enough heat to melt it.

Soldering Flux Selector	
METAL	**FLUX TYPE**
Copper	Rosin
Brass and bronze	Rosin
Galvanized iron	Acid
Tin	Acid
Steel	Acid
Stainless steel	Acid
Lead	Water-soluble organic type
Aluminum	Special flux for aluminum
Silver	Rosin
Zinc	Acid
Pewter	Water-soluble organic type

Flux removes the oxide from metals, making the metals bond better with solder. Flux also helps prevent further oxidation of the metals; it is important to always use flux when soldering metals.

Flux is classified as non-corrosive, mildly corrosive, and corrosive. Rosin flux, for example, is non-corrosive. Fluxes are sold in paste and powder forms, or in the cores of solders as detailed above. (See box, this chapter for more information.)

How it's sold

Solder is sold in packages of wire rolls, or bars. Sometimes it's sold by weight.

Flux is sold by the can or tube. Both paste and powder flux are very easy to use, so it's a toss-up as to which is best.

Rod solder is sold by the rod; prices vary according to the type; stainless steel is more costly than steel.

Brazing/welding outfits are now priced within most homeowners' budgets. If you normally make a lot of metal connections, consider buying a unit of this type; they use the rod solders described above.

Special order

Solders are so readily available that you probably won't have any trouble finding the type you want. Home centers and lumberyards may be limited to types; hardware stores and welding supply outlets generally stock full lines of solder.

If you can't locate the solder product you want, write the Consumer Information Director of:

Turner Company
Div. of Cleanweld Products
821 Park
Sycamore, Ill. 60178

Kester Solder Co.
Div. of Litton Industries
4201 Wrightwood Ave.
Chicago, Ill. 60639

M.W. Dunton Co.
350 Kinsley Ave.
Providence, R.I. 02901

PLUMBING PRODUCTS

At first glance, the plumbing department in many home centers may appear to be skimpy, with not much merchandise for sale. But don't be fooled; most plumbing departments in home centers are stocked in depth. Products that once were dumped into long, wide bins now hang on hooks in neat, compact packages. And, if a salesperson isn't to be found, you will have to do some exploring to find the repair item needed to stop a leaking faucet, fix a flush tank, or unstop a clogged drain. That's what this chapter is all about: finding the right plumbing products for those annoying plumbing breakdowns. You'll also find that doing the repairs yourself can save plenty and that most of them aren't difficult.

Although home centers have a wide selection of plumbing products, you may not always find the item you need. In this event, your other options are hardware stores and specialized plumbing outlets that cater to the consumer—and often the pro. You will find the latter category listed in the telephone book advertising pages under "Plumbing Fixtures & Supplies—New Retail." For emergency products, such as drain openers and pipe leak kits, don't overlook drug, grocery, and variety stores. Although the selection may not be complete, these retailers often have "make-do" plumbing products that will work.

There are *only* two problems to cope with in any home plumbing system:

1. *Clogged pipes or drains.* The solutions to these problems are simple and direct: First try putting a caustic soda compound down the drain or working a plunger—a plumber's friend—up and down over the drain. If these methods don't work, you'll have to take off the trap or open up the cleanout and use an auger. The next step is to call a professional. For any outside problems, call a plumber immediately.

2. *Leaks in pipes, valves, and fixtures.* These problems are caused by

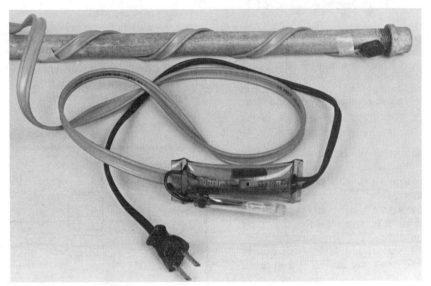

Pipes subjected to freezing should be wrapped with electrical heating tape that comes in various lengths. Quality

bad connections or defective parts. If leaks don't stop when you tighten the joints, then the defective joint or fixture must be replaced. Make sure you have identified the culprit accurately before you start to work.

Although plumbing may be complicated, it really isn't mysterious at all: Water and waste run through pipes to valves, which shut off or open the

tapes have a thermostat that automatically turns on the power when the temperature drops near 32°F.

pipes. The valves can be sink faucets or a rubber ball in a flush tank. These parts are all connected in one system that runs throughout the entire house.

How the system works

Take a minute to study how the water and waste pipes are connected in your home, as illustrated in this chapter. Familiarizing yourself with this plan

To stop pipe leaks, this clamp is one of the better devices to use. A rubber-type gasket is folded around the pipe after the water has been turned off.

Then the clamshell clamp is tightened against the gasket and the water turned on.

Epoxy putty is a good product to use to stop leaks around fittings. It is troweled around the threads with a putty knife or ice cream stick after the water has been turned on. It hardens in a few minutes and the water may be turned on.

from the various plumbing fixtures.

The soil stack is connected to the main sewer pipe. Both stack and the main sewer pipe have a cleanout access opening covered with a plug-type cap.

Water supply ranges from about ⅜ to 1 inch (inside diameter) in size. Drain or waste pipes measure from 1½ to 4 inches (inside diameter) in size.

Water pipes are always under pressure—usually 60 pounds per square inch (psi). Drain or waste pipes are never under pressure. They drain by gravity into the sewer system, which funnels the waste to a disposal plant or to a septic system.

Caution: *Before you make any repairs to the water system—including faucets, flush tanks, pipes, and pipe connections—make sure that the water is turned off at the main valve or at individual fixture shut-off valves under sinks, toilets, etc.*

If the system is opened without the valves being shut off, a flash flood can be expected immediately.

Plumbing terms

Plumbers and plumbing supply manufacturers have a set of terms that apply throughout the United States. For example, if you ask for a "union fitting," you'll get a union whether you're in Maine or California. Know-

will help you decide which products to buy when plumbing troubles arise.

Water probably comes into your home from a public utility. It passes through a water meter which keeps tabs on how much water the household uses. You are billed for this amount. If you have a well system, you don't pay for water, and therefore, there is no meter. However, the system will work the same from the entrance point on throughout the house.

At—or near—the meter or water entrance is a shut-off valve that controls the water flow for both hot and cold water. By closing this valve, the water is stopped completely.

The incoming water supply splits or divides just before the water heater. From that point on, there are two sets of water supply pipes—one for cold water and one for hot water produced by the heater.

If necessary, you can trace the pipes quickly, using the hot water heater as the base point. As you face the heater on the control side, the cold water pipe will be on the right; the hot water pipe will be on the left of the heater. Check carefully by touch. As the pipes snake through the house, they usually run parallel to each other.

Drainage pipes can be identified by size: they are always larger than water supply pipes. Drainage pipes, or waste pipes, channel water and sewage from the kitchen sink, lavatories, bathtub/shower, toilets, etc., in the house.

The largest pipe in this waste connection is the soil stack. The top of it sticks out of the roof to vent odors

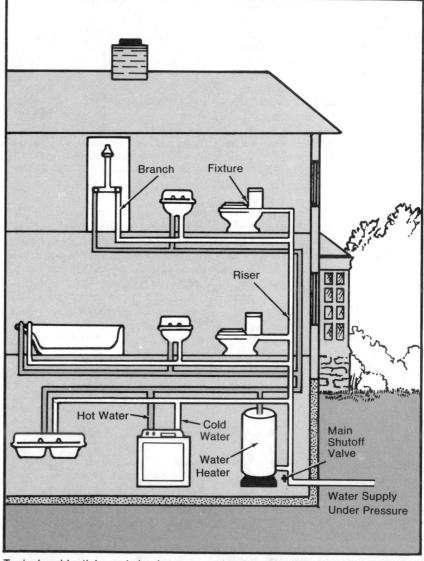

Typical residential supply hookup: Water comes in through meter and is then distributed throughout the house. The black lines denote hot water. The drawing shows how runs are connected, and where to look when problems with the water supply arise.

ing this nomenclature before you go shopping for any plumbing product can save you time and money.

Pipes, whether they carry water supply or waste, are classified by material: galvanized steel, copper, plastic, brass, and cast iron. Waste pipes are often stamped DWV for Drain-Waste-Vent, which describes their use. Other materials used for pipe—usually for waste systems—include vitrified clay, lead, asbestos-cement, and bituminized-fiber.

Fittings are pipe connections. These include unions, elbows, tees, reducing couplings, etc. (See chart, this chapter.) The types, of course, are matched to the pipes: galvanized steel, copper, plastic, etc.

Fixtures are the devices pipes connect to, such as toilets, sinks, wash basins, showers, etc.

Valves also are connected to pipes; these are the faucets or shut-offs that control the flow of water.

Risers are water supply pipes that channel water above the place where the water enters a house or high-rise building.

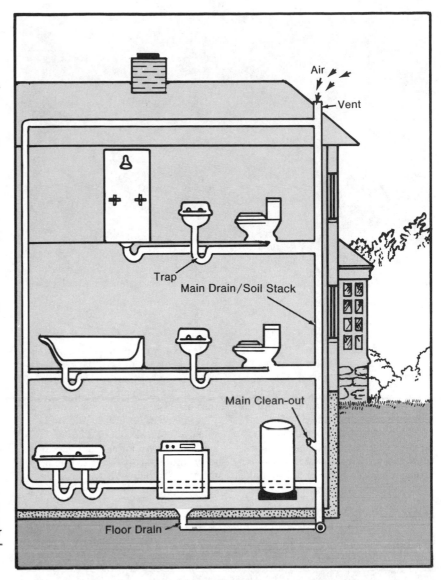

Typical residential drainage hookup. The sinks, lavatories, toilets, and tubs all have a P or S trap; the drain lines from the traps run to the main drain or stack. The drain lines may have cleanouts along the system, as well as at the main drain.

All About Pipe

The nominal size of a pipe is always determined by the inside diameter (i.d.). For example, a ¾-inch pipe will have a ¾-inch inside diameter or *approximately* a ¾-inch diameter. The actual size may vary slightly, but this is not important when buying pipe. Just ask for the nominal size you require. The standardized fittings and fixtures will fit the size that you specify.

The larger the pipe, the more water it delivers. Water supply pipes with a nominal size of ¾ to 1 inch (i.d.) are the workhorses that deliver the water

directly to the fixtures or to a smaller pipe, usually copper or plastic tubing, which may have an ⅛- to ¼-inch (i.d.) nominal size.

Smaller-diameter pipes are adequate for sinks, lavatories and toilets, while the larger sizes are best for faucets such as outside silcocks.

When buying pipes and fittings, be sure to match the metals: copper to copper, steel to steel, and so forth. Joining different metals causes a chemical reaction that can produce corrosion, rust, and eventually leaks. Two different-size pipes are joined

with reducing fitting. The hookup between different types of pipe—copper-to-plastic, plastic-to-galvanized steel, etc.—is made with an adaptor fitting, and it will be labeled as such in most stores.

Drain or waste pipe (DWV) also is measured by inside diameter, and the size may vary slightly. These pipes can be threaded, soldered, solvent-welded, clamped together with a gasket, or joined with lead, depending on the material from which they are manufactured. These techniques are explained later in this chapter under

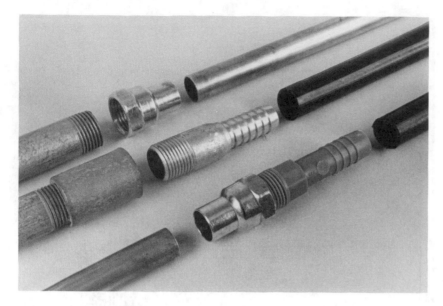

Standard adapters for converting pipe runs from steel to copper, copper to plastic, etc., include, from the top: galvanized steel to copper pipe; galvanized steel to flexible plastic tubing; copper pipe to plastic tubing or pipe.

specific pipe and fittings.

Plumbing supplies are located in the plumbing departments of most stores, although DWV pipe and fittings may be located in the hard materials department (cement, sand) or the lawn and garden department. Pipes and fittings are displayed together so you can thread or push the fittings on various-size pipes to make sure you have the item you want.

The best way to shop for single repair products is to take the old part—pipe, fitting, washer, cartridge, gasket—to the store and match it. Second best is to measure exactly the part you want to replace and even make a rough sketch of it so the salesperson will know what you are after. If the part has a brand name jot this down, along with any other information that may be embossed on the part. The more information, the easier it is to find the right replacement.

If you are adding plumbing to an existing run—or replacing an existing run—always take a sketch plan of the installation to the store. The sketch doesn't have to be fancy, but it should include dimensions so you go home with the right parts. Also, if the salesperson knows his business, he may suggest plumbing shortcuts that will save you time and money.

Most home centers stock galvanized steel pipe, copper pipe, and copper tubing. Depending on plumbing codes in your community, the store may also stock plastic pipe.

DWV pipe, with the exception of plastic and a small selection of cast-iron fittings, may not be stocked by some retailers; you can find it at specialty plumbing stores. Special DWV pipe such as lead asbestos-cement seldom is stocked by home centers, but it is a regular item at plumbing supply shops.

Galvanized steel pipe

Galvanized steel pipe is manufactured from steel, and galvanized to deter rust. A similar pipe is made for gas lines, but is colored black so you can tell the difference. Galvanized steel pipe costs less than copper; it is resistant to shocks such as blows from a hammer or other object. If your water supply is strongly alkaline, galvanized pipe will tend to accumulate lime and scale deposits, reducing the water flow.

Plumbing Pipe Selector

TYPE OF PIPE	PIPE USE	FABRICATION
Cast iron	DWV only	Bell and spigot ends of hub pipe go together with oakum and molten lead. No-hub is joined with plastic sleeves and clamps.
Copper/flexible	Hot and cold water lines	With solder, compression rings and nuts; by flaring.
Copper/rigid	Hot and cold water lines and DWV	Generally soldered.
Galvanized steel	Hot and cold water lines and DWV	Threaded.
Black steel	Gas lines; may be used for hot water	Threaded.
Brass/bronze	Hot and cold water lines	Threaded.
Plastic/CPVC/rigid	Hot and cold water lines	Solvent-welded.
Plastic PVC	Cold water and DWV only	Solvent welded.
Polybutylene/flexible	Hot and cold water lines	Special clamp-type fittings.
ABS/rigid	DWV only	Solvent welded.

Pipe measurements are made from face-to-face between fittings plus the length of the threads that go into the fittings (see chart, below.) For measuring pipe runs—where the pipe will go through walls and floors—figure from center-to-center between the pipe. Do this by measuring from one side of the pipe to the same side of the adjoining pipe. Center-to-center in this illustration would be 6¾ inches.

Basic sizes of galvanized steel pipe, although not always readily available in all sizes, include ⅛, ¼, ⅜, ½, ¾, 1, 1¼, 1½, 2, and 2½ inches. All connections are threaded for necessary fittings or adaptors.

To assemble or disassemble galvanized steel pipe these tools are needed: two pipe wrenches, pipe cutter or hacksaw, a metal file, pipe reamer, cutting oil, and pipe joint compound. If you thread the pipe yourself, you will need a pipe die cutter and a vise. These two tools often can be rented.

HOW IT'S SOLD. Galvanized steel pipe is sold by size, diameter and length. Standard lengths in home centers and hardware outlets may be limited to 2, 4, 6, 10, and 12 feet, with both ends threaded to accept fittings. Longer lengths—up to 22 feet—usually are available at plumbing supply shops; these lengths may or

may not be threaded.

Nipples are short lengths of galvanized steel pipe that measure from about 1½ to 12 inches long; nipples are threaded at both ends for fittings.

To determine the length of pipe needed, measure from the face (opening) of one fitting to the adjoining fitting. Add one inch to the overall dimension for pipe under one inch in nominal size; the threads turn into the fitting ½ inch at each end. If the pipe is from 1 to 2 inches in nominal size, add 1¼ inches to the overall dimension; the threads turn into the fitting ⅝ inch at each end.

Threads on galvanized steel pipe are slightly tapered. As the threads are turned into the fitting, the taper causes a tight fit between the pipe and fitting. Never overtighten fittings; overtightening can strip the threads or, worse, split the pipe or fitting.

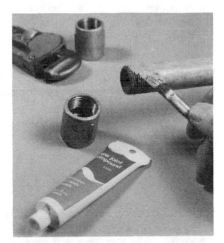

Pipe joint compound has the consistency of thin putty; it is smeared on the male threads of galvanized steel pipe before the pipe is turned into a fitting. The compound makes assembly easier and seals the threads to help prevent leaking.

Pipe Length Calculator		
PIPE SIZE	DISTANCE INTO FITTINGS	DISTANCE INTO DRAIN FITTINGS
½ inch	½ inch	None
¾ inch	½ inch	None
1 inch	⅝ inch	⅝ inch
1¼ inches	⅝ inch	⅝ inch
1½ inches	⅝ inch	⅝ inch
2 inches	¾ inch	⅞ inch
3 inches	None	1 inch
4 inches	None	None

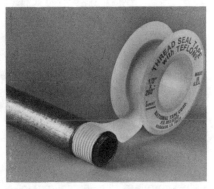

Plastic thread tape does the same job as joint compound—seals threads against leaks—but is less messy to use. It is available in several widths.

Two pipe wrenches should always be used in the assembly and disassembly of galvanized steel or threaded pipe. The jaws of the wrenches should be opposed, as shown here, for the proper turning pressure on the pipe and fitting. Go easy on the torque.

Galvanized steel fittings

There are many different galvanized steel fittings available, but you probably will be concerned with only seven of them: 45° and 90° elbows, tees, reducing couplings, straight couplings, caps, and plugs. The fittings are threaded inside and/or outside to match the threads on the pipe. If you are adding copper or plastic pipe to an existing galvanized steel system, you will need a copper or plastic adaptor fitting. These adaptor fittings are usually located with the standard fittings.

UNION FITTINGS. Standard galvanized steel pipe fittings—elbows, couplings, tees, etc.—turn *one* way. Therefore, when a pipe section is being repaired or a new section is being added to an existing section, a union fitting must be used so the pipe threads may be turned in the opposite direction. The union has three parts: two end pieces that screw into a common center. The end pieces have inside threads so the pipe may be connected like a straight coupling. Unions may be used almost anyplace along a plumbing run or section.

Threads on fittings are either male or female. Male threads are on the outside of the fitting; female threads are on the inside.

Common fittings and their specific uses are listed below:

Couplings are used to join two or more pieces of pipe in a run or section.

Reducing couplings join pipe of one size to a larger—or smaller—size.

Street elbow fittings with 45° or 90° angles have female threads on one end and male threads on the other end.

Regular and reducing crosses join four pipes in a single fitting.

Y-branches join two pipes end-to-end and a third pipe at a 45° angle.

Bushings change the diameter of a large pipe to a smaller one—or vice versa—where reducing elbows and couplings can't be used.

Return bends join two or more pipes that run parallel to each other.

Pipe joint compound or tape is placed on male threads to help prevent leaking after the pipe connections have been made. The compound, which is similar to putty, is smeared on the male threads in a thin coating. It may be purchased in a tube or can.

Union fitting almost always is used to assemble galvanized steel (and some copper) pipe because the threads on two opposing fittings turn in opposite directions. In this example, one straight piece of pipe couldn't be threaded into both 45° elbows; a union fitting is needed to make the connection.

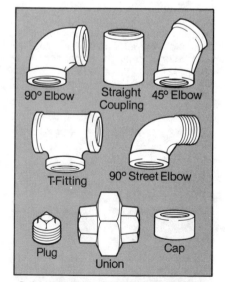

Galvanized steel pipe fittings. The ones used most in plumbing repairs, shown here, are all manufactured in different sizes. Other specialized designs are stocked at home centers and hardware stores. Most repairs require a union fitting.

90° Elbow   Straight Coupling   45° Elbow

T-Fitting   90° Street Elbow

Plug   Union   Cap

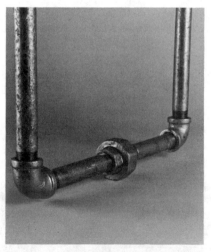

Once assembled with a union fitting, the pipe run looks like this. One half of the fitting has been screwed into one piece of pipe. Then the outer ring is loosely screwed onto that half. The other half of the fitting is threaded onto the other piece of pipe and then into the ring. Then the entire assembly is tightened with two wrenches.

Saddle tee fitting is used to quickly tap into a water supply pipe for a new water supply pipe, which can be galvanized steel, copper, or bronze. The water is first drained from the line, then a hole is drilled into the line, the tee is connected with a clamp and gasket, and finally the new line is connected.

Plastic pipe tape is wrapped around the male threads before the connections to fittings are made. A couple of layers of the extremely thin ribbon is adequate.

HOW IT'S SOLD. Fittings are sold by the piece. If the fitting has more than one part to it, such as a union fitting, it is sold as a unit. Most galvanized steel fittings are not packaged so that you have an opportunity to try the fitting on the pipe.

SPECIAL ORDER. Galvanized steel pipe and fittings are so commonplace that special-ordering it usually isn't necessary. If your regular retailer is out of stock on an item, you almost always will find it at another store.

If all fails, however, below are several companies that may be able to help with your specific problem. Write them in care of the Consumer Information Director:

U.S. Steel Corp.,
525 William Penn Pl.
Pittsburgh, Pa. 15219

Anaconda American Brass Co.
414 Meadow St.
Waterbury, Conn. 06702

Aluminum Co. of America
1501 Alcoa Building
Pittsburgh, Pa. 15219

National Clay Pipe Institute
1130 Seventeenth St. N.W.
Washington, D.C. 20016

Copper pipe and tubing

Copper costs more than its galvanized steel and plastic cousins, but copper pipe and tubing has advantages that may be worth it. Copper pipe, called rigid copper, and copper tubing are corrosion-resistant, lightweight, and easy to assemble and disassemble, using several techniques.

There are four types of rigid copper pipe: Types K, L, M, and DWV. There are two types of copper tubing: Types K and L.

There are no essential differences between rigid copper and tubing, except the tubing bends easily so it can be snaked around corners and splayed at slight angles.

Type K rigid is heavy-walled; it is used mostly for underground runs.
Type L rigid has medium-thick walls; it is best for interior plumbing runs.
Type M rigid has thin walls; it also is used for interior plumbing runs.
Type DWV (drain-waste-vent) is very thin-walled; it, of course, is used for drains, waste, and venting.
Type M and DWV may be restricted by plumbing codes in your area,

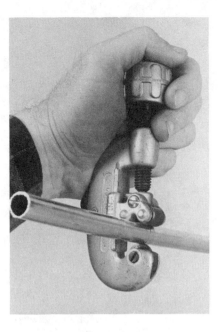

Cutter for copper pipe and tubing is rotated around the pipe or tubing, while cutting pressure is applied by screwing down the knob. The cutter is better than a hacksaw for this job because the cut ends are perfectly square, which they must be to fit properly into the copper fittings.

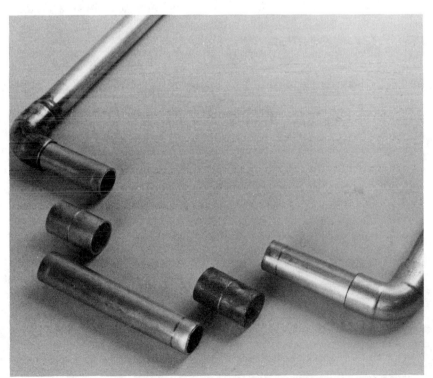

To replace a leaky run in copper pipe, you need two straight couplings and a length of pipe. By cutting into the run, disassembly and re-sweating of the 45° elbows is avoided; the straight couplings are easier to solder. The same technique is used for galvanized steel pipe. But instead of the couplings, a union fitting is used to connect the run.

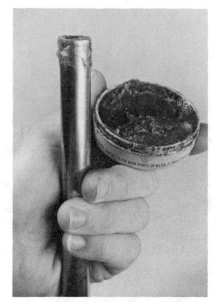

Non-corrosive flux must be used when assembling copper pipe with solder. The flux may come in a can, as shown here, or come in the core of the solder itself. The flux is marked ''for copper'' on most packages. Paste flux should be applied with an old toothbrush or an ice cream stick after the pipe has been buffed shiny clean with steel wool. Avoid touching the pipe with your fingers after it has been buffed: oil from your skin can produce a bad joint.

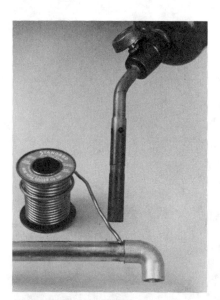

A propane torch, with replaceable gas containers, is the best heat source for sweating copper pipe. Heat from the torch must be directed to the fitting, while the solder is touched to the pipe or fitting at the joint. Through capillary action, the solder is drawn into the fitting, and a bead of solder formed around the joint. To disassemble a soldered joint, heat the fitting and pull the pipe out of it.

and, therefore, may not be available.

Type L is a standard stock item at most home center and hardware stores; Type K may be limited to plumbing stores.

Copper tubing is available in Type K and Type L. Although it may be bent at slight angles, the tubing can kink, so it must be handled with care. Both types usually are a stock item at most home center and hardware outlets.

PIPE SIZES. Copper pipe is available in 10- and 20-foot lengths; you may find it in shorter lengths—4, 6, and 8 feet—depending on the retailer.

Diameters are ⅜, ½, ¾, 1, 1¼, 2, and 3 inches, and the outside diameter of the pipe will be approximately ⅛ inch more than its nominal size.

When buying pipe, you must add the *depth* of the fitting to the length of the pipe. Since the depths of fittings can vary slightly, you can test the fitting on the pipe in the store so you can buy the material you need.

As a rule of thumb, you can safely add ½ inch to each end of the pipe for the fittings. Trimming it to size is no problem with a tube cutter.

Copper tubing is available in 15-, 30-, and 60-foot lengths. The shorter lengths usually are packaged in rolls. Standard diameters are ⅛ and ¼ inch.

JOINING. Copper pipe is assembled with solder; copper tubing with compression fittings.

A propane torch provides heat for soldering; you'll also need rosin-core solder or rosin flux (never acid), medium-grit abrasive or steel wool, a tube cutter or hacksaw, and (if possible) a metal-working vise or locking-type pliers.

For a mechanical joint—used mainly for flexible tubing—a flaring block is needed to flare the ends of the tubing to accept the compression fitting. Or, a ring-type compression fitting may be used. In this type, a ring is slipped over the end of the tubing and a nut snugs the ring and pipe tightly to a valve or fixture. The ring-type system is by far the easiest way to connect the tubing, if this technique can be used. A salesperson may be able to show you how it works. If not, manufacturers usually have detailed instructions printed on the backs of the compression nut packages.

An adjustable wrench is needed to assemble flared and compression fittings.

Standard copper fittings are similar to those manufactured from galvanized steel—except the type of metal. Types that you'll be mostly concerned with include tees, 45° and 90° elbows, street elbows, caps, plugs, and couplings.

Compression fittings are the best way to assemble copper tubing. The procedure is this: cut the tubing square. Slip the compression nut on the tubing and then the compression ring. Put the tubing into the fitting and tighten the nut on the fitting, wedging the ring against the sides of the fitting.

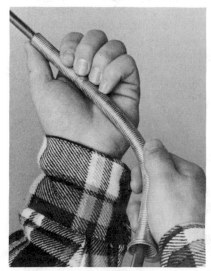

A tube bender, a spring-like device, is used to bend copper tubing for turns. The coiled spring is slipped over the pipe and the two are bent with your hands or over your knee. The bender works best if you overbend the tubing slightly and then carefully bend it back to the angle you want.

A flared fitting is used on copper tubing. The flare is made with a flaring tool called a block. To make the joint, the flare is pressed against the beveled fitting and held tight by a threaded nut. Inexpensive flaring blocks handle most standard sizes of copper tubing.

Adapters

Increaser

¼ Street Bend

Sanitary Tee with Side Inlet

Closet Flange

Sanitary Tee

Reducing Coupling

Drum Trap

⅛ Bend

45° Wye

P Trap

Cleanout with Plug

¼ Bend

Slip Coupling

Roof Flashing

Straight Coupling

Soil Pipe Adapter

Copper fittings used in most repair projects are shown here. More designs, to fit almost any plumbing situation, are stocked in home centers and hardware stores.

Copper pipe also uses union fittings so the run may be broken without disassembling pipes at soldered fittings.

The fittings have tiny shoulders that you can see inside the fittings; the pipe must fit against these shoulders so there are no leaks. Make sure the pipe is cut absolutely square. A tube cutter always does the job, if you handle it correctly.

Fittings for compression assembly include tees, 90° elbows, unions, female copper-to-steel adapters, and male copper-to-steel adapters.

HOW IT'S SOLD. Rigid copper pipe is sold by the length of the piece or by the linear foot.

Flexible copper tubing sometimes is sold by the length of the piece, but, most often, it is priced by the pre-packaged roll.

Most retailers won't cut pipe or tubing to your specific measurements. You will have to buy the entire piece or roll to get the material you need. The only exception to this is flexible tubing. Some specialized plumbing shops will cut small lengths from a master roll.

Fittings are sold by the piece. If you need a large quantity of fittings, a retailer may give you a discount, but you have to ask for it.

Copper pipe and tubing tools, such as propane torches, tube cutters, solder, and flux, are sold by the item and never in kits.

You should sketch the project you're undertaking before shopping for tools and materials. This way, you can be reasonably sure you'll get what you need in one trip. Include detailed measurements on the sketch.

Assemble the project without solder or nuts to make sure the plumbing run fits properly. This can save the time and work of breaking joints and re-soldering them.

The smartest trick in assembling copper pipe and tubing is to have as few fitting connections as possible. Correct measuring and double-checking the measurements before you buy is the way to do this.

SPECIAL ORDER. Copper pipe, flexible copper tubing, and standard fittings are plentiful. You shouldn't have any difficulty finding what you need for a specific project.

Unless a large quantity is involved, most home centers and hardware outlets will not special-order copper plumbing for you. Some specialty

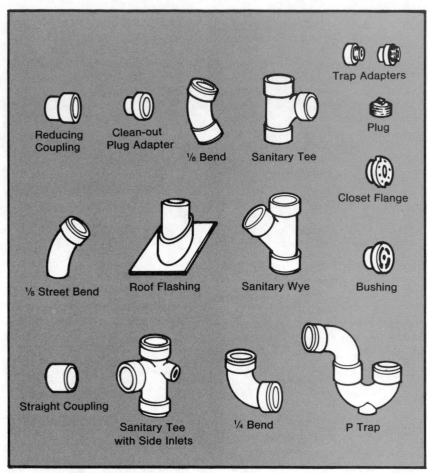

Plastic pipe fittings like these are used for most plumbing repairs and remodeling. Many more designs are available at most home centers and hardware stores. Before you buy any plastic pipe, make sure local codes permit its use.

plumbing shops will special-order, but you will pay extra for this service. Expect to wait from four to six weeks for a special order.

If you get into plumbing difficulty and can't find the proper products for the job, write to the Consumer Information Director of these companies:

Anaconda American Brass Co.
414 Meadow St.
Waterbury, Conn. 06702

The Plumb Shop
620 Fisher Building
Detroit, Mich. 48202

Nichols-Homeshield Inc.
15 Spinning Wheel Rd.
Hinsdale, Ill. 60521

Chicago Specialty Mfg. Co.
7500 Linder Ave.
Skokie, Ill. 60077

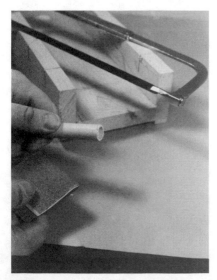

Remove all burrs with a file after cutting plastic pipe absolutely square with a hacksaw. The end of the pipe must fit squarely against a shoulder inside the fitting or the pipe will leak water.

Plastic pipe

If your local code permits, plastic pipe, tubing, and fittings are a do-it-yourselfer's plumbing repair and improvement dream. Plastic pipe runs go together in a twinkling of an eye; the fittings are solvent-welded onto pipes with cement applied by the tip of a small artist's brush. The fittings may also be strap-clamped to the pipe.

There are four standard types of plastic pipe available in most home centers, hardware, and specialty plumbing shops:

Chlorinated polyvinyl chloride (CPVC) is rigid pipe. It is used for both hot and cold water plumbing systems.

Polyvinyl chloride (PVC) is a rigid pipe used only for cold water supply systems.

Polybutylene (PB) is flexible tubing used for hot and cold water systems.

Acrylonitrile-butadiene styrene (ABS) is rigid pipe that is used for DWV purposes only.

Polyethylene (PE) pipe, popular for water supply to lawn sprinklers, irrigation, and other underground uses, is manufactured in several weights.

Styrene rubber (SR) is rigid pipe that is used basically underground.

Polypropylene (PP) pipe is rigid and may be used for draining systems, such as fixture traps, sink and lavatory tail pieces, and drain-trap extensions.

Two cautions: Do not use plastic pipe for natural gas distribution. Do not mix plastics; that is, do not connect ABS to CPVC. The chemical difference between the two products can set up a reaction causing the pipe system to crack and leak.

Most plastic pipe is stamped with a product label that will help you select the right product. A typical label will read: "CPVC, 100 PSI, Hot-Cold Water Pipe." This means that the plastic is chlorinated polyvinyl chloride; that it will withstand water pressure to 100 pounds per square inch (most utilities have a 60 psi factor), and the pipe may be used for both hot and cold water supply. The size of the pipe often is included in the label. It may read: "⅝" OD X ½" ID." This means that the pipe has a ⅝-inch outside diameter and a ½-inch inside diameter.

Fittings for plastic pipe are similar in type and construction to fittings for copper pipe. The fittings have tiny shoulders inside, and the pipe butts against these shoulders to make the system leakproof.

Fittings for the pipe will have size information marked on the product bins, not stamped on fittings. There-fore, be sure to test the fitting on the pipe to make sure they are the same size.

Basic fittings include tees, 45° and 90° elbows, 90° street elbows, couplings, caps, plugs, and plastic-to-steel and plastic-to-copper adapters. Unions are not used since the pipe is solvent-welded and simply stuck together. If you repair a run or add to the run, you must cut the section of pipe since a solvent weld cannot be disassembled.

Like copper pipe, plastic pipe must be cut perfectly square on the ends so the pipe fits tightly against the shoulders inside the fittings. Make sure the fit is as perfect as possible before applying the solvent cement to the pipe and pushing the pipe into the fitting. Once in place, the pipe cannot be removed from the fitting, since the solvent-weld is permanent.

ASSEMBLY. Plastic pipe is assembled with a solvent cement, but since there are different solvent cements for different plastics, make sure you buy the right cement for the plastic you're joining. The label on the solvent cement container will tell you what types it can be used on.

Flexible plastic pipe and tubing are assembled with clamps similar to those used on auto radiator hoses. A coupling is inserted in the ends of the tubing to be joined and the clamps are tightened against this coupling. The worm-drive clamps and couplings are sized and usually labeled as to what pipe they fit.

Tools for plastic pipe are limited to a hacksaw, miterbox, metal file, and sandpaper for smoothing the plastic pipe surfaces before they go into the fittings.

HOW IT'S SOLD. Plastic pipe, fittings, and accessories usually can be found in the plumbing department of most home centers and hardware outlets. The pipe is sold by the length or piece; it is seldom sold by the linear foot. A retailer won't cut a short length of pipe from a longer length to meet your measurement specifications; you will have to purchase the entire piece.

Fittings are sold by the piece, and the more complex the fitting, the more it costs. Size sometimes influences price.

Solvents, clamps, and the couplings for clamp assembly are sold by the item, and not in a kit.

SPECIAL ORDER. Retailers may be reluctant to special-order plastic

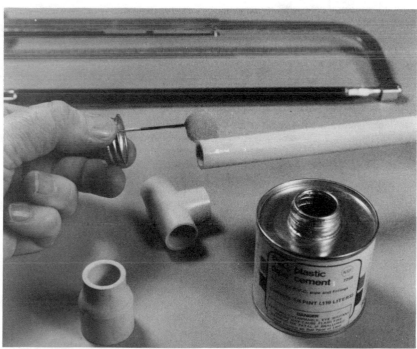

Plastic pipe is assembled with a specific cement that forms a solvent weld. Before the cement is applied, however, dry-assemble the pipe to make sure that it fits satisfactorily. Once solvent-welded, the pipe can not be disassembled at the welds; it must be cut.

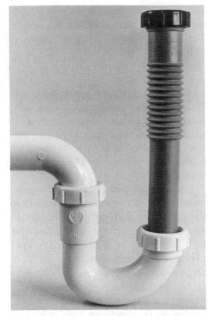

Flexible trap pipe is available in plastic systems so the pipe may be aligned without excess cutting and fitting. In drain lines, plastic can be joined with metal, usually without special adapters since there is no water pressure in the pipe.

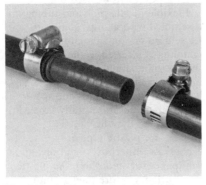

Flexible plastic pipe is joined with an inside fitting and clamps similar to those used for auto radiator hose connections. When buying clamps and fittings be sure to match the diameters of the pipe; mismatched connections will leak water.

pipe, fittings, and accessories for you since these materials are usually a standard stock item. You may be able to get a quantity discount if you purchase a lot of material; it's worth asking about.

If you can't find the product you want, contact the Consumer Information Director of these companies:

Can-Tex Industries
Division of Harsco Corp.
Box 340
Mineral Wells, Tex. 76067

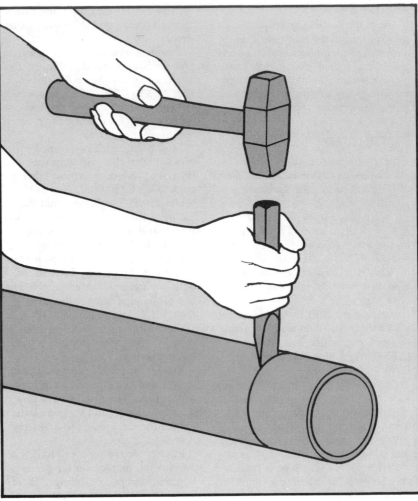

To cut hub-type cast-iron pipe, first score a line with a hacksaw. Then use a chisel and baby sledge to fracture the pipe. You may be able to rent a pipe cutter at a tool rental outlet. Cast-iron pipe is assembled with oakum and molten lead, which are placed in the hub, or bell, of the pipe.

Colonial Plastics Mfg. Co.
8107 Grand Ave.
Cleveland, Ohio 44104

DuPont de Nemours & Co.
Product Information Section
Wilmington, Del. 19898

Cast-iron pipe

For soil and waste stacks, cast-iron pipe is the favorite, and is reasonably easy for a do-it-yourselfer to assemble—especially no-hub pipe which goes together with plastic gaskets instead of with the molten lead used with hub pipe.

Both hub and no-hub pipe may be subject to code restrictions in your community. Be sure to check the codes before you buy and install either system.

Sizes of cast-iron pipe are 2-, 3-, and 4-inch diameters, in lengths of 5 and 10 feet. Because of weight, the short sections are easier to handle.

Cast-iron pipe is generally used for underground drainage systems, but it may be used for a drainage run from a toilet to a soil stack. It often is used as the soil stack instead of lead pipe.

Hub pipe has a bead—called a spigot—on one end, which goes into the adjoining pipe's bell-shaped hub. Then the hub is packed with oakum and calked with molten lead poured in to seal the joint. This is fairly easy to do on vertical joints, but on horizontal joints the project can become complicated. A special joint runner and clamp are used to funnel the molten lead around the joint.

In a vertical run, hub pipe must always be installed with the hub end facing up. In a horizontal run, the hub must face upstream.

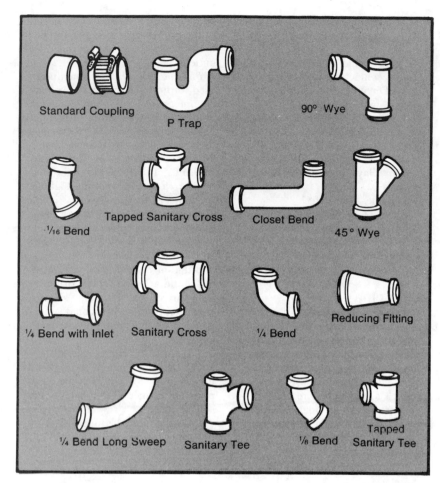

Standard Coupling

P Trap

90° Wye

¹⁄₁₆ Bend

Tapped Sanitary Cross

Closet Bend

45° Wye

¼ Bend with Inlet

Sanitary Cross

¼ Bend

Reducing Fitting

¼ Bend Long Sweep

Sanitary Tee

⅛ Bend

Tapped Sanitary Tee

ample), the higher the price. Pipe and fittings may be available in light- and heavy-weight grades; the heavy weight costs more.

Most retailers won't cut cast-iron pipe for you. If you need a length shorter than that stocked, you will have to buy the available length and cut it to fit.

Gaskets, clamps, oakum, lead, and joint runners are sold by the item, not in kits. Hangers are sold individually.

Before you shop for cast-iron pipe, determine the type you want to handle, and check the codes in your local community. Then make a sketch—with accurate dimensions—of how the pipe will be assembled, and draw up a list of all the fittings and lengths of pipe you need.

SPECIAL ORDER. Like other plumbing supplies, cast-iron pipe is plentiful in most areas. However, you may not find it stocked in some home centers and hardware stores. Specialty plumbing outlets, such as those that cater to the professional, almost always have a wide range of sizes and fittings to fill your needs; they also have any accessories needed, such as lead, gaskets, oakum, hangers, etc.

If you can't locate what you want, contact the Consumer Information Director of the following companies:

Triangle PWC Inc.
Box 711
New Brunswick, N.J. 08903

U.S. Steel Corp.
600 Grant St.
Pittsburgh, Pa. 15230

Jones & Laughlin Steel Corp.
3 Gateway Center
Pittsburgh, Pa. 15263

No-hub pipe fittings include these standard fittings. No-hub pipe is recommended for do-it-yourself assembly because it is easier to work with than hub-type, cast-iron pipe. No-hub can be spliced into an existing run of hub-type pipe; leaks at no-hub joints are easy to stop by simply tightening the clamp.

Hub pipe may be cut by scoring it with a hacksaw at the cut-off point to a depth of about ¹⁄₁₆ inch. A baby sledge and cold chisel are used to fracture the pipe, which breaks clean after a few taps.

No-hub pipe is better suited for do-it-yourself installation because the pipes are joined with a neoprene gasket and clamps, instead of oakum and molten lead. Cut-off pieces of pipe may be used instead of thrown away, and if the pipe becomes misaligned during assembly, the clamps may be quickly loosened and the pipe moved into the correct position.

Local codes permitting, no-hub pipe may be joined with hub pipe, and no-hub pipe may be used in underground drainage systems. No-hub pipe doesn't have a flow direction, so the pipe can be assembled almost in any way you want. However, the pipe openings should be as free-flow as

possible to prevent clogging; butt the ends of pipe sections up tight, but don't twist the gasket out of shape.

Connections or fittings for cast-iron pipe are similar to other pipe fittings with one important exception: the bends in fittings are not specified in degrees (45°, 90°, etc.) but in fractions of a circle; for example, a 90° turn is called a ¼ bend; a 45° turn is a ⅛ bend.

Standard fittings include Y-branches, double Y-branches, sanitary crosses, U-, P-, and S-traps, single and double ¼ bends, ⅛ bends, tees, and short and long sweeps.

HOW IT'S SOLD. Cast-iron hub and no-hub pipe are sold by the piece; the lengths available vary considerably. The fittings are sold by the piece also. The length of the pipe affects the price; the design of the fitting also affects the price: the more involved the design (an S-trap, for ex-

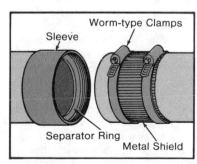

Worm-type Clamps

Sleeve

Separator Ring

Metal Shield

No-hub pipe connection consists of a sleeve and a shield. The sleeve, which is a neoprene plastic, slips over the pipe joint. The shield clamps are then installed over the sleeve; they hold the joint tight so it doesn't leak.

Vitrified-clay pipe

Since it is not damaged by acids, solvents, alkalies, or other household chemicals and solvents, vitrified-clay pipe is normally used underground, especially for septic systems. It is sometimes used for flue liners in gas heating systems.

There are two grades: standard and extra heavy; both are hub design; the joints are self-sealing—that is, they are wedged together—or are filled and sealed with regular Portland cement mortar.

Lengths are limited to 2, 2½, and 3 feet (standard) in the popular diameter of 4 inches. Slightly smaller and larger sizes may be available to satisfy codes.

Vitrified-clay pipe most often is sold at retailers specializing in plumbing pipes and fittings, and, sometimes, at companies selling concrete blocks, bricks, and other hard materials. Home centers and hardware stores may stock the product, but the stock will probably be limited, since it is considered a professional item.

Pipe and connections, which include Y junctions, tees, Y and T saddles, pipe reducers and increasers, running, P, and vent traps and elbows are sold by the piece. Both size and design determine price.

If your project calls for vitrified-clay pipe and you can't locate it in your area or find specific information about it, contact the Consumer Information Director at the following companies:

Columbus Clay Mfg. Co.
New Straitsville, Ohio 43766

Superior Clay Corp.
Box 352
Uhrichsville, Ohio 44683

National Clay Pipe Institute
1015 Fifteenth St. N.W.
Washington, D.C. 20005

Other pipe

Professionals use pipe and fittings made of the materials listed here more often than the do-it-yourselfer, because of weight, local codes, and the special equipment needed. But you should be familiar with these products and how they're used.

Concrete pipe is similar to vitrified-clay pipe with hub-and-spigot ends, and is assembled the same way. Standard lengths are 2, 2½, 3, and 4 feet and diameters are 4 to 24 inches (and larger). Look for it at shops catering to the professional plumber and at hard materials (concrete, brick, block) outlets.

Bituminized-fiber pipe sometimes is used for home drainage and sewers. It is impregnated with a coal-tar pitch that makes it waterproof. It is slightly flexible so it bends without cracking.

Standard sizes are diameters of 2 to 8 inches and lengths of 5 and 8 feet. The ends of the pipe are slightly tapered so a fitting (coupling) tightens the joints as they are hand-assembled. The coupling is simply driven onto the pipe with a baby sledge and wooden buffer block to protect the edges of the material.

Bituminized-fiber pipe is usually not found at home centers or most hardware outlets. Plumbing shops that cater to the professional generally stock this item, plus the necessary couplings.

Lead pipe sometimes is used for above-the-roof vents. It most often is used for closet bends, that piece of pipe that connects the toilets to the soil stack.

Lead pipe may be found at plumbing shops for the professional. You seldom will find it at home centers and hardware stores.

Plumbing Fixtures/Valves

At the end of a plumbing run, the pipe connects to the valves and fixtures—faucets, ballcocks, sinks, toilets, and so on. There are only two basic repair areas here: the valves (faucets) and the drains, which are connected to the fixtures to form self-contained units.

Therefore, when you have plumbing trouble, check the valves and drains at the fixture first for the cause, before ripping into the water supply pipes.

Valves and drain replacement parts are available in stores as individual parts or in kits. For example, you can buy a toilet ballcock assembly that contains all the parts for a complete flush tank overhaul. You can also buy a single part to repair a broken flush handle.

Since most plumbing valves and fixtures are standard designs, selecting thread sizes, diameters, lengths, etc., is fairly easy. The best way is to take the old part to the store and match it with a new part. The second best way is to make careful measurements of the old part and match the measurements with the replacement.

VALVE ANATOMY. The secret to repairing valves (faucets) is to know the anatomy of the faucet and buy the replacement part needed. This is not as difficult as it may seem; below you will find a basic parts list for different types of valves.

COMPRESSION FAUCETS. This valve has a removable handle, a packing or cap nut that screws to the faucet housing, a metal stem, and a washer at the bottom of the stem. The washer fits into a valve seat, which usually screws into the bottom of the faucet housing. Each part is replaceable; the parts that usually have to be

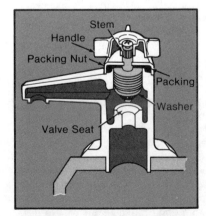

Anatomy of a compression faucet. Complete repair kits containing packing washers, valve seats, and stems are available, or you can buy each part separately.

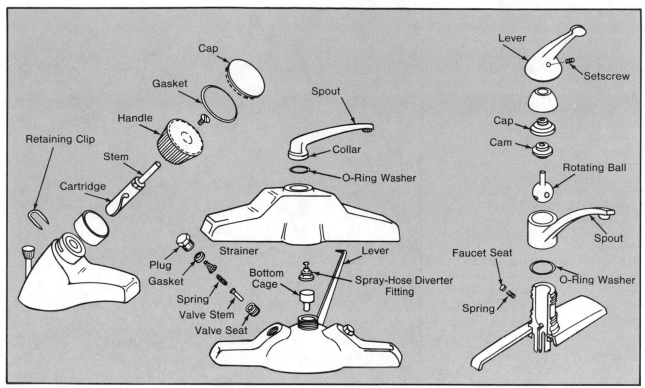

Typical cartridge-type faucets have many parts that can go bad, although most troubles can be traced to defec-tive gaskets and O-ring washers. The parts may be purchased as a kit or individually. Be sure you know what type faucet you are repairing before you go to the store: from left, rotating ball, single lever, and cartridge.

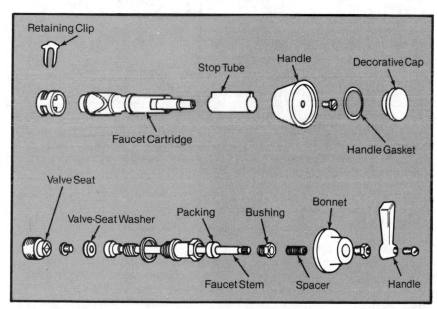

Horizontal faucets generally supply water in bathtubs and showers. At the top is a compression-type faucet; at the bottom is a cartridge-type faucet. The parts are sold as kits or they may be purchased individually. Washers and gaskets are usually the trouble parts.

replaced are the *packing washers* or *string* under the packing or cap nut, and the *seat washer* at the bottom of the stem.

The parts for compression faucets are usually sold individually rather than in kits or packages.

CARTRIDGE FAUCETS. These are advertised as "washerless" types, but they do have washers, called O-rings. All cartridge faucets have a handle or lever that is held by a set screw and/or a retaining clip.

Cartridge faucets are either hollow-ball type, or straight-cartridge type. If the faucet is a hollow-ball type, it will have a cap, cam, hollow ball, O-ring, faucet seal, and a spring. The parts that normally have to be replaced—the *hollow ball, O-rings,* and *cam*—are usually packaged in a kit; you should replace all these parts even though only one of them may be malfunctioning.

If the faucet is a straight-cartridge type it will have a decorative cap, gasket, handle, cartridge with O-rings, and possibly a seat washer, depending on the design. The parts that go bad and cause leaks in this faucet are the *O-rings,* which can be replaced separately. O-rings may be purchased individually or in a package of three or more. If the faucet won't work at all, you should replace the entire cartridge. Don't attempt to repair it; it's not worth it. Cartridges are sold individually, as are other parts of the faucet.

Important: Not all replacement parts for cartridge-type faucets are interchangeable; parts for a Delta faucet may not fit a Peerless faucet. Therefore, it is important to know the manufacturer of the faucet when buying replacement parts. If you can't identify the manufacturer of the faucet, be sure to take the old part to the store and match it with the replacement.

Drains

The parts of a sink drain assembly from the top down are: strainer, gasket, locknut, washer (rubber or plastic), coupling nut, tail piece, coupling nut, washer, and the trap. There are two types of strainers: The standard type is held in place with a locknut. The self-tightening type has a metal ring and a retainer; the ring is held with a retainer and thumbscrews. The retainer is installed from below so its notches align with tiny ridges on the bottom part of the strainer. By tightening or loosening the thumbscrews, the strainer may be installed or removed.

Trouble areas in sink drains are the *rubber washer* and the *trap.* Both can wear out and leak; both can clog, although the trap will have more clogging problems than the strainer.

If any strainer is replaced, the new strainer package will contain a rubber washer, which is pressed into place underneath the strainer's lip that goes around the opening in the sink. If no washer is supplied, use plumber's putty to seal the lip. If the sink is stainless steel, be sure to use stainless-steel putty for the repair—not regular plumber's putty. The package will note the type.

The trap assembly simply slips together and is held in place by coupling nuts. Since drains are not under pressure like water supply pipes, it is not necessary to forcibly tighten the nuts.

Traps wear out and leak along the

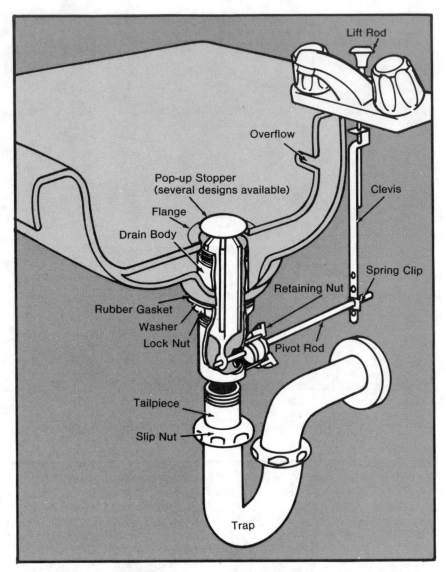

Labels: Lift Rod, Overflow, Pop-up Stopper (several designs available), Clevis, Flange, Drain Body, Spring Clip, Retaining Nut, Rubber Gasket, Washer, Lock Nut, Pivot Rod, Tailpiece, Slip Nut, Trap

Anatomy of a lavatory drain. These parts usually are sold individually, rather than in kits. Trouble spots include pop-up plugs, the trap, and the lift-rod assembly. When installing a new flange in a stainless-steel bowl, use stainless-steel putty to prevent spotting.

bottom curves. When this happens, replace the trap. Traps also may leak because the cleanout plug at the bottom of the trap is not tight or the gaskets between the coupling nuts are defective. Replace both with new parts.

Sink traps usually are 1½ inches in diameter. Wash basin traps usually are 1¼ inches in diameter. Replacements may be purchased in kits, which contain the strainers, gaskets, locknuts, couplings, and pipe. The parts may also be purchased separately. It is better to buy the entire kit if you are replacing a strainer. If you replace a trap, be sure to buy new coupling nuts and gaskets to go with

it. Don't use the old parts even if they fit.

Lavatory stoppers consist of a stopper and stopper control linkage. Replacement parts are available in a complete package, or as individual parts such as the stopper, horizontal, and vertical control linkage.

The problem part usually is the horizontal control linkage that is connected to the bottom of the stopper. This linkage consists of a *pivot ball, retaining nut, pivot rod,* and a *spring clip.*

Bathtub stoppers have a trip lever that slips into an escutcheon plate at the overflow level of the tub. The lever is connected to a lift linkage, spring, rocker arm linkage, and adjustment nut. The stopper fits over the adjustment nut. These parts may be purchased as separate items, rather than in kit form.

The usual trouble spots with linkage are just under the stopper at the adjustment nut, and at the lift linkage below the trip lever in the overflow pipe. By moving the nut up or down, the height of the stopper can be controlled so the tub is properly stopped or drained. By loosening the escutcheon plate, a dislocated lift linkage may be reconnected to the spring

arm, which, in turn, trips the rocker arm linkage. Replacement parts are seldom needed in this repair, although you can buy them. For replacement, the lift linkage can be pulled out of the overflow tube opening after the escutcheon plate has been removed. The rocker arm linkage comes out of the drain opening after the stopper has been removed.

Spouts

Water spouts, with or without diverter valves, are usually screwed to valve and faucet housings. They may have O-ring or gasket washers between the spout and the housing to prevent leakage. *Bathtub spouts* may be removed by turning them carefully counterclockwise. *Showerheads* also are threaded onto pipe and turn off counterclockwise. *Aerators* are threaded onto spouts and may be removed by turning them counterclock-

wise. Some aerators have replacement washers and screens; these must be matched with the aerator because designs are different.

Water supply shut-off valves

Located below sinks, lavatories, and toilets, these may be disconnected and replaced if they leak. There are two types: *angle* for wall or vertical mounting, and *straight* for through-the-floor installation. You should replace the water supply pipes to the fixture when the shut-off valves are replaced. These tubes—in chrome plate or plastic—usually are packaged in pairs, although you can buy them individually, in rigid or flexible metal and plastic.

Kits are sold containing all the parts needed for installing sinks, vanities, and toilets. For example, a double sink/vanity kit for a wall-

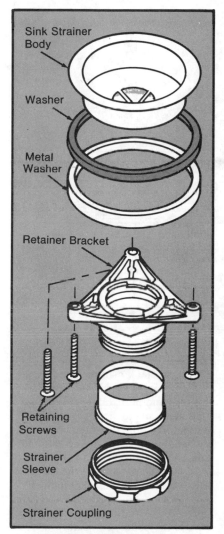

Anatomy of a kitchen drain. The retainer type (shown here) and the locknut type are common forms. The strainer coupling fits onto the tailpiece and trap of the drain. The parts are sold as a kit or individually. Be sure to use stainless-steel putty when setting the strainer body in a stainless steel sink. Regular plumber's putty may be used for setting the part in other fixtures.

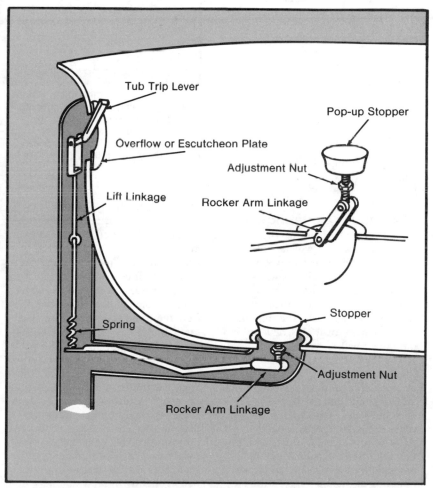

Anatomy of a tub or shower drain. The trouble points are the lift linkage and the adjustment nut under the stopper.

The parts are generally sold individually, although you can buy some pieces in a kit.

mounted unit, with center or end outlet waste, has a combination drain system including nuts and washers; a drain trap with wall mount, a plastic angle valve with a face bushing, plastic sink supply, plastic adapters, and joint tape.

As a rule, it's cheaper to buy parts in kits than individually. It usually is just about as easy to install all new parts as to replace a single part after the unit has been disassembled.

Special order

Plumbing repair parts are plentiful in most communities. Although home centers usually stock the basics, you will find a greater variety of items at hardware stores and plumbing specialty outlets that cater to the professional plumber. Hardware and plumbing stores will special-order plumbing parts, but you generally have to pay for the transportation. If you can't find what you want, and the retailers are reluctant to order for you, contact the Consumer Information Director of these firms:

Chicago Specialty Mfg. Co.
Box 1022
7500 Linder Ave.
Skokie, Ill. 60077

Hancock-Gross Inc.
401 North 21st St.
Philadelphia, Pa. 19130

The Plumb Shop
700 Fisher Bldg.
Detroit, Mich. 48202

Flush tanks/toilet bowls

Toilets have two main parts: the flush tank (water closet), which contains the valves and floats and water for the flush, and the toilet bowl, which has a built-in trap device that drains into the waste pipe and then into the sewer pipe. The flush tank may be wall-mounted, or it may be bolted to the toilet bowl.

The flush tank has a *ballcock* assembly that controls the water level in the tank. A *float* device, whether separate or built into the ballcock, regulates the *water-inlet valve* on the ballcock assembly. The *tank ball* controls the flow of water out of the tank into the toilet bowl. The tank ball is operated by the *trip lever* or handle mounted at the top edge on the outside of the tank.

TOILET PROBLEMS. Common toilet problems are described below,

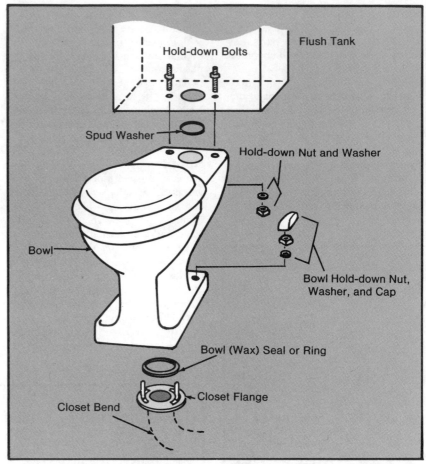

Anatomy of a flush tank toilet. When replacement is needed, the critical parts are the bowl (wax) seal, the hold-down bolts, and the closet flange. These parts often are packaged with the toilet bowl; they may be purchased as a kit or as individual parts. Flush tanks usually are sold with the ballcock assembly in place, although this unit can be purchased as a kit or as individual parts.

along with the likely solutions.

Running toilet usually is caused by a faulty *float ball* or *tank ball*. First, make sure that the float ball rod is straight and doesn't rub against the flush tank. If clear, check the float for water seepage. If the float has water in it, replace the float. It unscrews from the rod counterclockwise. The same rules apply for the tank ball. It should lift straight up and slide straight down in the guides when you trip the handle. If not, replace or realign the guides; they are fastened to the overflow tube with a single screw. If the tank ball contains water, replace it after unscrewing it from the lift rod. Also check the ball seat for roughness. If it is corroded, try smoothing it with steel wool so the ball fits tightly in the seat.

The tank parts needed to stop a running toilet are available in kits with both balls and other parts, or

may be purchased separately. The parts are standard design and will fit almost any tank manufactured.

Water won't shut off: In older tanks this problem probably is caused by a malfunctioning ballcock assembly. But before you replace the ballcock, try bending the float rod up carefully. This causes more water to enter the tank, which may shut off the ballcock valve. If this doesn't work, you can buy replacement washers for the ballcock (see illustration, this chapter), or replace the ballcock assembly entirely.

Two modern types of water control devices are available. One type has a combination valve and float cup attached to the shaft of the ballcock. The float rides up and down the shaft as the water goes in and out of the tank. A slightly different type that sits underwater on the bottom of the tank uses the water pressure inside the

How it's sold

Toilets and toilet parts are sold in a package or separately. For example, you can buy a complete flush tank kit that includes float balls, ballcock assembly, overflow tubes, etc., or you can buy each item as a part. Most retailers will not break a package to sell a single part.

Plumbing accessory items—plungers, augers, torches, washers, fittings, drain cleaners, etc.—are sold singly. There are so many accessory items available for toilets that limited space here prohibits listing them.

Special order

Retailers almost always will special-order any toilet item for you, provided the item is a brand name that the retailer stocks. However, keep in mind that toilets and parts are made in standard sizes, and special orders may not be needed. However, if you can't find the item that you want, write to the Consumer Information Directors of the manufacturers listed below:

Fillpro Division of JH Industries
980 Rancheros Drive
San Marcos, Calif. 92069

Kohler Co.
Kohler, Wis. 53044

Mansfield Sanitary Inc.
150 First St.
Perrysville, Ohio 44864

Septic systems

Simply put, a private disposal system (septic tank and field) runs from the house into the yard where the waste is absorbed into the ground. Parts of the system include a septic tank, concrete distribution boxes, clay tile or pipes, and, often, a grease trap system.

Because of the specialized equipment needed to service a septic system, you should call a professional service person when problems arise.

Component parts for a septic system are usually not stocked by home centers and hardware stores. Look for them at specialty plumbing outlets that cater to professional plumbers and home builders.

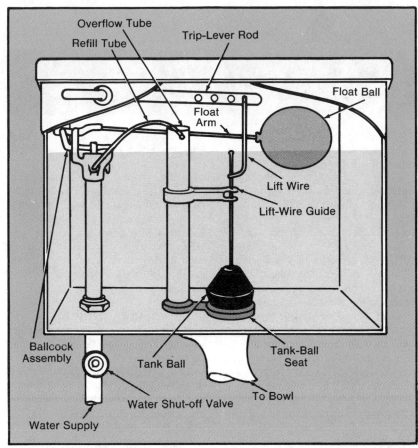

Anatomy of a flush tank. The flush assembly may be purchased as a kit or as individual parts, such as the tank ball, trip lever rod, or float arm. Common trouble spots are the ballcock assembly and the tank ball. The ballcock assembly shown here is standard. Low-profile models operate on water pressure alone, without a ballcock.

tank to open and close the inlet valve.

All three assemblies will fit any standard toilet; they come packaged with the necessary fittings, hardware, and instructions for installation.

No flush or *inadequate flush problems* can be traced to defects in these parts: *float rod, float ball, tank ball, ballcock,* and *nuts* that hold the ballcock in position.

First, try raising the water level in the flush tank by bending the float rod up gently. If this doesn't work, try moving the tank ball guide up so the tank ball can be raised higher by the flush handle rods. The next step might be to clean the ports around the underside of the bowl rim. If none of these work, a new ballcock and tank ball must be installed.

To stop outside leaks, try tightening the nuts on the pipe where the tank connects to the toilet bowl. Also, make sure the coupling nuts that hold the ballcock in the tank are tight. If not, you may have to replace the ballcock or the water supply line and nuts to the ballcock.

If the bowl or flush tank is cracked and is leaking water, these units must be replaced; they can't be satisfactorily repaired. The critical measurement to make when buying a new tank or bowl is along the floor from the center of the waste pipe (at the bottom of the toilet bowl) to where the tank is installed.

If the bowl will be replaced, make sure you buy new hold-down bolts, caps for the bolts, and a wax ring. Do not use these old parts with the new fixture.

4

ELECTRICAL PRODUCTS

The electrical circuits in a home distribute and control power much like the plumbing system handles the water supply. But instead of pipes, there are wires that carry the electricity. Instead of faucets, there are switches that turn the supply on and off. Instead of sinks and toilets, there are lights, ranges, and other appliances that use the power.

Electrical products to repair electrical breakdowns and improve the system are plentiful in most home centers, hardware outlets, and electrical supply shops that cater to the professional, although the inventory list may not be as long as for paint and painting accessories, and for lumber and millwork items.

Special and fancy lighting fixtures, however, may not be available at these stores. You'll have to search for them at specialty outlets such as lighting and department stores.

The electrical codes

Almost all communities have codes that govern the use of electricity. If a community doesn't have its own code, the National Electrical Code may apply. These codes protect you against misused electrical products and faulty electrical installation techniques that can cause electrical shock and fires. A local code won't prohibit you from repairing a plug on the end of a lamp cord, changing a switch or replacing a burned-out fuse, but you may need a permit to make wiring changes in your home, such as adding a new circuit to the main electrical entrance.

The retailer who sells you electrical products may know the procedures involved in obtaining a permit, and he should know where and how the products should be used. If he doesn't, or if you have any doubts whatever, call the building department of your local government. You can also seek the advice of a professional electrician in the community. Since the pros usually don't want to bother with handyman repairs, they may feel free to instruct you. It's worth a try.

If the work you do does not comply with local electrical codes, your home insurance may not cover you if an accident occurs. By following the codes, you're a winner in both technology and safety.

Contrary to popular belief, an electrical product stamped with an Underwriters Laboratory listing (UL) does not necessarily comply with the electrical codes. Underwriters Laboratory is a testing facility that assures the consumer that products will do what the manufacturer claims they will do. UL is not connected with any government agency or any regulatory group. However, the UL label does indicate that the product may be safely used as it is intended. In fact, some communities even specify the use of UL-listed electrical products for home wiring systems.

Do-it-yourself projects

You can make many electrical repairs yourself without special knowledge or skills. You can even wire new circuits without difficulty if you know something about basic electricity. If you do this, have a professional electrician check your handiwork before the power is turned on.

Caution: electricity is dangerous. If you are careless when working with electricity, it becomes one of the deadliest hazards in your home.

You can completely eliminate this danger by following just one simple rule: *Turn off the power before making any repairs or improvements to your home's electrical system; pull the plug before working on any home appliance. If you doubt your ability, call a professional.*

How Electricity Works

Before you buy any electrical products for repairs or improvements, you ought to know how electricity comes into your home and how it is divided at the main switch box. Here's a short, simplified course on the subject.

Electricity from a public utility is distributed through electrical substations. You've probably seen them: large rectangular boxes with big wires sticking out the tops. The sub-stations reduce the original high voltage generated at a dam, an oil- or coal-burning plant, or a nuclear power facility to 2,400 volts. From the sub-station, electricity goes to a transformer located on a power pole in your neighborhood.

The transformer then doles out the power to the main switch box in your home at either 115 or 230 volts. In some communities the power may be 120 or 240 volts, but for standard electrical calculations the National Electric Code sets 115/230 volts as the standard rate. In this chapter, all data will be based on the 115/230 figure, unless otherwise noted.

Products for electrical repairs and improvements that are most commonly available are designed for a 115/230 volt power supply. If you do not have this service, the utility company will install it free of charge up to the main switch box. However, you

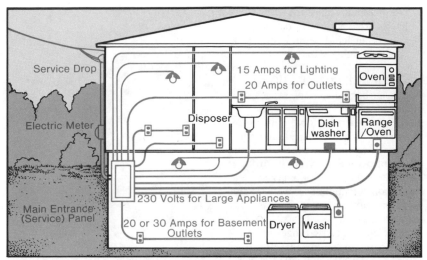

House wiring found in most residences is shown here. Individual circuits are formed at the main entrance panel. Some older homes may have more than one main entrance panel; check before making any repairs or improvements.

chine, and a television set.

Electrical power is controlled by fuses, or circuit breakers, and by switches. For example, one circuit may supply power to the kitchen and dining room, including the lights, a food blender, the refrigerator, and a can opener. You flip a wall switch and the lights go on; you flip a switch on an appliance and it goes on. But suppose all the switches are on at once. If this demands more power than the circuit—the wires—can safely carry, a fuse blows out or a circuit breaker snaps off. This stops the power flow and prevents an overload on the circuit that could start a fire. Overloaded electrical wires built up large amounts of heat; the fuse or circuit breaker is simply a watchdog: When the load is too heavy, the fuse or circuit breaker stops everything before trouble starts.

If fuses blow or circuit breakers pop frequently, it's likely the electrical wiring in your home is not adequate. Check with the utility about this; inadequate wiring can cause fires.

RESETTING CIRCUIT BREAKERS. A circuit breaker is usually a toggle switch. When a breaker trips off, you simply flip the toggle back to reset the circuit. The system is safe and simple. Don't touch a circuit

must pay for any wiring changes inside the house. If the utility is now supplying 230-volt service, check the main switch box for a label that specifies the amp service. If you are getting 60 amps, service is in the low range; most electrical codes call for 100-amp service. If you own power tools and large appliances, the system should be upgraded to 150/200 amps. The utility will also help you with

this improvement; you pay for any inside wiring change.

At your main switch box, the electrical power from the transformer is divided into circuits. One circuit will supply 230 volts to large appliances such as an electric range, a heat pump, and a clothes dryer. The other circuits supply 115 volts to lights and small appliances such as an electric shaver, a food blender, a washing ma-

Selected Wattage Ratings for Comparison

PRODUCT	APPROX. WATTAGE RATING*
Room air conditioner	800 to 1,500
Central air conditioning (230 v.)	5,000
Can opener	150
Clock	13
Clothes dryer (230 v.)	4,000 to 5,000
Clothes iron	700 to 1,000
Dishwasher	1,100
Portable electric drill	200 to 400
Food freezer	300 to 600
Gas furnace	800
Oil furnace	600 to 1,200
Garbage disposer	500 to 1,000
Hot water heater/electric	2,500 to 5,000
Range	5,000 per burner
Range oven	4,500
Refrigerator	150 to 300
Color television	200 to 450
Black and white television	50 to 100
Table saw	600
Vacuum cleaner	300 to 600
Clothes washer	600 to 900

*To determine amps, divide watts by volts.

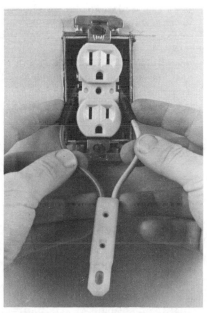

Testing for power with a voltage tester. Touch one probe of the tester to the positive (power) wire and the other probe to the negative wire. If the bulb in the tester lights, the power is on.

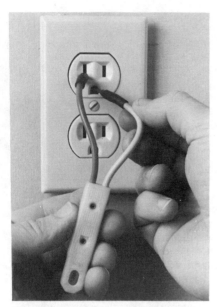

To check an outlet ground, place one probe of a voltage tester in the grounding slot and the other into the elongated (prong) slots. If the tester does not light, the receptacle is *not grounded* and is dangerous. Check the inside wiring.

breaker if your hands are wet or even damp. Keep your other hand behind your back when touching the switch.

REPLACING FUSES. Burned-out fuses have to be pulled or unscrewed from a socket. Here are the safety rules for changing a fuse:

1. Stand on a block of dry wood or piece of plywood when the floor below the fuse box is damp or wet.
2. Use a fuse puller to remove and install cartridge fuses. Touch only the rim of a screw-in fuse, not the box.

3. Never replace any fuse if your hands are wet or even damp; keep your other hand behind your back when changing a fuse.

APPLIANCE FUSES. Washers, dryers, garbage disposers, ranges, and other household appliances usually have their own additional built-in fusing system. When one of these appliances fails to work, the main fuse box or circuit breaker may not be at fault. Look for a small button marked "reset" on the appliance control panel or on or near the motor. Push it firmly to start the appliance.

Some older electric ranges have fuses located in the top rear of the oven or under a back heating element at the top of the range. This fuse is in addition to the one in the entrance box.

If your range has an appliance outlet on the control panel, there will be a 15- or 20-amp fuse for this circuit somewhere on the range. An older house may have more than one fuse box or circuit breaker panel. These additional power entrances may have been added to handle a new dryer, air-conditioner, furnace, or other large appliance. If there is no problem at the main service entrance, look for additional fuse systems elsewhere.

CIRCUIT POWER. The rate at which electricity flows is measured in amperes, usually called *amps*. Electrical circuits provide different amperage, or amp ratings, to match power demands.

Lighting circuits to lighting fixtures are commonly 15 amps.

Outlets, into which you plug radios, clocks, hair driers, and similar appliances, are on 20-amp circuits.

Cover plate grounds are checked by touching one probe of the voltage tester to the cover plate screw and inserting the other probe into the elongated slots. If the tester doesn't light, the cover plate isn't grounded and is dangerous. Check the inside wiring.

Dishwashers, washing machines, refrigerators, and other large appliances are on 30-amp circuits.

Caution: Do not replace blown fuses with fuses larger than the circuit specifies. For example, do not put a 30-amp fuse in a 15-amp circuit. If you do, and the circuit becomes overloaded, the larger fuse may not blow out; this will let the wires overheat and may cause a fire.

Never put a copper penny behind a blown fuse to restore power.

Fuses and How They're Sold

Most home centers, hardware outlets, electric specialty shops, drug stores, grocery markets, and variety stores stock and sell fuses. There are four types of fuses, three of which are *plug fuses*—those that screw into a socket similar to a light bulb socket—and one type that is held by clips.

Standard fuses have a glass top and a threaded metal base. The amperage is printed on the face and embossed

on the metal tip of the base. Under the glass top is a tiny metal wire that melts when the circuit is overloaded, thus breaking the circuit. When the fuse blows, the glass top appears black or burned.

A-Type S fuses are similar to standard fuses, but are designed for greater safety. The base of the fuse will fit only an adapter that matches the amp rating of the fuse. For exam-

ple, a 15-amp adapter is screwed into a 15-amp circuit in the fuse box. Since the adapter will accept only a 15-amp type S fuse, you are prevented from using the wrong fuse.

The fuses and fuse base adapters are sold separately. The adapters may be replaced if they become burned or corroded.

Time-delay fuses or time-lag fuses are designed to take a heavy surge of

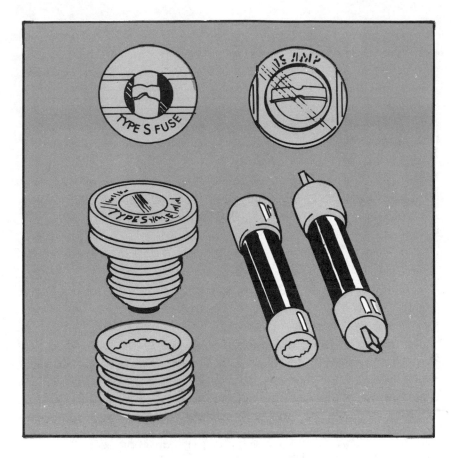

Types of fuses include (from left) Type S with safety adapter; standard glass top; cartridge. Fuses are usually sold two or more to a package. Buy the right amp fuse (15, 20, 30, etc.) to replace a blown fuse. Do not interchange amp ratings.

electrical power for a short period without blowing out. For example, when you turn on a table saw, it pulls 600 amps of power instantly. This surge of power would cause a standard or A-Type S fuse to blow. With a time delay fuse, the solder strip that completes the circuit resists melting long enough for the surge to pass, thus preventing the blowing action. If the power surge continues, however, the strip will melt, breaking the circuit. D (delay)-type S fuses are commonly available.

Cartridge fuses look like shotgun shells with a metal band at each end. Cartridge fuses rated between 10 and 60 amperes have slightly rounded ends.

Cartridge fuses used in large-capacity circuits for heavy appliances are rated at 60 to 600 amps. These fuses are similar to the ones described above, except that the ends are finned.

When buying cartridge fuses, check the labels carefully for the amp ratings. The packages of low- and high-amp fuses often appear to be identical.

Fused receptacles are standard outlets or receptacles that have a separate built-in fuse system. The fuse is located under a hinged metal shield directly above the outlet opening. This receptacle is used in workshops where overloads caused by power tools are common. Instead of blowing fuses in the main fuse box or tripping circuit breakers, the fuse in the receptacle pops when the circuit overloads. Use a time delay fuse in this system; the fuse amp rating should match circuit rating—usually 20 or 30 amps.

Circuit Breakers and How They're Sold

Circuit breakers look like thin toggle switches and are sold individually at home centers, hardware stores, and electrical specialty shops. They're available in three types: single, double, and extra thin. They have different amp ratings, just like fuses. And

there are two styles: one, similar to a wall plug, is simply plugged into a slot in the breaker box and is automatically seated. The second style also plugs into the breaker box, but you must then connect the positive

(black) power wire to a terminal screw at one edge of the breaker.

Circuit breaker packages look alike; check the amp rating, the type, and the style before buying. You must match the breakers already installed.

Electrical Wire

Electrical wire falls into several classifications and sub-classifications. Type T wire (T for thermoplastic insulation) is used for residential wiring. *Type T* is a general classification under which are these sub-classifications:

TYPES OF WIRE. Type NW is only for indoor use under dry conditions.

Type UF is for sheltered outdoor use.

Type TW is for outdoor use where damp and wet conditions prevail.

Type SPT is only for lamp cord.

Type HPN, or HPD, is only for heater cord.

Bell wire must be used only in doorbell circuits. It's rated for 25 amps.

Speaker wire must be used only for wiring radio and phonograph speakers.

Type AC cable is used where codes require metal-clad wire.

Type CO-ALR is aluminum wire that must be used only with 15- and 20-amp aluminum fixtures.

Type CU-AL is aluminum wire for ratings larger than 20 amps.

Caution: Always use aluminum wire with aluminum fixtures. Never connect aluminum wire to copper terminals or copper wire to aluminum terminals. Connecting different metals causes a corrosive action that can lead to an electrical fire.

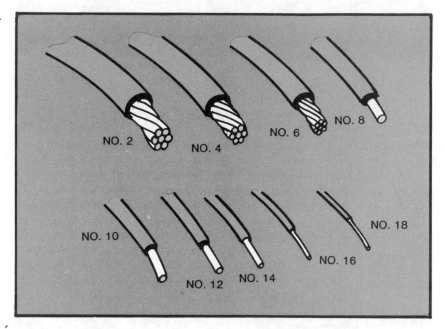

Wire sizes are identified by number: the larger the number, the smaller the wire. No. 18 wire is available both as stranded wire and as solid wire. Bell cord is solid wire for low-voltage systems. Match wire size to the volts and amps the circuit carries.

WIRE NUMBERS. The size of electrical wire is identified by the numbers in the AWG (American Wire Gauge) system. (It has nothing to do with wire type.) The larger the number, the smaller the size of the wire and the lower the amp rating. For example, No. 18 wire is small in diameter and can carry only 7 amps. No. 10 wire is larger and carries 30 amps. Here's a complete list.

No. 18 wire	7 amps
No. 16 wire	10 amps
No. 14 wire	15 amps
No. 12 wire	20 amps
No. 10 wire	30 amps
No. 8 wire	40 amps
No. 6 wire	55 amps

You'll often see the AWG number stamped on the insulation of wires along with the type, such as UF, NW, etc.

In fusing or circuit breaker systems, use Nos. 16 and 18 wire in a 15-amp circuit, Nos. 10 and 12 wire in a 20-amp circuit, and Nos. 8 and 10 wire in a 30-amp circuit.

For general repair and improvement work, use Nos. 14, 12, and 10 wire. Do not use Nos. 16 and 18 wire except for low-voltage systems, such as lamp cords, doorbell wire, speaker systems, and intercom systems.

Use No. 14 and 12 wire for 120-volt circuits. Use No. 10 wire for 120-volt circuits to which heavy appliances such as refrigerators, window air-conditioners, and power tools are connected. Use No. 8 and No. 6 wire for 230/240-volt circuits.

How wire is constructed

The electrical codes in your community probably permit three varieties of

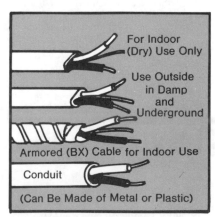

For Indoor (Dry) Use Only

Use Outside in Damp and Underground

Armored (BX) Cable for Indoor Use

Conduit

(Can Be Made of Metal or Plastic)

Wires are marked for use as required by local codes. Power wires have black or white insulation; ground wires may be bare or have red or green insulation.

Wire Selection Guide		
AWG COPPER WIRE NO.	AMP RATING	AWG ALUMINUM WIRE NO.
6	55	4
8	40	6
10	30	8
12	20	10
14	15	12
16	10	(not available)
18	7	(not available)

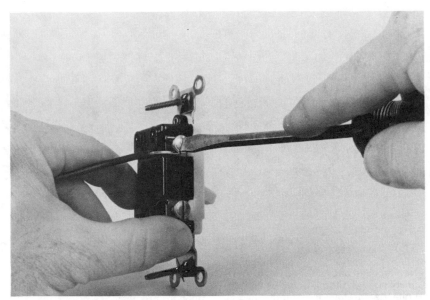

The power wire (positive) has black insulation and is connected to the brass-colored terminal. White wire (negative) is connected to the silver-colored terminal. Bare, red, or green ground wire is connected to the green-colored terminal. If two positive wires are connected, use one black and one red with a green wire for ground.

Some switches and outlets have wire holes as well as screw terminals for connections as shown here. Inside the holes are spring clamps to hold the wire in place. To release a wire from its hole, a screwdriver is inserted into the slot next to the hole. Many fixtures are marked like this one with recommended wire sizes and stripping guides.

Conduit Selection Guide

TYPE	LENGTHS	DIAMETERS (in.)
Rigid Aluminum	10 ft.	½; ¾; 1; 1½; 2; 2½; 3; 3½; 4; 5; 6
Thin-Wall Steel (EMT)	10 ft.	⅜; ½; ¾; 1; 1¼; 1½; 2; 2½; 3; 4
Rigid Steel	10 ft.	½; ¾; 1; 1¼; 1½; 2; 2½; 3; 3½; 4; 5
Rigid Plastic (PVC)	10/20 ft.	½; ¾; 1; 1¼; 1½; 2; 2½; 3; 4

Note: PVC or high-density polyethylene that will be left in sunlight should be painted with two heavy coats of latex paint to stop deterioration. A dark color such as black is recommended.

wire construction. You will find these at home centers, hardware outlets, and electrical specialty shops.

Plastic sheathed cable comes in NW and UF types. It's ideal for the do-it-yourselfer because it is highly flexible and may be snaked through walls, around corners, up, down, and through foundations.

Flexible armored cable—sometimes known as *BX*—is NW type; it must not be used in damp locations. This product has a shiny galvanized metal sheath through which the power wires run. Armored cable is easy for the handyman to use since it can be snaked.

Before you buy flexible armored cable, however, check your local codes; some codes prohibit its usage anywhere.

Thin-wall rigid conduit looks like galvanized steel water pipe without the threaded ends. This product is only a sheathing for the wires that you thread through it—such as flexible plastic-sheathed.

Rigid conduit is approved by most codes, although it's smart to check the codes before buying.

Conduit is frequently used for new electrical wiring; it is difficult to use in some applications simply because it is rigid. You can buy connections (couplings and elbows and offsets) for the straight conduit. Conduit also may be bent—with a conduit bender—to gentle curves and slight angles.

Inside insulated wire you'll find two kinds of wire: stranded and solid.

Stranded wire is made up of many very thin hair-like wire components clamped together; it is intended only for lamp cords and carries AWG number 18. Solid wire consists of just one solid wire in AWG Numbers 8 through 18. In wires numbered 0 through 6, you'll find multiples of solid wire encased in the insulation.

READING WIRE SYMBOLS. Wire sold in most stores is labeled as to size, type, and other characteristics. Metal cable is labeled on the package (usually a box); non-metalic wire is labeled on the package and on the insulation of wire large enough (Numbers 6 through 10) to take the imprint. Here is a typical example:

*14/2 WITH GROUND TYPE NM Cu
600 V UL AWG*

Here's what the numbers and symbols mean:

14 is the wire size.

2 means that there are two insulated No. 14 wires inside the sheathing: one positive (black insulation) and one negative (white insulation) wire. (If there are three wires inside the insulation it will be labeled 14/3.)

WITH GROUND means that there is a third wire in the sheathing which is to be used as a ground wire. This wire probably will be bare—without insulation; if it is insulated, it will be colored green or red.

TYPE NM means that the wire may be used only in dry locations. Dry means *dry*—no dampness or wetness is permitted.

Cu means that the wire is made of copper.

600 V means that the wire is rated for use in 600-volt systems.

UL stands for Underwriters Laboratories. (The chapter introduction explains this symbol.)

AWG means that the wire has been sized according to the American Wire Gauge system.

MATCH THE CABLE YOU BUY.
Do not mix varieties of cable in any repair or improvement work. If the cable already installed is BX, use BX. If the cable is plastic-sheathed, use only plastic-sheathed.

Buy the right type
As pointed out previously, cable is specified for different locations—dry, damp, or wet. The electrical codes call this "circumstance." Here are the definitions of these *code circumstances:*

Dry: completely dry and above ground level. For interior use where *no* dampness or wetness ever occurs.

Damp: some moisture is permitted, such as may occur in a basement.

Wet: locations in outdoor areas, underground, next to concrete slabs, patios, walks, and driveways that may become water logged.

Measuring wire for a specific job is simple. Just measure the length between fixtures and the power source and add 5 feet to the measurement.

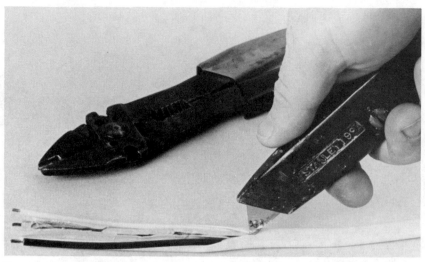

Non-metallic cable is stripped with a utility knife (bottom). If you use a knife, be careful not to cut the insulation on the wires inside. About 8 inches of outside sheathing must be stripped to expose the wires for connections.

Example: for a measurement of 20 feet, buy 25 feet of wire. The extra is for terminal connections, a margin for error, for wire bends, stripping, and so forth.

How it's sold
Plastic-sheathed cable is sold by the roll in 25-, 50-, and 100-foot sizes. As a rule, the larger roll costs less per foot than the smaller rolls.

Lamp cord is sold by the linear foot. It usually is stored on a large spool; you cut off the length required for the project. However, some stores sell lamp cord by the package containing 10, 15, 20, or 25 feet. There may be a price break on quantity, but it will be slight.

Bell and speaker wire is sold by the linear foot from a roll and by the package. The package is precut wire to a specific length, usually 65 feet.

BX cable (armored) is sold in boxes containing 25, 50, and 100 feet.

Thin-wall conduit is priced by the linear foot. The standard length is 10 feet. Connectors are sold as single items. They're priced by type: a simple connection costs less than a complex connection.

Special wire, such as range and clothes dryer connection, is packaged and sold by length. The standard length is 5 feet, although other lengths are readily available.

Extension cord wire is cut to specific lengths and sold in packages of 5-, 10-, 25-, 50-, and 100-foot lengths.

You can also buy round, rubber-covered cord and make your own extension cord by simply adding a plug on one end and an outlet on the other end. When buying extension cord, consider what the cord will do; the wire must be large enough to carry

Wire insulation is removed with wire strippers that resemble pliers. The holes match the wire gauge; you simply squeeze the strippers on the wire and pull off the insulation. Strippers also are equipped with wire cutters.

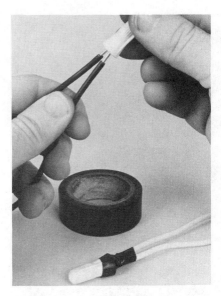

All splices are secured with wire nuts. After the wire has been twisted with pliers, turn the wire nut down, tight around the splice. Electrician's tape may be wrapped around the wire nut splice for added protection (bottom). Wire nuts are available in assorted sizes to match wire sizes.

the power demanded by the appliance. Here are some guidelines:

For large appliances and power tools, buy No. 14 wire for 25 ft.; No. 12 wire for 50 ft.; No. 10 wire for 100 ft.

For small appliances, buy No. 16 wire for 25 ft.; No. 14 wire for 50 ft.; No. 12 wire for 100 ft.

For lamps and small-amp fixtures, buy No. 18 wire for 25 ft.; No. 16 wire for 50 ft.; No. 14 wire for 100 ft.

Single wire is sold by the roll in packages of 25, 50, and 100 feet. It may sometimes be purchased from an open roll and priced by the linear foot. If you buy lots of wire, you may be able to get a price break, but you have to ask the retailer for it.

If you buy solid wire to thread through thin-wall conduit, the wire must be color-coded to show its function. Use black insulated wire for the positive (power) line.

Use white insulated wire for the neutral or negative line.

Use red or green insulated wire for the ground wire.

If the project calls for a second power wire (in addition to the black one), buy red insulated wire for this power line and use green insulated wire for the ground. These colors are a standard in the electrical world and should always be correctly installed for safety's sake.

Wire hangers: Metal electrician's staples and preformed hangers are used to support cable wire in its run between the main power entrance and the fixtures. Both staples and hangers are sold by the package in small quantities. Staples are easier to use than hangers; there is little price difference between the two types.

Splicing wire

Wire must be spliced only within a junction box—not along the main run of wire. Most codes permit only splicing with wire nuts. The wires are twisted together and the nuts are turned down on the completed splice.

To splice stranded wire with solid wire, first twist the stranded wire around the solid wire, leaving a half-inch of solid wire free. Bend the solid wire back and compress it with pliers. Then screw a wire nut around the splice and wrap it with electrician's tape.

To make a more secure splice, wrap electrician's tape around the wires and the nut.

Wire nuts are available in a variety of sizes to fit various wires. They are usually in packages of a dozen.

Electricians' tape is made of plastic or cloth; the plastic tape conforms better to the shape of the splice. Tape is sold by the roll; the standard size is 25 feet, but other lengths are available.

Junction Boxes

Fixtures such as switches and outlets are mounted on junction boxes, which are made of metal or plastic. All wire splices, whether end-of-the-run or middle-of-the-run, are made inside a junction box. Junction boxes are designed to fit almost any wiring situation indoors and outdoors; they usually are fastened to framing members (studs, rafters, joists, sills), although special clips are available for securing the boxes to gypsumboard and wall paneling without the support of framing.

Box measurement

The size of junction box is important to the project you're undertaking. According to the codes, the number of wires that can be run into a junction box is determined by the size of the box. For example, a 4 × 1¼-inch ceiling box is limited to six connections of No. 14 AWG wire or five connections of No. 12 AWG wire. The number of connections doesn't include ground wires that may be connected to the box, or to the switches, outlets, or other fixtures that may be con-

nected to the box. Use the wire connection chart in this chapter to determine the size junction box you need.

Ganging wall boxes

Wall junction boxes are sold as a single unit, but they may be easily ganged, or combined, into multiples to handle two, three, four, five, and even six switches or outlets. Boxes are ganged by removing the screw that holds the side of the box to the top and bottom. Then the side may be removed with a slight twisting action.

To gang metal wall boxes, the sides of the boxes are first removed, as shown here. Then the boxes are fastened together with the screws that held the sides. The round plugs in the sides of the boxes may be knocked out to make wire connections. Note clamps inside for securing cable.

		MAXIMUM NO. OF WIRES (EXCLUDING GROUNDWIRES)			
TYPE	**SIZES (in.)**	**#8**	**#10**	**#12**	**#14**
Ceiling	4 × 1½ round/octagonal	5	6	6	7
	4 × 2⅛ round/octagonal	7	8	9	10
	4 × 1½ square	7	8	9	10
	4 × 2⅛ square	10	12	13	15
	4¹¹⁄₁₆ × 1½ square	9	11	13	14
	4¹¹⁄₁₆ × 2⅛ square	14	16	18	21
Utility (major)	4 × 2⅛ × 1½	3	4	4	5
	4 × 2⅛ × 1⅞	4	5	5	6
	4 × 2⅛ × 2⅛	4	5	6	7
Basic switch or receptacle	3 × 2 × 1½	2	3	3	3
	3 × 2 × 2	3	4	4	5
	3 × 2 × 2¾	4	5	6	7
	3 × 2 × 3½	6	7	8	9

Junction Box Selector

The opposite side of a similar second box is then removed, and the two boxes are joined with the screws to produce a double box. More multiples may be added by removing the sides and joining the boxes. Note: Ceiling and major utility boxes may not be ganged together.

Cable connectors

Wire is connected to junction boxes with different kinds of clamps, depending on the type of cable.

Internal clamps or internal saddle clamps fit inside on the back of the box to secure plastic-sheathed cable. The clamp is held by a screw. The wire is threaded through the U-shaped channel knockout in the box, then in back of the clamp, and secured by tightening the clamp against the back of the box.

Two-part clamps for cable and conduit fasten the wire to the box through a knockout hole on a side. The large part of the clamp is inserted over the wire and then positioned in the hole. The second or smaller part of the clamp is then slipped over the bottom section of the wire and threaded onto the larger part of the clamp.

Plastic rings that slip into knockout holes are used to protect wires from damage. To connect thin-wall conduit to junction boxes, a metal nipple is attached to the box with a locknut inside the box at the knockout hole. A plastic insert is used over the connec-

tor to protect the wires from damage.

The various connector parts sometimes are included with the junction boxes. If not, you can buy them separately.

Junction box accessories include internal wire clamps, expansion and offset hanger straps, depth rings, grounding screws with pigtails, grounding clips, knockout blanks, and a variety of covers in all shapes and sizes. Some of these accessories may be part of the box. Others have to be added to the box as the job requires.

Separate accessories are individually priced.

Junction box use

Boxes are designed for use in different locations. The kinds you'll find at most home centers and hardware stores are described below.

BOX WITH SIDE CLAMPS. Use this box for installation in paneling and wallboard where the box can't be secured to a framing member such as a stud. Small clamps on the top and bottom of the box are tightened and

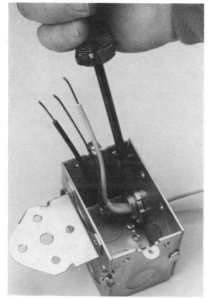

Left: Non-metallic cable fastener clamp is screwed to the cable, as shown here, before it is connected to the junction box. The locknut is on the right. *Right:* The cable fastener is con-

nected to the junction box with a clamp outside (not seen here), and the locknut is screwed tightly around the fastener from the inside, using a screwdriver.

loosened by turning a nail-like rod with a screwdriver. Once the box is wired and in position, the clamps are tightened to hold the box securely to the wallcovering material.

BOX WITH ADJUSTABLE EARS. This standard junction box has tabs at the top and bottom of the box through which screws may be driven into framing members or wallcovering materials such as plaster, gypsumboard, and wood and hardboard panels. Nails may be used instead of screws. The box may be installed as purchased in plaster wall construc-

Plastic junction boxes cost about half as much as metal boxes. They are nailed to framing members, as shown; the nails are usually packaged with the boxes.

This standard metal junction box has a side flange with prongs that are driven into a wood frame with a hammer to hold the box lightly before it is nailed or screwed in position. Many different flange and fastening devices are available for wall and ceiling boxes.

tion. To mount it in other wall materials, you will need two side brackets per box for additional support. The side brackets are sold separately.

BOX WITH SIDE FLANGE. This style is used on open framing where the studs are exposed. The box is attached to the framing with screws or nails driven through the flange that runs along one side of the box.

BOX WITH FLANGES AND TEETH. The flange that runs along one side of the box has metal teeth punched from the edge of the flange. The box is held to framing members by hammering the teeth into the wood. The flange also has holes through which screws or nails can be driven for more support.

SHALLOW BOXES. An addition to the electrical products market is a shallow junction box that is designed for installation behind wall paneling that has been furred out ¾ in. from a finished (gypsumboard, lath-and-plaster) wall. Only one fixture may be installed in a shallow box and there is no space for any extra wire. The box may be attached to the finished wall with nails, screws, or hollow wall fasteners (toggle or Molly bolts).

CEILING BOXES. There are two basic styles: adjustable bar hanger and flanged.

The adjustable bar hanger is nailed or screwed to the ceiling joists after a screw inside the box has been loosened so that the hanger may be spread the width of the joist. The box also slides on the hanger so it may be positioned anywhere between the joists. The box is held in position by tightening the screw.

The flanged box is held by a side flange which is nailed or screwed to the joist.

MAJOR UTILITY BOXES. Also called 4-square boxes, these are simply nailed or screwed to a wall surface or framing member. No flanges and bars are needed. Hollow wall fasteners may be used. To attach the box to a masonry wall, use lead or plastic anchors.

Major utility boxes are designed to accept either plastic-sheathed or armored cable; the only difference between the two is the internal cable-holding device. For armored cable, a round support is used. For plastic cable, a double-clamping device is used.

Weatherproof boxes and accessories

Weatherproof receptacles, connections, and fixtures are required for all exterior electrical hook-ups. The se-

Plastic ceiling boxes cost less than metal boxes and are available with different flanges and clamps for mounting. When installing plastic boxes, be

careful hammering in fasteners: a hammer blow can damage the box so it won't function properly.

Adjustable brackets for ceiling boxes (left) can be mounted between framing members. A screw inside the box loosens and tightens the bracket and box so both may be positioned where you want them. A non-adjustable off-set bracket is shown at right.

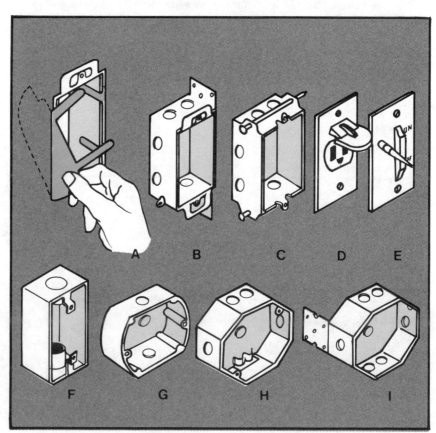

Types of wall and ceiling boxes available at most home center and hardware stores include: (A) sidewall flanges for gypsumboard; (B) stud flange for gypsumboard; (C) top-and-bottom nailer for gypsumboard; (D) waterproof outlet with snap cover; (E) waterproof switch with outside toggle; (F) standard waterproof junction box; (G) plastic wall or ceiling box; (H) metal ceiling box with internal wire clamps; (I) ceiling box with side flange for joist and rafter mounting.

lection of these products may be limited at home centers and some hardware outlets, but you will find a complete inventory at specialty electrical shops and some stores specializing in garden supplies or outdoor furniture.

The basic fitting is the LB (for L-shape) connector, which is installed where wires go through the outside wall and turn toward the outside ground. The fitting is threaded to accept conduit; it has a waterproof gasket that is sandwiched between the fitting and an access plate that is fastened to the fitting with screws. Other conduit components for external wiring include offsets, T-bodies, C-bodies, and corner elbows. All are sold individually.

Waterproof receptacles, made of heavy metal castings, consist of three parts: box, gasket, and cover. The box has holes that are threaded for metal conduit. The gasket is sandwiched between the box and the cover for protection against water. The screwholes are countersunk to further provide protection from moisture. The cover plate has small gasketed doors over the outlets and switches.

OTHER WEATHERPROOF FIXTURES. Some switch box designs have a toggle positioned outside the cover plate to trip the switch toggle inside the box. A waterproof light fixture that uses a gasket to seal out the weather is also available.

None of these weatherproof fixtures is designed for submersion under water such as in a swimming or reflecting pool. For such installations you have to buy components with watertight construction.

Switches and Outlets

The basic types are single-pole and three-way switches, and these can't be interchanged when you are replacing them. Most of the switches are embossed with the letters AC-DC, or AC ONLY. AC ONLY means the switch may be used only for alternating current, the housepower furnished by a utility. AC-DC means the switch can be used in both alternating current and direct current circuits.

Switch type

Most home centers and hardware stores stock the following types of switches for both single pole and 3-way wiring.

Snap switches make a snapping noise when the toggle is tripped. The snap comes from a spring that controls the contacts inside the switch. Snap switches are the standard household switch, and usually cost less than other types.

Quiet switches, or mercury switches, do not snap when the toggle is tripped. Quiet switches may be connected to AC-DC systems; they cost about 20 percent more than standard toggle switches.

Dimmer switches are designed for either fluorescent or incandescent lighting. They can be used in either single-pole or three-way connections. Dimmers have a rheostat that lets you reduce the wattage used by the lights. There are three types of dimmer switches: high-low, rotary, and push-rotary. A high-low switch has three switch positions: off, low, and high. At the low setting, the light is about half wattage. The high-low is the cheapest type of dimmer switch. The rotary dimmer has a knob that in-

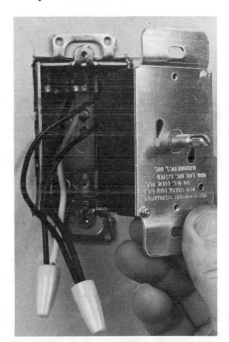

Dimmer switches lower the wattage supplied to lamps when a control knob is turned. The shaft for the friction-fitted knob is seen here in the center of the switch. On this model the light may be turned on and off by pushing the knob down. After a dimmer switch has been wired into a standard junction box, as shown here, a cover plate slips over the shaft and is fastened with screws.

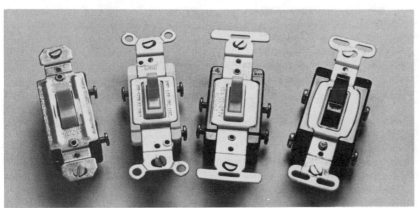

Types of switches that fasten to wall junction boxes include, from left: single-pole; three-way; four-way; and double-pole. You can tell the difference by the number of terminals on the switch. The four-way and double-pole switches look alike but usually are labeled.

creases or decreases the wattage to the lamp. It may be set to off and up the scale to high. A push-rotary switch, the most expensive type, has a rotary dimmer control and a separate toggle switch. The light may be turned on by pushing in the dimmer control or by flipping the toggle.

Before buying a dimmer, check the label on the switch package; it will give you data on the maximum wattage of the light bulbs that can be used with the switch. Dimmers can cause interference with radios, television sets, and stereo sets. You can solve this problem by simply plugging the equipment into a circuit not connected to a dimmer. Power line filters that stop dimmer interference are available at radio and television stores.

Rocker switches use almost all of the cover plate as a toggle to turn on and off lights. Some rockers glow in the dark. Prices are about 20 percent more than silent switches.

Lock switches lock with a key. They

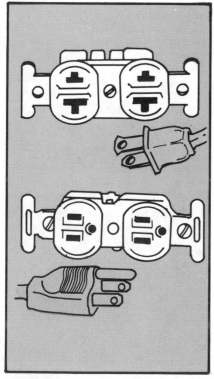

Two basic types of outlets are, at top, a polarized outlet that has one slot larger than the other, and, at bottom, a three-pronged outlet that accepts a grounded, or three-pronged plug. A polarized outlet accepts only a plug with prongs of different sizes in order to properly ground the fixture in the outlet. Both of these outlets are side wired.

are installed the same way as a conventional switch. Prices are about the same as for a quality dimmer switch.

Time-delay switches keep a light burning for a few moments after the switch has been turned to the off position. They do not automatically turn *on* the lights.

Adjustable time-delay switches may be set to delay the light from being turned off for any period from 45 seconds up to 12 hours. These are similar to the switch described above, except they have two settings: off and delay.

Time-clock switches automatically turn the lights on and off at prescribed intervals. These switches are costly and may require a deep junction box to provide room for the clockworks. Read the information on the label before buying.

Special switches not often stocked by home centers and hardware stores include four-way switches that work in tandem with two- and three-way switches to control a light from three locations, and double-pole switches for 230-volt fixtures. Check these switches before buying: double-pole and four-way switches look alike.

Wire terminals are found in different locations on switches; check your installation before buying switches.

Side-wired switches have terminal screws on one side only. Front-wired switches have terminal screws on the front of the switch—one on top and one on the bottom. End-wired switches have terminals on the top and bottom. Back-wired switches have holes in the back into which short lengths of bare wire are inserted. Next to the wire holes are small slots; if you want to remove the wires, you release the spring clamp that holds the wire by pushing a screwdriver into the slot. Some back-wired switches also have terminal screws on the side of the switch. Three-way backwired switches have a hole marked COM; this is the power wire connection.

Receptacles

The three basic receptacles, or outlets, commonly stocked by home centers and hardware stores are described below. Special receptacles such as a receptacle-and-switch combination may also be found at electrical stores.

Grounded receptacles have three slots for a three-prong, or grounded, plug. One slot is connected to the

A waterproof box has seamless joints and cable openings that are threaded to keep out water. Gaskets are inserted between the receptacle and the box covering, and inside the small doors to keep moisture out.

positive (hot) wire, one to the negative wire, and the third to the ground wire. According to the codes, no new wiring may be installed without a ground wire. Standard grounded receptacles are side-wired with a top or bottom grounding terminal.

Back-wired receptacles are wired like back-wired switches, as described above.

Polarized receptacles have one wide and one narrow slot. The plug on a polarized appliance has one prong wider than the other, so that it fits only into a polarized receptacle. The purpose of this system is to prevent

High-voltage, heavy-duty appliance cords have special plug and outlet shapes so they can't be connected to the wrong circuit. These items are stocked at most home centers and hardware stores. When buying replacements, take the old cord to the store so you buy the right item.

electrical shock. You can't insert the plug the wrong way into the receptacle; therefore, the grounding system reduces the shock hazard.

How they're sold
Switches and outlets are priced individually. They are marked as to power capacities and other data, and most of them bear a UL listing. Standard colors are black, dark brown, and ivory.

Standard cover plates, priced individually, are available to cover the switches and outlets. The standard colors are black, dark brown, and ivory. You can also buy decorative plates, which are more expensive. Plates also may be painted to match room colors, or they may be covered with wallpaper, contact paper, and decorative tape.

Lighting Fixtures

Home lighting is produced by three systems: incandescent, fluorescent, and HID (high-intensity discharge). The bulbs and fixtures for these types cannot be intermixed.

Incandescent lighting
Incandescent lighting is produced by bulb with glowing tungsten filaments—the familiar type invented by Thomas Edison nearly a century ago. Styles of incandescent fixtures are seemingly limitless; they can be mounted directly to a ceiling or wall box or plugged into a receptacle. Or the fixtures may be recessed, on a track, or pendant type. We can't possibly list them all in this chapter. You can find the best selection at lighting-fixture stores; most home centers and hardware outlets have only a limited selection. Electrical shops and home furnishing departments of general merchandise stores also stock them.

Portable lamps (those that sit on tables, dressers, desks, etc.) have a bulb socket made of brass or plastic. The sockets are connected to standard No. 18 lamp cord and the end of the cord has a plug for a receptacle. The parts—sockets, insulation, housing, plugs—are standard and may be replaced individually.

Track lighting
The system uses incandescent fixtures that slide on open or closed channel tracks that are fastened to the ceiling with screws, toggle, or Molly bolts in almost any configuration that you want. The tracks are usually wired to a ceiling box for power.

The power flows through a metal strip in the tracks. The fixtures plug into and slide along the track. Open tracks let you set the lights anywhere you want by simply sliding the light along the tracks. Closed channel tracks position the light fixtures more or less permanently in one position.

Some types of track lighting don't have to be connected to a ceiling box; they use a cord and plug combination that is plugged into a regular wall receptacle. Also available are fittings that let you connect track lights to the grid system of suspended ceilings, along with T, X, and L couplings that serve as junctions to direct the track anywhere in the room.

Track lights are usually sold in a kit, although you may be able to buy additional lights, track, and fittings separately. Selection may be limited at home centers and hardware stores; light specialty shops, home furnishing departments of department stores, and electrical specialty shops stock a complete line of track products.

Fluorescent lighting
Because it takes less power to operate, fluorescent lighting is a bargain. The fixtures themselves, however, cost as much as incandescent fixtures. There

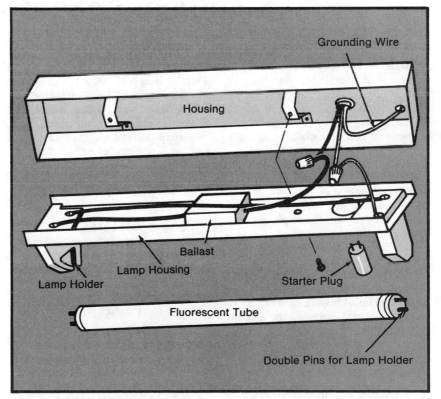

Grounding Wire

Housing

Ballast

Lamp Housing

Lamp Holder

Starter Plug

Fluorescent Tube

Double Pins for Lamp Holder

Fluorescent light fixtures are easy to install and repair; you can buy separate parts—as well as the tubes—at almost any hardware store or home center.

is a variety of fluorescent fixture styles, sizes, and shapes: strip lights, under-cabinet lights, round lamps, and units that are recessed in ceilings, under soffits, behind valances, and in suspended ceilings.

Fluorescent fixtures are connected to ceiling or wall junction boxes; some models have power cords that are plugged into regular house power outlets; still others are screwed into light sockets. The junction-box mounting technique, however, is the most popular technique.

The parts of a fluorescent fixture include: the metal housing, ballast (a kind of transformer), lamp starters, lamp holders, and lamp tube. All are replaceable separately. To buy a replacement part, you must first know what part is malfunctioning. This diagnosis chart can help you:
FLUORESCENT LIGHT FAULTS.
No light: If the fixture is receiving power, first check the electrical connections—the lamp holders and the wire connections from the ceiling box to the ballast hook-up. If these aren't

the problem, replace the starter, tube, and ballast in this order.
Light is partially on: Replace the starter; if this fails, replace the tubes.
Light flickers: Try reseating the starter. Then try reseating the tube. If the light is new, it may flicker for an hour or two. If the light is old, it may flicker just before it burns out. Any light may flicker if the temperature in the room is below 50°F.
Hum: Go right to the ballast. The connections are probably loose. If not, replace the ballast.

HID lighting fixtures
HID lighting is generated by mercury-vapor, sodium-vapor, or metal halide devices. The fixtures have a ballast similar to a fluorescent unit. Flood and spot lighting are available, although usually in limited fixtures at home center and hardware stores. The lights range in wattages from 50 to 1,500; they are generally cheaper to operate than incandescent lights, and the bulbs last longer than incandescents.

For the most part, HID lighting is used outdoors to flood a landscape at night with light or to spotlight a yard feature such as a beautiful tree or garden or swimming pool.

The lights are sold in kits with lamp posts or as individual parts. The kits usually are less expensive than the parts.

Low-voltage lighting
Low-voltage lighting uses a transformer to reduce regular house power to 6 to 10 volts, to operate doorbells or small outdoor lights.

The system usually is sold in kit form, although you can buy separate components and assemble them; you can make kit repairs with separate components. Bell cord is used to distribute power from the transformer to the lights, which are clipped to the cords without special connections, junction boxes, or splicing. The bulbs are 25- and 50-watt size. The basic hook-up is simply plugging the transformer into a regular house power circuit.

Electrical Accessories

Surface Wiring
You can add lighting to your home without ripping into walls and floors to install electrical circuits and fixtures: surface wiring can be attached to walls, ceilings, baseboards, along countertops—almost anywhere. It consists of wires running through a metal or plastic raceway. The wires can be connected directly to a junction box, such as a wall switch or outlet, or they can simply be plugged into an outlet.

Surface wiring is covered by national and local codes; be sure to check the codes in your community before buying any surface wiring products. Local home centers or hardware stores may not stock the product if local codes do not permit its use. If it is available, the system is generally sold in kits that include the raceways and proper connections. You also can buy add-on raceways and connections to enlarge an installation. The kits usually are less expensive than buying the system piece by piece.

Lampposts
Exterior lampposts are a problem to install for most homeowners if the wiring has to be run under a walk or driveway. The lamp components must be waterproof and specified for exterior use. Trenches for buried cable should be 12 inches deep. Outdoor receptacles should be elevated 18 inches from ground level, if the receptacle is on a support post.

Smoke detectors
There are two types: battery operated and those connected to house power. The battery types are simply fastened to a wall or ceiling. Those operated by house power are connected to a junction box just like you would connect a ceiling light.

Ground fault interrupters
In high-moisture areas such as bathrooms, kitchens, and pools, the National Electrical Code requires that ground fault circuit interrupters (GFIs) be installed, even though the electrical system is connected to a

three-wire grounding hook-up. The codes apply to new home construction, but it's smart to install GFIs in these moisture areas even if you live in an older home.

A GFI is an inexpensive device that detects electricity leaking from the wiring system. In a normal situation a small leakage is harmless, but if you are standing in moisture and touch a leaking circuit it could kill you. If the GFI detects as little as .005 amps of leakage, it automatically turns off the power within 1/40 of a second. This can save your life: it takes less than 1/10 of an amp of electricity only two seconds to kill a person.

A GFI can be added to an existing outlet, wired into the main electrical service entrance, or installed in a new outlet junction box. You may be able to install a GFI in an existing box, but call a professional electrician to hook it to the main power entrance or add it to a new outlet box. The cost is not prohibitive; home center, hardware, and electrical supply outlets sell GFIs.

Tools for Electrical Work

Several tools are needed for electrical repairs and improvements.

You probably already have the basics: a hammer, standard and Phillips-head screwdrivers, pliers, a utility knife, gypsumboard saw, hand brace or portable electric drill, spade bits, masonry bits, and auger bits with an extension attachment for them.

Specialized tools and supplies are inexpensive and are available at most home centers and hardware dealers. They include a voltage tester, fish tape (for pulling wires through walls and floors), lineman's pliers, long-nose pliers, wire strippers, metal shears (straight cut), wire nuts, electrician's tape, and a conduit bender. If your home is equipped with cartridge fuses, buy a fuse puller.

Special order

Other than lighting fixtures, most electrical supplies and equipment are readily available at home centers, hardware stores, and electrical specialty shops. These retailers will special-order parts for you, but you will probably have to pay the freight costs. Be prepared to wait up to six weeks for delivery.

Answers to special problems are available from the following associations and manufacturers. Address your request to the Consumer Information Director.

NFPA 70-1981
National Electrical Code
National Fire Protection Association
Quincy, Mass. 02169

General Electric, Lamp Division
Appliance Park
Louisville, Ky. 40225

Leviton Manufacturing Co., Inc.
59-25 Little Neck Parkway
Little Neck, N.Y. 11352

General Electric
Wiring Device Department
95 Hathaway St.
Providence, R.I. 02940

5

CEMENT AND CONCRETE, BRICKS AND STONES

Concrete blocks, bricks, and building stones are called *masonry units.* Concrete mixes stick these units together, patch them, decorate them, or form their own surfaces such as driveways, walks, patios, retaining walls, and stucco. Cement is *cement* until it is mixed with water; then it becomes *concrete.* All tools used to work with cement and concrete and masonry units are called *masonry tools.* Knowing this will enable you to buy masonry tools and products, instead of woodworking tools and products.

For regular maintenance of masonry materials in and around your home, you will find the necessary mixes, units, and tools at most home centers and some hardware outlets. If you are building a new room addition or placing a new concrete patio, driveway, or walk, you will need materials in quantity that a home center or hardware may not be able to provide at a reasonable cost. Your second stop is a hard-materials retailer—a dealer in concrete and masonry products such as a Ready-Mix cement company, or a block and brick manufacturer. These dealers are listed in

Weight Calculator for Hard Materials			
PRODUCT	APPROX. WEIGHT	PRODUCT	APPROX. WEIGHT
Masonry cement	70 to 85 lbs. per bag	Gravel	96 lbs. per cu. ft.
Portland cement	94 lbs. per bag	Crushed stone	50 lbs. per bag/100 lbs. per cu. ft.
Cement pre-mix	80 lbs. per bag		
Mortar pre-mix	80 lbs. per bag		
Sand pre-mix	80 lbs. per bag	Slag	70 lbs. per cu. ft.
Blacktop mixture	70 lbs. per bag		
Dry sand	97 to 118 lbs. per cu. ft.	Water	8.33 lbs. per gallon

your classified telephone directory. Most deliver the heavy masonry products and accessories.

Most masonry maintenance and repair jobs are exempt from local building codes. You may need a permit, however, for construction projects. Check the codes before you buy any materials and start working. You also should check Federal Housing Authority (FHA) and Veterans Administration (VA) minimum property and

construction standards. Your home will have to meet these standards if you ever plan to sell it.

Local codes will apply to footings, interior load-bearing walls, exterior walls, solid masonry such as walks and driveways, hollow masonry units (concrete blocks), and some types of interior non-load-bearing walls. Local codes also govern footing depths, the type of concrete mix required for footings, grout and mortar mix, type of concrete block units, and reinforcing.

Concrete Blocks

Concrete blocks or masonry units are available in a variety of sizes and shapes. The blocks include stretchers, corners, jambs, channels, and partition units. Concrete blocks also come in decorative units such as screen blocks. Some screen units may be used as structural blocks, as well as for decorative purposes.

Standard-weight concrete blocks

are made from a mixture of cement, sand, and coarse aggregate such as gravel. The mixture is placed in block molds. Lighter-weight blocks use other aggregates such as pumice, shale, or cinders. Since these aggregates are of lighter weight, the units are easier to handle. However, you must comply with the codes if these lighter-weight blocks are used.

The most common hollow-core construction block is labeled 8×8×16 inches, but the dimensions are nominal. The actual size of the unit is 7⅝×7⅝×15⅝ inches. The ⅜-inch difference is for the mortar that holds the units together. Other block dimensions (nominal size) include blocks that are 4 or 8 inches wide; 4, 8, or 12 inches high; 8 or 16 inches

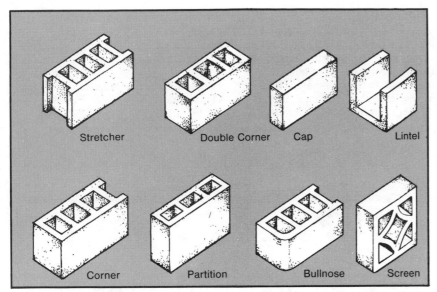

Typical concrete block masonry units are shown here. For specialized projects, such as window and door lintels and sills, other blocks are available.

Several types of aggregate are used in block manufacturing, including sand and gravel, pumice, and cinders.

long. For foundation walls, blocks 12 inches high often are used.

Measuring for the number of blocks you need for a project isn't as complicated as it might seem.

Lay out the job in multiples of 8 inches to save yourself the trouble of cutting blocks. These figures also will be important:

Type of block sometimes can be determined by its texture. Cinder blocks (shown) tend to be porous, while concrete blocks are dense in texture. The hollow cores may be filled with loose-fill insulation to increase the R-value (heat resistance) of the masonry wall.

- There are about 113 blocks per 100 square feet.
- The area (length × width) of one standard block is 0.878 square feet. Therefore, the number of blocks you need will be the area (length × width) divided by 0.878.
- Corner units are necessary for the ends of each course of block. Assuming 8-inch blocks will be used, divide the height of the wall by 4 (inches). The answer is the number of blocks required for the project. Add three more blocks to this figure to make up for any damage during cutting and fitting.

For maintenance and repair projects, you need only buy the units required for replacement.

Masonry tools necessary for maintenance and repairs include a mortar-mixing tub or bucket, shovel, mason's hammer, brick chisel, joint strike, tuckpointing trowel, and a pointing trowel (triangular).

Tools you'll need for masonry construction include the ones above, plus a level, line level, masonry string, line stretchers to support the string, a story pole marked at 4- and 8-inch increments to check the height of each course (row) of block, and a mortar board (plywood) to hold small amounts of mortar for the joints.

Proper storage of concrete blocks before they are used is important: Cover the blocks with a tarp or plastic sheeting to keep rain from soaking them. Unlike bricks, concrete blocks are set up dry. The excess mortar is scraped from the block faces immediately after the blocks are set. The joints also are struck (smoothed) after each course is set.

A standard mortar mix for concrete blocks is three parts sand to one part cement. Use a stiff mixture (not too much water) and mix small amounts of mortar at one time. For small jobs, you can buy ready-to-mix mortar mix in 80-pound bags. Mortar mix has been specially formulated for laying brick, stone, and block. It also may be used for stuccoing and tuckpointing damaged mortar joints. You just add water to the dry mixture and stir it until thoroughly mixed.

How they're sold

Concrete masonry units are sold by the piece or block.

Cement is sold by the 100-pound bag, although smaller-weight units

Cap blocks complete a free-standing concrete wall. Cap blocks also may be used for garden paving; they are available in colors.

may be available and priced accordingly.

Ready-to-mix concrete mix is sold by the bag.

Sand and gravel are sold by the ton, by the cubic yard, or by the pound.

If your project is a large one, you may be able to get a price discount on quantity. Ask the store manager.

Special order

Concrete blocks are not special-ordered because of their weight. If the home center or hardware outlet doesn't have the type of block you need, look for a hard-materials dealer in your area. You will be limited to the dealer's products, but a fairly wide variety of shapes and sizes usually are available. For special help, contact the Consumer Information Director at:

Portland Cement Association
Old Orchard Road
Skokie, Ill. 60076

Bricks

Bricks come in a wide variety of sizes, colors, and textures. They are also made for interior or exterior use, so you should buy the type that fits your project. If you are replacing only a few bricks, you may have trouble finding an exact match; take an old brick with you if you can.

Firebricks are quite different from building bricks. They are manufactured from a clay mixture that will withstand extreme heat, and appear quite dense and heavy compared to building bricks.

Common bricks are available in three grades for different weathering conditions: NW grade for no weathering, MW grade for medium weathering, and SW grade for severe weathering.

Common bricks are available in only a few shapes, sizes, and colors and are roughly finished.

Facing bricks are available in two grades: SW and MW. These bricks are available in a variety of shapes, sizes, and colors and are a higher quality, smoothly finished brick.

Veneer bricks may be real bricks or simulated bricks (plastic or ceramic) that are used to build veneered walls next to an existing wall surface such as framing and sheathing. Veneered walls are not structural; that is, they aren't designed to support heavy weight, such as a roof.

Paving bricks for driveways and roads may be slightly larger than common bricks. These units are known as *pavers* and should be ordered by name. (Patio bricks usually are not pavers, but are manufactured from weaker concrete instead of fired clay.)

Used or reclaimed bricks that you can buy from a wrecking site or a

Firebricks are very heavy and dense, and ivory or buff in color. Concrete bricks are similar to concrete blocks in density; they are solid like standard clay bricks. Patio blocks are also made from concrete, with the same density.

hard-materials dealer are just as good as brand-new bricks. However, choose only bricks that are sound, clean, and not cracked or chipped.

Brick construction—with the exception of maintenance and repair—is subject to local codes similar to those governing block construction. Be sure you check with local authorities before building with bricks.

Common or standard bricks have a nominal size of 2¾×4½×8½ inches. Their actual size is 2¼×3¾×8 inches. The smaller measurement allows for mortar joints. Standard mortar joints are ⅜ and ⅝ of an inch thick.

The spacing difference increases the amount of mortar needed; see the estimating chart on page 79.

A good rule of thumb when estimating brick needs is: You need approximately 8 bricks per square foot of area. First calculate the area to be bricked—length × width in feet—and multiply by 8.

Brick types include solid bricks, which are recommended for general work, and cored bricks, which give mortar better holding power. Electrical wires can be run through some types of cored bricks.

Artificial brick is a brick veneer that is fastened to a horizontal or vertical surface with adhesive. It is manufactured from clay, mica, and cement, and engineered for both interior and exterior use. To break a brick, score it with a hacksaw and snap it over a straightedge such as a pencil.

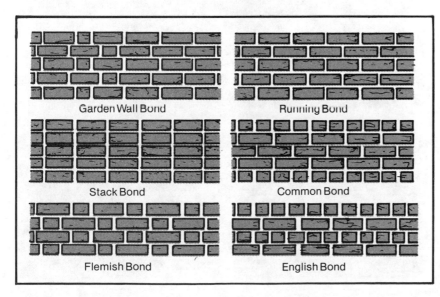

Garden Wall Bond | Running Bond

Stack Bond | Common Bond

Flemish Bond | English Bond

Standard designs or bonds for bricks are shown here. The easiest for a do-it-yourselfer are the common and running bonds.

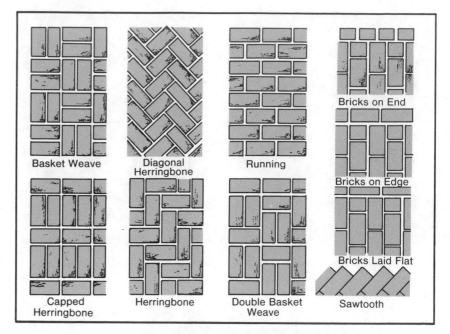

Basket Weave

Diagonal Herringbone

Running

Bricks on End

Bricks on Edge

Bricks Laid Flat

Capped Herringbone

Herringbone

Double Basket Weave

Sawtooth

Paving brick designs can be quite varied. The easiest for most do-it-yourselfers are the basket weave and running designs. Most paving bricks are laid on a sand base; a concrete base may also be used.

Metal wall ties, which are galvanized sheet steel, help hold bricks into position along parallel walls. The ties are sandwiched in mortar between bricks and nailed to framing members or the sheathing.

Bricks Needed for Specific Wall Areas and Thicknesses

AREA (sq. ft.)	4-IN. THICK	8-IN. THICK	12-IN. THICK
100	756	1,512	2,268
200	1,512	3,024	4,536
500	3,780	7,560	11,340
1,000	7,560	15,120	22,680

Note: These minimum estimates do not include allowances for breakage and cutting.

Estimating the number of bricks for a project depends on the design of the project. The following are guidelines:

☐ Exterior walls require concrete footings. This includes brick retaining walls that are over 2 feet high. The footings must have a base below the frostline in your area. The National Weather Service will give you frostline depths in your area if the retailer where you buy bricks doesn't know. The footing should be twice the thickness of the brick wall. It also should be level and smooth.

For exterior walls, a SW (severe weathering) type of brick is recommended. Retaining walls also use a SW brick, but MW and NW bricks and reclaimed bricks may be used, codes permitting.

☐ Brick paving may be set on sand or concrete; the base must be level and smooth. If it's sand, the sand should be moistened with water, tamped, and then leveled.

If the bricks will be divided with wooden strips or edged with wood, the wood should be treated with chemicals to prevent rotting and weathering. Or, you can use redwood, cypress, or cedar for the strips. This wood will not rot (see Chapter 1 for recommendations).

☐ Brick driveways are subject to code restrictions and FHA and VA standards.

Also to be considered for estimating purposes is a flare design at the entrance/exit of the driveway for vehicles.

Most driveways paved with bricks must have a concrete base that is at least 4 inches thick and reinforced with steel mesh or reinforcing rods. The slope of the driveway should be limited to 2 inches per foot if possible. Any humps or dips should be de-

signed so that the undercarriages of vehicles don't hang up on the road surface.

If your driveway is fairly level, the surface should have a cross pitch of about ¼ inch per foot for adequate drainage. A driveway should be at least 8 feet wide, and preferably 10.

☐ Brick sidewalks should be from 2 (minimum) to 3 feet wide. They are also subject to local codes and FHA and VA requirements, so check this out before building—especially if the walk will be used by the public. Private garden walks are not as critical in design requirements.

Walks should slope no more than 2 inches per foot. If the slope is more than 2 inches, you should build steps. If the walk is level, give the surface a cross pitch of about ½ inch per foot for drainage.

If the bricks are to be laid on a sand base, the base should be at least 2 inches thick, watered, tamped, and leveled. If the bricks are laid on a concrete base, the concrete should be at least 3 inches thick and reinforced with steel mesh or rod.

If you will mortar bricks on a concrete base, the base also should be at least 3 inches thick and reinforced.

☐ Brick patios may be laid on a sand or concrete base. A sand base should be at least 2 inches thick—watered, tamped, and leveled. A concrete base should be 3 inches thick—reinforced and smooth and level.

Provide about ½ inch per foot pitch to the patio surface for drainage—if laid on level ground—and pitch the surface away from the house, toward a drain, if possible.

Masonry tools needed for brick repairs and maintenance include a mixing tub or bucket, pointing trowel (triangular), tuckpointing trowel, joint strike, shovel, tape measure, and stiff broom.

For brick building projects, you will need the tools mentioned above plus a brick chisel, mason's hammer, mason's string, line level, carpenter's level, and corner blocks to hold the mason's line at the ends of the various brick courses. A story pole marks each course of bricks. The pole can

Mortar mix is a premixed formula of cement and fine sand used to stick blocks, bricks, and stones together. Unless your job is a very large one, it will pay you to use this mix instead of mixing your own mortar from cement and sand.

Sand mix is similar in texture to mortar mix, but this product is more suitable for filling cracks, grouting, and tuckpointing. Mortar mix may be used for these purposes, too, but it is higher priced than sand mix.

Paving Bricks and Mortar Necessary for Specific Areas

AREA (sq. ft.)	BRICKS	MORTAR (cu. ft.)
50	208	2
100	419	3.2
200	838	6.4
500	2,095	16.0
1,000	4,190	32.0

Mortar Formulas by Volume

TYPE	CEMENT	LIME/LIME PUTTY	TYPE II CEMENT	DAMP MORTAR SAND
High strength (M)	1 part	¼ part	—	3 to 3¼ parts
Medium strength (N)	1 part	—	1 part	4½ to 6 parts
High bond (S)	1 part	¼ to ½ parts	—	3½ to 4½ parts
Grout	1 part	—	—	2 parts sand; 3 parts pea gravel
Parging	1 part	—	—	3¼ to 4½ parts

be made with a length of 1×4 with an extremely straight edge. Handy tools to have are a mortar board and a line level. The board can be a square of plywood.

Standard mortar mix for laying or tuckpointing for bricks is three parts sand to one part cement. The consistency should be fairly thick—not too soupy. Mix small amounts of mortar at one time; it dries out quickly, especially during the hot summer months.

For small jobs, you can buy ready-to-mix mortar mix. See the preceding section for details.

How they're sold

Bricks are sold by the unit. If the project calls for a lot of bricks, you may be able to get a lower price. Ask the retailer for it; he won't offer.

For a small quantity of bricks, a home center or hardware store may be your best shopping source for type and variety. For big jobs, a hard-materials retailer probably will be the best source because the retailer will deliver the heavy load. The hard-materials dealer also will have large bulk quantities of aggregate such as sand and bags of Portland cement. He also will stock metal reinforcement, concrete coloring mixtures, and may have concrete power mixers for rent. Concrete tools usually are not sold by a hard-materials retailer; buy them at a home center or hardware store.

Special order

You may be able to special-order bricks, although from a price standpoint, you'll fare better by buying the units in your local community.

Simulated bricks, made from a mixture of clay, cement, and mica, may be special-ordered, usually at no extra cost.

Also available on special order are fire bricks and brick tiles that are decorative and fireproof. These products are similar to simulated bricks, which may be used outdoors.

Concrete colors, bonding agents, and chemical additives, called *admixtures,* that control hardening, can be special-ordered; but check several retailers in your area before placing an order.

For special materials and questions about brick and mortars, write the Consumer Information Director of these companies:

Barclay Industries Inc.
65 Industrial Rd.
Lodi, N.J. 07644

Pine Hall Brick & Pipe Co.
Box 11044
Winston-Salem, N.C. 27106

Z-Brick Co.,
Division of VMC Corp.
Woodinville, Wash. 98072

Republic Powdered Metals Inc.
(colors)
2628 Pearl Rd.
Medina, Ohio 44256

Flintkote Stone Products Co.
Executive Plaza IV, Dept. PM
Hunt Valley, Md. 21031

Stone and Crushed Stone

Limestone, sandstone, granite, marble, slate, and bluestone are the types of stone sold for construction work. Some home centers sell all six types; most home centers stock only two or three varieties, usually slate, limestone, and marble.

Stone also is classified according to shape as: ashlar, rubble, and trimmings. As a rule, rubble is less costly than ashlar and trimmings.

Ashlar is any type of stone cut on all four sides to resemble bricks, but the sizes of individual pieces vary considerably. The cuts may be smooth or rough; the rough cuts usually are less expensive than the smooth.

Rubble is uncut stones with random shapes. Rubble is usually stacked without mortar.

Trimmings are pieces cut on all four sides for specific uses, such as molding, sills, and lintels above doors and windows. The cuts usually are very smooth and the shapes are exact.

Here are descriptions and uses of several common types of stone.

Limestone: Soft to fairly hard, this product is idea for walls, steps, paving, and garden walks. It offers color variation—from a buff color to shades of brown. The price is moderate.

Marble: This stone is hard and may be polished with a stone abrasive. Polished, it can be used for tabletops, fireplace mantels and facings, and for floor tile. In some sections of the country, the stone is moderately priced. Otherwise, it is in the expensive class.

Slate: This stone is brittle and cracks easily. It can be split into veneer for lamination to concrete bases. Three colors are usually available: black, green, and gray. It can be used for floors, veneer facings, and roofing; always set it on a flat side over a solid base. Don't set it on edge.

Sandstone: It's stronger than you might think, and can be used for window and door sills and veneering. Colors range from buff to brown. Many soft spots in the stone indicate poor quality. The price ranges from inexpensive to moderate.

Granite: Extremely hard, granite—like marble—may be polished for decorative use. Colors are white, gray, green, reddish, and pinkish. The price ranges from inexpensive to expensive, depending on the quality of the material, color, and sizes of the blocks.

Bluestone: It is blue to black in color, and is recommended for veneers and paving. It often is used as a garden walk and for stepping-stones.

Most stone is also described and sold in these three classifications: dressed, semidressed, and undressed. Dressed stone (such as trimmings) is cut to your requirements. Semidressed stone has the rough edges knocked off and is in approximate sizes. Undressed stone (such as rubble) is sold just the way it came from the earth, with no labor value added.

Crushed stone is available for walkways and garden paths and is used for garden decorating. Marble and granite chips are frequently used for built-up roofs.

Masonry tools needed for stone repair and maintenance include a brick chisel, cold chisel, baby sledge hammer, tuckpointing trowel, rubber mallet, a portable electric drill with a masonry disc, and a mixing tub or bucket for cement.

For large building projects with stone, you need the tools mentioned above plus a level, mason's string, pointing trowel (triangular), and a slate cutter (if you are using slate).

Caution: When cutting, polishing, and drilling stone, always wear safety glasses and heavy gloves. The tiny chips generated by striking stone materials can harm eyes.

Mortar for stonework should be mixed to this formula (by volume):

1 part white Portland cement. (Do not use gray Portland cement.)

3 parts damp, clean mortar sand.

¼ part hydrated lime.

Add water carefully as you mix, until the mortar has the consistency of foamy shaving cream or a stiff cake batter. Mortar should show only a slight slump when dropped off a trowel.

How it's sold

Stone is sold by the piece and sometimes by the weight. Most retailers will let you pick the stones that you want, although dressed stone may not be selected.

Stone chips are sold by the bag—usually 50 pounds—and by total weight.

If a large quantity of stone is needed, you may be able to get a dis-

count on the material. But you must ask.

Special order

Stone may be special-ordered, but most retailers will be reluctant to order it for you. Be prepared to pay high freight costs on special orders. Simulated stone, made from clay, cement, and mica—is readily available by order, and you may not have to pay the freight charges.

If you can't find the stone that you want in your community, or if you have a special building problem with the material, write the Consumer Information Director of the companies listed below:

Bloomington Limestone Corp.
Box 250
Bloomington, Ind. 47401

Corning Glass Works,
Pyram Products
Oneonta, N.Y. 13820

Decro-Wall Corp.
375 Executive Blvd.
Elmsford, N.Y. 10523

Miami Brick & Stone Co.
Box 879
Miami, Okla. 74354

Concrete

Concrete is cement and aggregate (sand and gravel) mixed with water. It is available everywhere in all the textures and designs you can imagine.

In residential housing, concrete is used for foundations, walks, driveways, floors, retaining walls, patios, screens, and so forth.

For small maintenance and repair jobs, you can buy ready-to-mix concrete in 80-pound bags, or, you can buy the cement and aggregate and mix the concrete yourself. But be prepared for lots of hard, dirty work. There's a time element, too: concrete has a short work time—usually an hour.

For large jobs, it's easier to order already-mixed concrete from a Ready-Mix company or a hard-mate-

rials retailer. Most home centers and hardware stores do not sell already-mixed concrete, but some rent concrete mixers if you want to tackle the mixing job yourself.

Poured concrete work—such as a driveway, walk, patio, retaining wall—usually is governed by local building codes. You may also need a building permit to place concrete; be sure to check regulations set down by the FHA and VA.

The specifications you must provide for a building permit will likely include slope data, subgrade preparation, materials for forms, concrete thickness, reinforcement and composition, color restrictions, and curing and hardening information. These basic standards—and others, too—are

available at the building department of your local government. The standards can help you in designing the project.

Any concrete construction requires several steps in succession. These include preparing the grade or base for the material, constructing a base, building the forms, placing the concrete in the forms, finishing the concrete, and curing the concrete. The materials used include crushed stone for the base; dimension lumber, plywood, or hardboard for the forms; 2×4s for form stakes; the concrete itself; material, such as plastic sheeting, burlap, and straw, to cover the concrete during curing.

Information on crushed stone may be found above. Data on forms may

Pre-mixed concrete (or ready-to-mix) is useful for small- to medium-sized concrete repair, maintenance, and building projects. Add water to the mixture and stir. An 80-pound bag yields about 1/3 cubic yard of concrete.

be found in the Lumber and Plywood chapter; information on plastic sheeting and burlap may be found in the Specialty chapter of this book.

Buying already-mixed concrete is easier than mixing it yourself, although you may pay slightly more for it. The type of concrete you order depends on what you are building with it. For example, a patio project may require a slightly different mix than a driveway. But don't concern yourself with this problem when you order from a company that sells ready-mixed material. They will handle the details. Just provide them with this information:

- The length and width of the project that will be concrete.
- The thickness of the concrete.
- Whether or not the concrete will be reinforced. The company may sell steel reinforcing mesh and/or rods. You can buy these from them or at a home center or hardware store. The big advantage of ordering from the concrete company is that the company will deliver the reinforcing materials to the job.
- Whether or not the concrete will be colored. You add the color mix when you finish the material.
- The access route to the job site.
- The time you want the concrete delivered to the job site.

Many concrete companies have a minimum order which usually is 3 cubic yards. If your project will take less concrete than this (see the estimating chart) you will have to mix it yourself. While a few concrete companies will sell less than the minimum, be prepared to pay a premium for the material.

Be ready with the base and forms in place at the hour the concrete will be delivered. The driver will wait a few minutes for last-minute alterations and for you to place or elevate reinforcing, but he will want to dump the load and get to the next job.

Check the first pour out of the revolving truck drum. If the mixture is too dry, have the driver add some water. But go easy on the water: Too much can weaken the mixture and delay finishing. If the weather is cold the day the concrete is placed, ask the driver to add a chemical to the mixture which will speed its curing time or help prevent damage from freezing.

Mixing concrete yourself will involve renting a concrete mixer if the project is fairly large—such as a driveway or 50 feet of sidewalk. If the project is a small one, you can mix the material in a plastic tub, a wheelbarrow, or even on a sheet of plywood. Some home centers and hardware stores have small-capacity concrete mixers for rent. If you can't find one there, try a tool-rental outfit. It's cheaper to rent this equipment than buy it, unless you are constantly working with concrete.

If you are mixing small batches of concrete, you will have to plan the placement job in sections. Set up the mixing operation near the forms and have the sand and gravel dumped near this site. Mix batches to fill sections of forms completely. Don't leave a small amount of concrete to dry in a form; fresh concrete poured later will not bind well with the old remnant.

The best all-around formula for mix-it-yourself is this:

3 parts gravel mix
2 parts sand
1 part cement

After you mix the ingredients thoroughly, run a trowel across a mound of the mixture. The trowel should leave a smooth and solid track indicating that everything has been evenly mixed. Then add water slowly to the mix. You have to guess at the amount of water, but you will know when the mix is right by its consistency: like cake batter or fairly stiff whipped cream. Too much water will make the mixture weak; too little water will make the mixture difficult to float and trowel to a smooth finish. Adding water to the mixture after it has been placed in the forms will weaken the concrete. Complete all mixing before the concrete is placed and finished.

Another formula that has been used successfully contains *con-mix* gravel, which you can buy at many hard-materials outlets. The con-mix is a combination of sand and gravel:

4 parts con-mix
1 part cement

Concrete also can be mixed by weight, but the part formula (one part of this to three parts of that) is easier to figure for most do-it-yourselfers.

Estimating concrete needs

Quantities of concrete are measured in cubic yards, or simply *yards*. Here's the formula for finding the number of yards of concrete needed for a project:

Pigments for Coloring Concrete, Mortar, and Stucco

PIGMENT	COLOR
Black iron oxide; carbon black; mineral black	Black to gray tones
Yellow iron oxide	Buff, ivory, cream
Red iron oxide	Red (dense)
Chromium oxide; phthalocyanine green	Green (medium dense)
Brown iron oxide; raw and burnt umber	Brown
Cobalt oxide; ultramarine blue; phthalocyanine blue	Blue

Note: Pigment is added to the mixture by the weight of the cement, as indicated on the container. (Aggregate is not included in the weight.)

Concrete Estimator (Cubic Feet)				
CONCRETE THICKNESS (in.)	AREA TO BE COVERED (sq. ft.)			
	20	50	100	200
2	3.3 cu. ft.	8.3 cu. ft.	16.7 cu. ft.	33.3 cu. ft.
4	6.7 cu. ft.	16.7 cu. ft.	33.3 cu. ft.	66.7 cu. ft.
6	10 cu. ft.	25 cu. ft.	50 cu. ft.	100 cu. ft.

☐ For squares and rectangles, multiply the length by the width of the thickness of the area in feet.

☐ If the project is a circle, multiply the square of the radius in feet by 3.14 and then by the thickness desired. Then divide these volumes by 27 to get cubic yards.

Ready-mixed concrete is sold by the yard. Premixed formulas you buy by the bag in a store—concrete, mortar, and sand—contain about ⅓ yard per 80 pound bag.

The estimating chart in this chapter will help you determine the amount of material needed for surface areas and thickness.

Pre-mixes

Although more costly than mixing concrete, sand, and gravel together yourself, the bagged pre-mixes are convenient, fairly easy to handle, and ideal for small jobs where only a yard or two of concrete is needed. There are three types of pre-mixes that are found in almost all home centers and hardware stores and even some drug stores:

Concrete mix has coarse aggregate (gravel or crushed stone ranging in size from ¼ to 1½ inches) and is used for projects where strength is needed. Since the mixture's strength exceeds 4,000 pounds per square inch, it is the best mix to use for walks, patios, and some light-support foundations.

Mortar mix (mentioned earlier in this chapter) has a sand aggregate that will sift through ¼-inch screen wire. Its strength is 1,250 pounds per square inch. Use it for laying bricks, block, and stone, and for tuckpointing damaged mortar joints.

Sand mix has a strength of more than 5,000 pounds per square inch. The aggregate is fine—similar to mortar mix—and the material may be used for grouting, patching cracks, tuckpointing, topping or veneering concrete, and setting stone goods.

Concrete tools

For routine repair and maintenance of concrete, you will need a mixing tub or bucket, shovel, wooden float, concrete-finishing trowel, and a length of 2×4 with a straight edge for leveling (screeding) concrete.

For large jobs—walks, patios, retaining walls, and such—the tools listed above are necessary, along with a rented concrete mixer, if you're going to mix it yourself, wire cutters, hacksaw, hammer, scaffolding nails, sledge hammer, concrete edger and divider, and a concrete tamper, which you can also rent.

Other equipment, which you probably already own, includes a garden hose, water buckets, a rake, and a stiff-bristle broom.

How it's sold

Already-mixed concrete is sold by the cubic yard. Premixed cement is sold by the bag; each one weighs 80 pounds. The type of mix—patio mix, driveway mix, etc.—determines the price, both for already-mixed concrete and bag goods.

Reinforcing mesh is sold by the roll, which may vary as to width, length, and gauge of wire. Reinforcing rods are priced by the diameter and the length of the rod. Standard lengths are 10 feet.

Sand and gravel are sold by the cubic yard or by weight. You can buy sand and gravel separately or sand and gravel mixed at hard-materials outlets. Many home centers and hardware stores sell sand and gravel or sand/gravel mixes in 80-pound bags similar to the premixed cements. The type and quality of the aggregate also is a price factor. Washed sand, for example, costs more than unwashed sand.

If you buy huge quantities of concrete components—for example, a driveway or a foundation wall—you may be able to get a discount. Otherwise, the price you see is the price you pay. If you ask, however, you

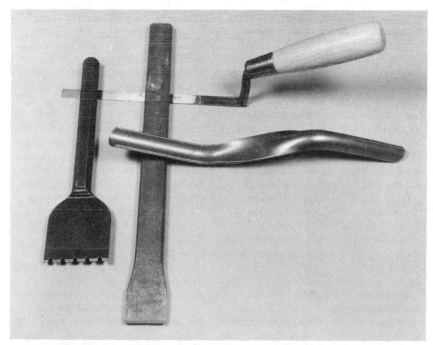

Basic tools needed to maintain and repair concrete around the home include a brick chisel with notched blade or a narrow brick or stone chisel; tuckpointing trowel (top); a joint strike. Total cost is less than $6.

may get a price break on broken-bag goods from home center and hardware retailers.

Special order

Since concrete materials are so plentiful in most communities, there is no need to special-order them. If a home center or hardware retailer doesn't have the product you want, you usually can find it at a hard-materials dealer or at a ready-mixed concrete company. This is especially true of concrete admixtures and coloring compounds; most home centers simply don't have a demand for them and, therefore, do not stock them.

If you have any questions about concrete, aggregates, special designs, load-bearing data, and so forth, write to the Consumer Information Director at:

Portland Cement Association
Old Orchard Road
Skokie, Ill. 60076

This organization of concrete and cement manufacturers has a large selection of free, or low-cost literature that can be most helpful in the design and placement of concrete products.

Concrete forms

Forms hold concrete in position while it is being placed, finished, and cured. They can be made of almost any material that is sturdy enough to withstand the thrust of the concrete against it.

Dimension lumber (2×4s, 2×6s, 2×8s) generally is used to make forms for driveways, walks, patios, and slabs. Boards also can be used for forms (1×4s, 1×6s, 1×8s) for small jobs such as a garden pathway or individual forms for stepping stones. Plywood (Plyform) is excellent for large forms such as those used for retaining walls. Hardboard (tempered) is the material to use when irregular shapes and curves are included in the design.

Most forms are nails together with scaffolding nails (double-headed) and staked with short lengths of 2×3 or 2×4.

If you intend to use the forming material more than once, buy a concrete form oil to brush on the inside and top of the wooden surfaces. Form oil prevents the concrete from sticking to the wood so that the forms may be reused.

Control joints

Slabs of concrete expand and contract as the weather changes. This movement, if not controlled, can crack and break the concrete.

Three methods are used to prevent cracking. The simplest: a tool called a divider is drawn across the finished concrete, making an indentation about an inch deep. On a sidewalk, for example, you draw the divider across the slab every four feet or so.

A better method uses expansion joints—strips of asphalt material ½ inch thick and 4 inches wide—that are inserted into the finished concrete every three or four feet. Slice down into the concrete with a trowel, after it has been placed, and force a piece of expansion joint into the crack; then finish the concrete. You should place a piece of expansion joint against an existing structure, such as a stair step or foundation wall, before placing concrete against it.

Expansion joints are available at most home centers, hardware stores, and hard-materials dealers. Ready-mixed concrete companies also stock them.

Permanent forms

A third way to prevent cracking is to create a grid design in concrete, wooden strips or forms sometimes are left in place after the concrete hardens and cures. These forms serve as expansion joints to help prevent concrete from cracking and breaking. Standard expansion-joint material is not necessary against the sides of the forms, although expansion joints may be used at foundation walls, steps, and other house parts against which the new concrete butts.

The permanent forms should be made with wood that doesn't rot— redwood, cedar, or cypress. Pressure-treated boards and dimension lumber offer some rot resistance, but should be considered a second choice if redwood, cypress, or cedar can be used. Never use untreated wood.

Precast concrete

Some home centers and many hard-materials dealers carry precast concrete components such as stair steps, splash blocks for gutter drainage, and patio blocks. These products vary in size, so take measurements to the store. The individual components are sold by the unit and are seldom tailor-made to your specifications; that cost would be too great.

Veneers, sealers, and patches

Standard accessory items, for concrete products include concrete topping or veneer mixes, sealers, concrete patch and plugging pre-mix, anchoring cement, and asphalt maintenance and repair compounds and formulas.

For veneering, where you want to hide a cracked, broken, or crazed concrete surface, a topping mixture is used. This material, sold in bag form, contains a latex base that serves as a bonding agent.

This topping can be troweled to a feather edge less than ¼-inch thick and still stick without cracking or loosening from its base. This expensive product is sold in 20-pound bags at home centers and hardwares.

For veneering walks with flat stones—slate, bluestone, flagstone—a 1-inch bed of mortar (premixed or mix-it-yourself) may be used. The joints should be filled with mortar and smoothed to deter loosening.

Ready-to-use concrete patch, available in plastic pails, is ideal for small tuckpointing and patching jobs in concrete, concrete block, and stone and brickwork. This is a costly product; it comes in quart and gallon containers at home centers and hardware stores.

Concrete anchoring cement is formulated especially for setting bolts and other fasteners into holes drilled into concrete and brickwork. Sold in quart and gallon containers, it is fairly expensive. Even so, it is easier to use than old-fashioned melted sulfur and without the mess and heat involved with sulfur.

Concrete sealers, usually clear without colored pigment, are used to seal the porous surfaces of concrete and brick. The sealers are put up in one- and five-gallon containers; they are moderately priced. Seal the surfaces of artificial brick and stone—especially if they are used outside—to make the surfaces resistant to stains, dirt, grease, and the weather.

Hydraulic cement, available in quart and gallon containers, is used to plug basement foundation and floor cracks that are leaking water. The cement sets extremely quickly, but it may be troweled smooth for appearance purposes. Most home centers and hardware stores stock it; it is expensive.

Concrete patch cartridges for caulking guns is ideal for repairing small cracks and breaks in concrete, and

Joint control prevents concrete from cracking and breaking. An expansion strip (held at left) was not inserted between the walk and steps shown above when the concrete was placed. The walk has pulled away from the step, permitting rain and snow to freeze and thaw in the crack and damage the concrete.

may be used to tuckpoint mortar joints if the job isn't too large. Inexpensive, it is best used as a quick-fix for hairline fractures in concrete.

For asphalt (blacktop) surfaces such as driveways, walks, and access paths, several patching and sealing products are available at most home centers and hardware stores. The prices of these products are low enough for you to apply them annually for preventative maintenance of all asphalt surfaces.

Blacktop sealer in caulking-type cartridges is tailored especially for small cracks in asphalt surfaces. The patching technique involves cleaning the crack, partially filling the crack with clean sand, and then topping the sand with the sealer. The material is effective in cracks up to about ⅛-inch wide. For larger cracks, the sealer can be mixed with sand to a thick paste and then forced into the fracture with a putty knife or trowel.

Blacktop coating, sold in five-gallon containers, is spread thinly over the asphalt surface. Apply the coating every two years to asphalt that is exposed to the weather. A combination

squeegee and brush is used for application.

Although similar to blacktop coating, asphalt roofing and foundation cement should not be used for resurfacing. It has a different formula that will not perform satisfactorily.

Blacktop patch, sold in 70-pound bags, is used to patch large holes in asphalt. It is ready to use out of the bag and resembles the material public road maintenance crews use to fill potholes. The repair procedure involves cleaning the hole, pouring in the mix, and tamping it down. A good way to tamp it is to cover the patch with a piece of hardboard or plywood and then drive your car over the cover. After the patch has weathered for six months or so, it should be sealed with blacktop coating.

Stucco

Stucco may be patched or repaired with concrete patching cement, if the repair isn't too large. For large areas, you can mix your own patch:

1 part white cement
3 parts white sand

Blend this formula thoroughly and then add water—a little at a time—until the mix has the consistency of putty or glazing compound. Then fill the area, using a wall scraper or pointing trowel.

If the stucco is colored, add mortar coloring, available at hard-materials dealers. If you want a close color match, mix a small amount, let it dry, and compare it to the original stucco. Most mortar pigments will fade as much as 60 to 80 percent as they dry, so use more pigment at the outset than you think you should. However, the pigment should not exceed approximately 3 percent of the mixture's total volume. More pigment will weaken the mixture.

Concrete paints

Concrete paints are more for decorative purposes than structural repair, although they will hide hairline cracks in reinforced concrete and concrete block walls. Large cracks must be cleaned and pointed with mortar.

Concrete paints will damp-proof concrete; they won't waterproof concrete, since the water pressure comes from behind the structure and pushes the paint off the surface. If water is a problem, a coating should be applied to the outside of the wall, not to the inside of it.

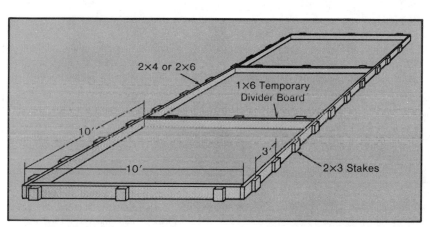

Most forms are fabricated from dimension lumber. For big surfaces, such as steps and retaining walls, plywood and hardboard forms are used. If the job is light and the concrete thrust not too great, boards may be used for forming. Hardboard is ideal for curved surfaces, since it can be bent to a fairly tight radius.

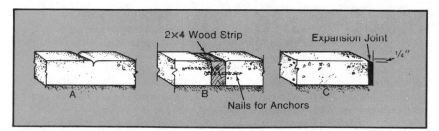

Types of control joints include: (A) grooved joint made by a divider tool; (B) wooden form (redwood, cypress, cedar) left in the concrete; (C) a fiber expansion joint.

6

ROOFING AND SIDING PRODUCTS

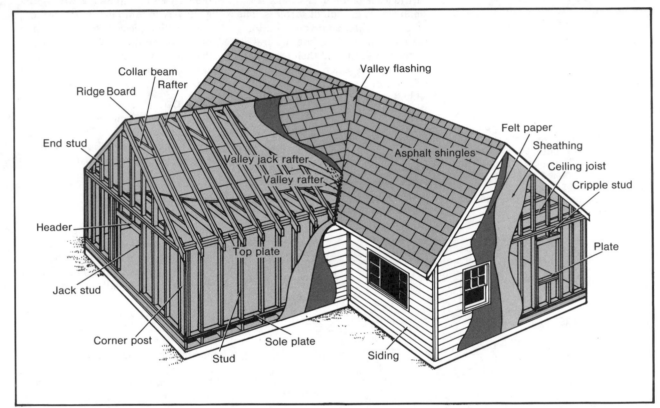

Roofing and siding products involve more than shingles and shakes. A roof also has chimney and valley flashing, sheathing, asphalt building paper, and a rain-carrying system—gutters and downspouts. Siding products also include sheathing (discussed in the Lumber and Plywood chapter), casings, and a waterproof base—usually asphalt paper. All of these products are standard items at home centers and lumberyards that cater to the professional. The roofing and siding application guide (above) shows where and how the different roofing and siding materials are used. Roofing is always applied from the eaves to the ridge board; siding is always applied from the foundation to the top plate.

Roofing Shingles and Coverings

Shingles may be made of cedar, asphalt, slate, or tile. You can repair a cedar or asphalt roof—if the roof is not pitched too steeply for you to work on it. Slate and tile roofs should be installed and repaired only by a professional. You should not attempt to do this job yourself; it requires expensive and specialized equipment.

Cedar shingles and asphalt shingles are sold by the bundle or by the square. A square is 100 square feet. Cedar roofing shingles are sold four bundles to the square. Asphalt shingles are sold three bundles to the square. Prices may be quoted in bundles or squares; divide the square price by the bundle price to find out if it is less expensive to buy the roof covering by the square or by the bundle.

Cedar roofing shingles are available in 16-, 18-, and 24-inch lengths. No. 1 grade has clear and edge grain. No. 2

Typical wood shingle roof gives a rustic appearance to this home. Wooden shakes, similar to wooden shingles, also may be used for roofing.

grade is mostly clear with a flat edge grain. No. 3 grade, which is utility, often is used for shims.

Asphalt roofing shingles—also called strip shingles—are priced according to weight, and the heavier the shingle the higher the price. Average shingles weigh from 210 to 240 pounds per square. Heavy shingles weigh from 300 to 400 pounds per square. Asphalt shingles are also known as 3-tab shingles; they have ½-

inch notches cut at 1-foot increments. Other designs available include no-tab shingles, double-layer laminated shingles, and irregular-butt shingles. All types are approximately 3×1-foot in size.

Fiberglass roofing shingles look like asphalt roofing shingles, but they have a combination fiberglass-and-asphalt base; asphalt shingles utilize an asphalt base. Fiberglass shingles have greater resistance to wear, as well as a better fire rating. They usually cost more than asphalt shingles.

Cedar roofing shingles, asphalt, and fiberglass roofing shingles must always be used on a sloped or pitched roof—never on a flat roof. (Metal and tar and gravel coverings for flat roofs are discussed later in this chapter.)

Roofing shakes are somewhat thicker and more heavily textured than cedar roofing shingles. They are sold in bundles of either 18- or 24-inch lengths. Five bundles cover a square (100 sq. ft.). No. 1 grade is hand split and resawn. No. 1 taper split and No. 1 straight split are reverse split in a cutting block.

The butts of hand split shakes are from about 1¼ to 1½ inches thick. The butts of tapersplits are about ¾-inch.

Estimating wooden shingle needs

The number of wooden shingles needed to cover any roof depends on two factors: the area of the roof and

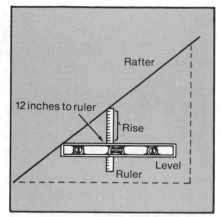

To determine the pitch of a roof, first measure 12 inches from one end of a carpenter's level and mark this point. Hold the level horizontal with the marked end against a rafter in the attic, and measure straight up from the 12-inch mark on the level to the rafter. This measurement gives you the pitch of the roof. Example: If the ruler reads 5 inches, the pitch is 5 inches in 12 feet. This figure is used to estimate shingle needs, as explained in the text.

the slope, or pitch, of the roof. As a rule of thumb, the steeper the roof, the less the shingles are overlapped, and therefore the fewer shingles that are needed.

MEASURING A ROOF. Here's a way to find the area of your roof, without having to climb up on it—a risky business for most people. First, go up in to the attic and measure the roof pitch. Mark the frame of a carpenter's level 12 inches from one end. Hold the level horizontal with the marked end against a rafter. Measure from the 12-inch mark straight up to the rafter. This measurement gives the pitch in inches. For example, if the vertical measurement is 5 inches, the roof rises 5 inches every 12 inches—that is, the pitch is *5 in 12*.

Then measure the roof outside in

Typical asphalt shingle roof looks like this up close. Roll roofing instead of metal flashing was used for the valleys.

Wood Shingle and Shake Estimator

| | EXPOSURE | | |
	4 in.	5 in.	6 in.
100 sq. ft.	900	720	600
Waste	10%	10%	10%
No. needed to cover 100 sq. ft.	990	792	660
3d nails	4 lbs.	3 lbs.	2½ lbs.

Asphalt Shingle Selector							
SHINGLE TYPE	WEIGHT (lbs.)	LENGTH (in.)	WIDTH (in.)	TOP LAP (in.)	HEAD LAP (in.)	EXPOSURE (in.)	SIDE LAP (in.)
2–3 tab square butt	230	36	12	7	2	5	0
Hexagonal	195	36	11⅓	2	2	5	0
Staple/lock	145	16	16	2	2	5	2½
American	330	16	12	11	6	5	0
Dutch lap	165	16	12	2	0	10	3

feet, along the eaves from one end to the other, and *horizontally* from the eaves to the point directly below the ridge. Multiply these two figures together; then multiply the answer by the conversion factor given in the chart below for the pitch of your roof. Add 10 percent for cutting and waste. Divide this answer by 100 to find the number of squares in your roof.

Example: The pitch is 5 in 12. The outside measures are 20×10 feet, or 200 square feet. Multiply by the factor 1.09; the product is 218. Add 10 percent (22) and the sum is 240. Divide by 100. You require two squares (100 square feet each) plus two bundles (25 square feet each) of wood shingles to cover your roof. Since you always round off the estimate to the next higher whole number, there will be some shingles left over. You'll probably need them for patching the roof after a storm.

Roof Pitch	Factor
1 to 3 in 12	1.03
4 in 12	1.06
5 in 12	1.09
6 in 12	1.12
7 in 12	1.16
8 in 12	1.20
9 in 12	1.25
10 in 12	1.30
11 in 12	1.36
12 in 12	1.45

EXPOSURE OF WOODEN SHINGLES. The method described above for estimating wooden shingle needs assumed that your roof had a pitch of 5 in 12. The shingles would be installed with an exposure shown on the first line of the chart below. If your roof is shallower than 4 in 12, you must lay up shingles with less exposure, as shown in the second line. In this case, add 25 percent to the estimated quantity of shingles needed.

The part of the shingle that shows is called the *exposure.* The following chart gives the exposures to allow for wooden shingles of different lengths when they are installed on roofs of different pitch.

Roof Pitch	Exposure		
	16 in. Shingles	18 in. Shingles	24 in. Shingles
4 in 12 or steeper	5″	5½″	7½″
3 in 12 to 4 in 12	3¾″	4¼″	5¾″

Estimating asphalt roofing needs
To estimate asphalt roofing needs, find the area of your roof in square feet. If you don't want to climb up onto the roof, use the measuring method described in Estimating Wooden Shingle Needs. Since the standard exposure for asphalt roofing is 5 inches at any pitch, unless otherwise specified on the package, you do not need to buy more roofing for shallower-pitched roofs.

Example: A roof that measures 30 × 12 feet has 360 square feet. Therefore, you need three squares (100 square feet) plus two bundles (33⅓ square feet each) of asphalt roofing. If your estimate comes out to an exact number of squares or bundles, order one extra bundle to allow for waste.

Buying roofing
When you purchase roofing, consider its life expectancy. Of course, if your home is already covered with asphalt shingles, you probably don't want to switch to cedar. But if you are adding a new addition, or building anew, here are several guidelines that may help you decide:
- Asphalt shingles are inexpensive. They may be applied to slopes or pitches with a minimum of 2 in 12, and will last from 12 to 25 years.
- Wooden shingles and shakes are fairly expensive. They may be applied to pitches of at least 3 in 12. If you reside in a humid climate, the pitch may be steeper. Wood shingles will last from 15 to 30 years. Shakes will last from 25 to 75 years. (The large range in life expectancy is caused by climate. In a dry climate, the shingles will last longer than in a humid climate with lots of freezing and thawing.)
- Built-up roofing (tar and gravel) costs more than asphalt, but less than wooden shingles. It is applied only to flat roofs (0 in 12), and can be expected to last from 10 to 20 years before it has to be renewed.
- Metal roofing costs about the same as built-up roofing. It may be applied to pitches of 2 in 12 minimum. Durability is rated at 25 to 50 years.
- Roll roofing is inexpensive. The minimum pitch is 1 in 12; it will last from approximately 10 to 15 years.
- Slate and tile are very expensive. They can be applied to roofs with a 4 in 12 minimum pitch. Life expectancy is from 75 to 100 years or even longer if they are maintained.

FASTENERS. Both asphalt and fiberglass roofing are nailed in place with large-headed roofing nails. Wooden shingles are nailed with shingle nails. Metal roofing needs a nail with a rubber gasket under its head. All these fasteners are described in the Fastener chapter.

SHINGLE COLORS. Wooden shingles are sold in their natural state. Asphalt and fiberglass shingles are made in a wide range of colors; the standards are off-white, black, brown, and green—all in many tones. Most retailers have samples of a complete line of shingles. If you pick a color other than the standards, you probably will have to wait from four to six weeks for delivery. There usually isn't a freight charge for this service.

Roof construction

The anatomy of a roof is quite simple. The rafters are covered with a sheathing such as plywood or sheathing boards. The sheathing is covered with asphalt-impregnated felt paper, commonly called *asphalt building paper*. The metal flashing, around the chimney and vent stacks and in the valleys of the roof, is installed over the felt, and then the shingles or roof covering are installed.

REROOFING. You can put new asphalt shingles over worn-out asphalt shingles, and you can add wooden shingles and shakes over asphalt shingles. You can also add new shingles and shakes over old shingles and shakes. The techniques are not difficult.

To install asphalt shingles over old shingles, butt the first course of new shingles against the bottoms of the old shingles, and nail them in place.

If the old shingles are damaged, they must be removed entirely, or removed in fairly large areas before the new shingles are applied. This keeps the surface uniform and smooth over the roof area. The cap shingles at the ridge must be removed before the rest of the roof is reshingled.

Don't use the old shingles to guide the installation of the new shingles. Instead, snap a chalkline and follow the line mark. Work completely across the roof with two or three shingle courses, and then snap another line.

Wooden shingles may be applied over asphalt roofs or over old wooden shingles with furring strips. The strips can be 1×3s or 1×4s nailed to the roof sheathing, through the old shingles. The strips should be spaced to match the width of the new shingles. With shakes, start the first two or three courses over a layer of building felt nailed over the old shingles. The rest of the shakes are furred like regular wooden shingle applications.

Specialty roofings

Roll roofing materials, as well as metal, plastic, and tar and gravel roofing, are stock items at most home centers, and at lumberyards that have a roofing department.

ROLL ROOFING. Roll roofing is asphalt-impregnated felt with mineral granules affixed to the felt on the side that will be exposed to the weather. Standard size rolls are 36 feet long by 3 feet wide. The product is sold by

Corrugated metal roofing is made of aluminum or galvanized steel. It is installed with roofing nails that have gaskets under their heads to help deter water leakage down the nail shaft and into the wood rafters below.

the roll and by weight. Weights are between 50 and 90 pounds; the heavier the material, the more it costs. Roll roofing is best for roofs with slight pitches (1 in 12). It must not be used on flat roofs. It is applied with roofing nails; the joints are lapped about 3 inches. It's a good idea to buy asphalt roofing compound in a bucket or caulking tube at the same time you buy roll roofing. The compound should be applied to every nailhead after the nails are driven. The laps also should be cemented along the edge. This procedure adds more durability to the roof and makes it waterproof.

METAL ROOFING. There are two standard types: corrugated and ribbed. Both may be made of aluminum, galvanized steel, copper, or terne, which is steel coated with a tin and lead alloy. The roofing is sold in panels that vary in size, depending on the type of roof. Standard sizes are 4 feet wide by 24 feet long, although narrower and longer pieces are available by special order.

Metal roofs usually have to be laid over thick furring strips called purlins that cross the rafters at right angles; 2×4s are often specified for purlins with spacing from 16 to 36 inches. Follow the roofing manufacturer's specification for spacing.

Flat sheet metal roofs are laid over standard sheathing, which should be covered with asphalt building paper first.

All exposed nailheads in metal roofs should be covered with solder. Seams of metal roofs sometimes are soldered, too, but this is a job for a professional.

PLASTIC ROOFING. These panels are usually used for lightweight patio and shed roofs; they are seldom specified for regular residential roof coverings.

Plastic roofing is made from fiberglass. The panels may be corrugated or ribbed since these configurations

Nail Lengths for Asphalt Shingles		
USE	ON 1-IN. SHEATHING	ON 3⁄8-IN. PLYWOOD
Asphalt re-roofing	1½ in.	1 in.
Over wood shingle re-roofing	1¾ in.	Do not use
In new construction	1¼ in.	⁷⁄8 in.

Fiberglass roofing panels, either corrugated (shown here) or ribbed, are usually applied to patio, deck, and other lightweight roofs where snow loads are not heavy.

make the material much stronger. The panels come in 30-inch widths and various lengths; the standard length is 14 feet. Colors and color combinations are available.

Plastic roofing should be backed with wooden strips that have been cut to fit the configuration of the panels; the strips are nailed to the roof sheathing or rafters and the panels are nailed to the strips. Roofing nails with gaskets are used to fasten the plastic panels. In most stores, the nails are kept near the paneling stock.

BUILT-UP ROOFS. Also known as tar-and-gravel roofs, these roofs are always flat from the bottom. The parts of a built-up roof are: sheathing or wood decking, several layers of asphalt felt nailed down, a mopped-on coat of hot asphalt, alternate layers of felt and mopped asphalt, and then, finally, gravel or slag embedded into the top felt and asphalt topping.

Constructing a built-up roof is a job for a professional since special equipment is needed to apply the different products. However, you can patch a built-up roof with asphalt roofing compound and gravel. Remove the damaged section, trowel the compound over the area, and embed the gravel into the compound. If large areas of the roof are in bad shape, call a professional.

Roof flashings

To keep water from running down the sides of chimneys and vent stacks into the house, a metal flashing is bent and fastened to the roof and to the vertical projections. Flashing also is used in the roof valleys where two gables meet. In older homes, an 18- or 24-gauge galvanized sheet metal usually was placed in valleys for flashing. However, today roll roofing is used instead of the metal. Roll roofing sometimes is used around vents and chimney structures, although metal is preferred by many professional builders.

Flashing does not have to be replaced when a new roof is added over the old roof. In fact, it is better to leave the flashing material intact and coat it with asphalt roofing compound.

Metal flashings are made of aluminum and copper. They are sold in rolls (coils); standard widths are 14 and 24 inches; the standard length is 50 feet. The choice between aluminum and copper is personal preference; both do a good job. Copper is more expensive than aluminum.

At the eaves, a double layer of asphalt building paper should be fastened to the sheathing as a flashing. The paper should extend up the roof at least 36 inches. For example, if the overhang is more than 36 inches wide, the paper should overlap 6 inches and be cemented in place. This will form a band of flashing about 66 inches wide at the eaves. Apply plastic asphalt roofing cement with a notched adhesive spreader to stick the paper down and together. The paper flashing serves as a drip cap along the edge of the fascia and prevents water from running back under the roofing and damaging it.

Flashing is an aluminum or copper piece that goes around the base of vents (shown here) and chimneys to help prevent roofs from leaking. As a rule, the flashing does not have to be replaced when the roof is re-roofed. However, the flashing must be kept properly sealed with asphalt roofing compound at all times. The compound may be brushed onto the surface or applied with a caulking gun.

NAIL SIZE	NAIL LENGTH (in.)	SHINGLE LENGTH (in.)
3d	1¼	16–18
4d	1½	24
5d	1¾	16–18
6d	2	24

Nail Lengths for Wooden Shingles

Note: 3d and 4d nails are used for new construction only.

Preformed metal and plastic drip cap is available in 12-foot lengths. The cap is fastened to the sheathing along the eaves of the roof with nails. Shingles butt against a ridge in the cap.

How it's sold

Roofing is sold by the square (100 square feet), at many home centers by the bundle (33⅓ square feet), and, if the bundle is broken, by the piece. Shim shingles are sold by the bundle or by the shingle.

Roll roofing is sold by the roll. Metal and plastic roofing is sold by the sheet. Slate and tile is sold by the piece or by the square. Most home centers don't stock slate and tile roofing.

Special order

Many home centers and lumberyards will special-order shingles for you if the quantity is at least three squares.

If you can't find the products you want, or need special information about roofing materials and techniques, write the Consumer Information Director of the following manufacturers and associations:

Red Cedar Shingle & Handsplit
  Shake Bureau
5510 White Building
Seattle, Wash. 98101

GAF Building Products Div.
140 West 51st St.
New York, N.Y. 10020

Johns-Manville Co.
Greenwood Plaza
Denver, Colo. 80217

Celotex Corp.
1500 North Dale Mabry
Tampa, Fla. 33607

Asphalt Roofing Mfgrs. Assn.
757 Third Ave.
New York, N.Y. 10017

Bird & Son Inc.
Washington St.
East Walpole, Mass. 02032

Roof Skylights

There are two types of skylights: curb-mounted and flush-mounted. Both are easy for a do-it-yourselfer to install, and for some installations the job may be completed entirely from inside the attic. The hard part is cutting a hole in the roofing and roof sheathing.

Curb-mount skylights fit over a curb of 2×6s nailed into a rectangular hole cut through the roof; they are nailed to the sheathing around the hole. Roofing cement is applied to all joints and the curb is flashed with roll roofing or metal that is sealed with roofing compound. The skylight is then attached to the curb and sealed with standard weather stripping.

Flush-mount skylights fasten to the roof sheathing after the shingles have been trimmed away for the mounting flange of the skylight and a hole is cut through the roof. The skylight is sealed to the roof with roofing felt flashing and asphalt roofing cement.

How they're sold

Skylights usually are sold in kits containing the necessary framing and flashing materials. Individual parts are available, but they cost more than the kits. Most manufacturers furnish complete installation instructions.

Special order

Home centers and lumberyards may be reluctant to special-order skylights; if they do, you may have to pay the freight charges; A more expensive skylight, however, may ride from the factory to you free.

If you can't find the skylight you want, write to the Consumer Information Director of the following companies:

Baxt Industries Inc.
Addison, Tex. 75001

Skymaster Div.
413 Virginia Dr.
Orlando, Fla. 32803

Keller Companies Inc.
Box 327
Manchester, N.H. 03105

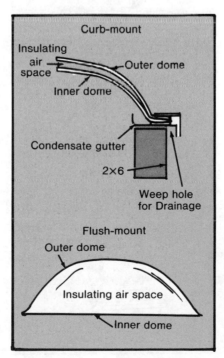

Curb-mount
Insulating air space
Outer dome
Inner dome
Condensate gutter
2×6
Weep hole for Drainage

Flush-mount
Outer dome
Insulating air space
Inner dome

Skylights are flush-mounted directly to the roof sheathing (under the shingles), or attached to a curb made of dimension lumber such as 2×6s. Curb-mounts usually are installed on flat roofs (built-up roofs), although they may be added to pitched roofs. Installation is easy with the complete instructions that come with skylight kits.

Rain-carrying Systems

Roof drainage system includes gutters, downspouts, and accessories to connect the system. The gutters and downspouts pictured here are vinyl; the products also are available in prefinished aluminum, copper, wood, galvanized steel, and stainless steel.

Gutters and downspouts are sold at home centers and lumberyards in two types: rectangular (aluminum or vinyl), and half-round (galvanized steel and vinyl). Wooden gutters are sold by some roofing contractors or roofing retailers. Stainless steel and copper gutters are sold by some specialist shops.

Downspouts (sometimes called *leaders*) are made from the same metals and vinyl in a corrugated rectangle and round shape. The basic types usually are preprimed with white paint.

Here is a list of the many parts of a rain-carrying system:

Gutters are available in standard lengths of 10 feet.

Inside miters are short pieces of gutter that form inside corners of the system. These pieces are interlocked with straight gutter pieces.

Outside miters are short pieces of gutter that form outside corners. They interlock with straight pieces.

End caps, marked *L* for left and *R* for right, interlock with the ends of straight pieces to close the gutter.

D end pieces have a built-in connection for the downspout that slips into a length of the downspout.

Downspouts, or leaders, are available in standard lengths of 10 feet.

A and B elbows fit the bottom of downspouts, to lead water away from the house.

Pipe straps are used to fasten the downspout to the house structure.

Wraparound hangers are used to fasten the gutter to the roof and fascia, the vertical board that is nailed to the ends of the rafters.

Spikes are also used to hang gutters; they are 7 inches long and made from aluminum.

Ferrules fit around the gutter spikes inside the gutter to help prevent debris from clogging the gutter. The ferrules are 5 inches long.

Slip joint connectors join straight lengths of gutters.

Strainers are inserted into the tops of downspout openings to prevent debris from clogging the pipe.

Measuring for gutters is very simple; just measure the length of the eaves

Gutter and downspout components are shown here. Always match materials: copper-to-copper, aluminum-to-aluminum, steel-to-steel, vinyl-to-vinyl. If you don't, the mismatch can set up a corrosion process and ruin the system.

for gutters; measure the drop from the eaves to about six inches from the ground for downspouts.

Hangers or spikes are placed every three to four inches; the gutter is pitched down toward the downspout at ¹⁄₁₆ inch per foot. For example: If the gutter is 20 feet long, the downspout end is 1¼″ lower than the other end. The maximum span between a high point and the downspout should be about 25 feet.

Downspouts should be supported by pipe straps placed at three-foot intervals. The downspout should empty onto a splashblock that is at least 3 feet long and pitched away from the foundation of the house. The downspout may be connected to a dry well or underground drainage system.

If metal gutter is not preprimed, it should be left outside to weather for about six weeks before a primer and a finish are applied. If it has been primed, the gutter should be degreased with a degreasing solution and then painted.

How they're sold

Gutter and downspout components are sold by the piece. Aluminum components and vinyl components are the least expensive. Galvanized steel components cost more than those of aluminum and vinyl. Copper components and wood components cost more than those of galvanized steel, aluminum, or vinyl.

A roof heating cable is used in heavy snowfall areas to melt snow and ice and to prevent roof, gutter, and downspout damage. The heating cable is clipped to the eaves of the roof over the shingles; a thermostat turns it on when the weather drops below freezing and snow and ice are present. The cable is plugged into an outdoor outlet.

Special order

Most home center stores and lumberyards will not special-order gutters. If a special metal piece is needed, a professional roofer may make it for you; this craftsman has the bending and forming equipment necessary to make special shapes.

If you can't find the rain-carrying system you want, or need any specialized information, contact the Consumer Information Directors of the following firms:

Hunter Douglas
Hunter Douglas Inc.
Durham, N.C. 27702

Genova Inc.
Building Products Division
7034 East Court St.
Davidson, Mich. 48423

Bieler-National Division
Revere Co.
11440 West Addison St.
Franklin Park, Ill. 60126

Soffit Systems

A soffit is the underside of the eaves or the roof overhang; soffits cover the ends of the roof rafters. They are made from hardboard, plywood, tongue-and-groove boards, and perforated aluminum. They are held in place by a piece of trim fastened on the back side of the fascia and the siding. The soffit may also be dadoed, or grooved, into the back of the fascia. In some cases, the soffit is held by clips attached to the house, the rafters, or fascia board.

Wooden soffit materials often rot and decay because they are next to the rain-carrying system (gutters) and take the brunt of moisture vapor coming out of the attic space.

The soffit, which is usually in short lengths, may be removed and replaced by removing the fasteners. If the soffit is plywood, it should have an exterior glue bond; a good buy is ¼- or ½-inch (MDO) exterior grade. If you're using hardboard, buy tempered material ¼ inch thick. Tongue-and-groove boards installed at right angles to the house should be primed on the tongues, grooves, backs, and edges, and given a prime and finish coat on the exposed surface. Metal soffits are sold in strip, rolls, or panel sections and the metal—usually aluminum—is preprimed.

SOFFIT VENTS. Moisture collecting under soffits can be eliminated by installing round or rectangular soffit vents in the soffit material. Standard sizes are 2 to 4 in. in diameter, or 6 × 10. If the attic is insulated, the soffits must be vented. The formula is one square foot of soffit vent as well as one square foot of gable vent for every 300 square feet of attic space that is insulated *without* a vapor barrier.

If the attic is insulated *with* a vapor barrier, there should be one square foot of inlet vent in the gables and one square foot of outlet vent in the soffit vents for every 600 square feet of attic ceiling area. There should be an average of three soffit vents on each side of the house.

Exterior Shutters

Non-functional, decorative window shutters are made of plastic and wood. The louvers usually are fixed—they don't open or close. Wood shutters must be primed and painted.

Plastic shutters are available painted in standard black, white, and brown and may also be painted to suit your home's color scheme. See the Painting chapter for details.

Standard sizes of exterior shutters are ¾ inch thick by 14 inches wide by 24, 31, 35, 39, 43, 47, 51, 55, 59, 63, 67, 71, and 80 inches long. They are sold individually.

Exterior Sidings: Non-wood

Exterior sidings fall into three broad categories: strip siding, panel siding, and shingle siding. (Brick and block siding products are discussed in the Masonry chapter. Stucco is another type of siding in the Masonry class.)

Sidings in each of these categories are made from plywood, hardboard, vinyl plastic, steel, and wood. Most home centers and lumberyards that cater to professional builders stock all types. You may not find a wide variety of siding colors in steel and plastic at retail stores, but since a siding job is a big sale, most retailers will be happy to order what you want. Be prepared to wait six weeks or so.

Aluminum siding
Aluminum siding is always prefinished with two coats of baked-on enamel. The siding comes in a limited choice of colors including white; any difference in price is based on the quality of the paint.

Siding is sold in squares, as shingles are; it is packaged to cover 100 square feet—for example, 20 pieces of 5-inch siding cover 100 sq. ft. You also can buy single strips or panels of siding if you need a small amount for repair purposes.

Aluminum siding comes in two thicknesss: 0.019 gauge is standard; thicker 0.024-gauge strips, panels, and shapes should be used where there are more than five inches of flat area without backing, or backer board. Backer board looks like fiberboard sheathing, but comes in narrow strips instead of 4×8-foot panels. Backer board is used to support aluminum siding; it has little sound-deadening or insulating qualities.

Aluminum siding comes in standard 4- and 8-inch widths. The 8-inch-wide strips produce a modern siding look; the 4-inch-wide strips have an old-fashioned clapboard look.

Aluminum siding requires several accessories for installation. These include: drip cap or window head flashing; undersill and general purpose strips; door and window trim strips; narrow (2-inch) outside corner post trim; wide (4-inch) outside corner post trim; insider corner post trim; and starter strips. You'll find these accessories next to the siding display area.

Vinyl siding
Vinyl siding costs about the same as aluminum. It comes in both horizontal and vertical panels. Colors are somewhat limited: white is the most popular; there are six pastel colors. As vinyl siding becomes more popular, you can expect to find a wider range of color choices.

Vinyl siding panels come in 12½-foot standard lengths with an 8-inch exposure on horizontal bevel styles and a 4-inch exposure on double bevels (a bevel down the center of an 8-inch-wide panel). The vertical panels also can be used as soffit panels; see details above.

Accessories for vinyl siding include starter strips; J-channel trim; inside and outside corners; fascia covers; undersill trim, soffit frieze runners. Two other accessories are available, but may have to be special-ordered from the manufacturer: covering strips for window and door frames and batten strips.

Vinyl siding is sold by the square or by the piece.

Steel siding
Steel siding sizes and accessories are similar to aluminum siding. Since steel is a high-quality product, it costs considerably more than aluminum and vinyl. Many home centers and lumberyards that cater to the do-it-yourselfer do not stock steel siding.

Special order
Retailers will seldom order a brand of siding different from the one they normally stock. Most of them will special-order colors at no extra charge. If non-stocked special accessories are needed, the retailer will order these for you; you may have to pay freight costs, unless the special order is included along with a regular shipment from the manufacturer. Expect to wait from four to six weeks.

If you can't find the siding you want, or have any special installation problems, the Consumer Information Director at the following companies may be able to help.

Bird & Son Inc.
Washington St.
East Walpole, Mass. 02032

B.F. Goodrich Chemical Co.
6100 Oak Tree Blvd.
Cleveland, Ohio 44131

Alcoa Building Products Inc.
2 Allegheny Center
Pittsburgh, Pa. 15212

Bendix Modern Materials Co.
16000 West 9 Mile Rd.
Southfield, Mich. 48075

Exterior Sidings: Wood

Plywood siding

Plywood panel siding is a do-it-yourselfer's delight to install because you can cover a lot of square footage at once with a standard 4×8-panel. There are seven standard styles used for exterior siding: Texture 1-11 (grooved); kerfed rough-sawn; brushed; plain rough-sawn; channel groove; reverse board-and-batten, and MDO or Medium Density Overlay. (See Chapter 1, on lumber and plywood.) Each panel face has its own characteristics.

Texture 1-11 has shiplap edges and parallel grooves that are 1/4 inch deep and 3/8 inch wide; the grooves are on 4- or 8-inch centers. The material is available in 19/32- and 5/8-inch thicknesses in Douglas fir, cedar, redwood, southern pine, and other species of wood. Although they may have to be special-ordered, panel faces in this style are available in scratch-sanded, rough-sawn, overlaid, and brushed surfaces. Panel size is 4×8 feet.

Kerfed rough-sawn has sawblade-wide grooves that are 4 inches on center. You can order panels with grooves in multiples of 2 inches on center. The panels are 11/32, 3/8, 1/2, 19/32, and 5/8 inch thick. Standard panel size is 4×8 feet.

Brushed panels accent the natural grain of the wood. The soft part of the wood is brushed so it exposes the hard grain in the panel. Available in redwood, Douglas fir, cedar, and other species, in 11/32-, 3/8-, 1/2-, 19/32-, and 5/8-inch thicknesses. Panels are 4×8 feet.

Rough-sawn panels have a rough texture on the face; they are available with or without grooves, and in lap sidings. Most wood species are available in 11/32-, 3/8-, 1/2-, and 19/32-inch thicknesses. Panels are 4×8 feet.

Channel groove siding panels have 1/16 inch deep by 3/8 inch wide on 4- or 8-inch centers. Redwood, Douglas fir, cedar, and southern pine species are generally available. The 4×8 panels are in thicknesses of 11/32, 3/8, and 1/2 inch.

MDO, or Medium Density Overlay, panels are smooth or with V-grooves spaced 6 and 8 inches on center; they're available in Texture 1-11, and in reverse board-and-batten, in thicknesses of 11/32, 3/8, 1/2, and 19/32 inches. MDO also is available in precut widths for horizontal lap siding with 12- and 16-inch widths and 3/8-inch thickness. Lengths up to 16 feet may be special-ordered. Preprimed panels also are available.

Reverse board-and-batten panels have wide grooves in coarse-sanded, brushed, and rough-sawn surfaces. The grooves are about 1/4 inch deep, 1 inch wide, and are spaced 12 or 16 inches on center. Panel size is 4×8 in 19/32- and 5/8-inch thicknesses.

The panels made according to the standards of the American Plywood Association are marked with a span rating, a group number, and a face grade designation; those points are explained in the Lumber and Plywood chapter.

HOW IT'S SOLD. Plywood siding is sold by the piece. If you place a large order, you probably can get a price break; ask the manager of the store. You also may have to arrange for delivery of a large amount of the material to your job site.

SPECIAL ORDER. Many of the textures and patterns described above are special-order items. Many home centers and lumberyards will order these panels for you at no charge, if you are willing to wait for delivery—usually four to six weeks. If you can't locate the material you want, or have any special installation questions about it, write to Consumer Affairs at:

American Plywood Association
Box 11700
Tacoma, Wash. 98411

Hardboard and particleboard siding

Hardboard siding is similar to plywood siding in types of textures available; many of these are special-order items.

The basic siding panels are 4×8- and 4×9-foot; the standard thickness is 3/8 inch; those with special grooving or integral battens are usually 7/16 inch thick. Horizontal lap siding comes in 9- and 12-inch widths, 7/16-inch thickness, and lengths of 16 feet. Most hardboard siding products come prefinished; some are completely finished in a choice of several colors. The textured styles are available prefinished or prestained.

Both 4×8- and 4×9-foot panels and lap siding are easy for a homeowner to install on new construction or over old siding.

Although hardboard is a manufactured product, hardboard is real wood that has been chipped and whipped into a cake-batter consistency and then pressed into the various sheet configurations. These materials have been impregnated with a compound that produces a very dense and grainless material that won't split during installation. The products take stain and paint and other finishes just as well as, if not better than, other wood products.

If the siding you buy is already primed, but not finished, the surface must be finished within 60 days of installation to protect the hardboard from the weather. If the siding is unfinished, it should be primed as soon as possible after installation—no later than 10 days—and the finishing coats applied within 60 days of the prime coat.

Bevel siding made of hardboard creates a traditional look to architecture. The butt, or thickness, of the siding determines the shadowline that the siding produces.

Panel siding usually is grooved, with a rough-sawn (above) or smooth face for texture preferences.

Is this stucco siding? It looks like it, but it is really hardboard that has been textured to appear like stucco.

Particleboard sidings are similar in sizes and textures to hardboard sidings. The material is dense and takes finish very well. Installation techniques for particleboard are the same as for hardboard and plywood sidings.

HOW IT'S SOLD. Hardboard and particleboard siding materials are sold by the piece. If the order is a large one, you may get a discount; ask for it. Hardboard lap siding may be packaged with several strips per unit; you may get a price break on the package.

SPECIAL ORDER. Most hardboard and particleboard sidings are standard stock items at home centers and lumberyards. Some special panels, however, will have to be ordered; be prepared to wait several weeks for delivery.

If you can't locate the siding you want and it can't be special-ordered by the retailer, try contacting the Consumer Information Director of the following manufacturers. Also, if you have any special installation problems, the firms below will be able to help you with them.

Acoustical & Board Products Assn.
205 West Touhy Avenue
Park Ridge, Ill. 60068

Masonite Corp.
29 North Wacker Drive
Chicago, Ill. 60606

Abitibi Building Products Div.
3250 West Big Beaver Rd.
Troy, Mich. 48084

Temple Industries
Diboll, Tex. 75941

Wood siding

There are eight basic types of wood siding: board, drop, bevel, bungalow, Dolly Varden, tongue-and-groove, channel rustic, and log cabin. Home centers and lumberyards that cater to the professional builder usually stock drop, bevel, bungalow, tongue-and-groove, and board.

Board siding is made with a smooth-
or rough-textured surface. A minimum overlap is one inch, unless battens are used to cover the joints. It may be applied vertically or horizontally to sheathing and furring strips.

Bevel siding may be plain or rabbet beveled; the plain type may be used with either face showing for a smooth or textured surface. Minimum overlap is one inch.

Bungalow siding is the same as bevel siding except the pattern is thicker and wider. This product also is known as Colonial siding.

Dolly Varden siding is similar to bungalow and bevel siding. It is thicker than bevel siding and has a rabbeted edge.

Tongue-and-groove siding—sometimes called drop siding—is made in smooth and rough textures. One edge is grooved to accept the tongue of the opposite edge. It may be installed vertically or horizontally over sheathing or furring.

Channel rustic siding in some areas is known as board-and-gap siding. It has rabbets cut along each edge; one cut is ½-inch lap, and the other cut is 1¼ inch. It may be applied vertically or horizontally to sheathing and furring.

Log cabin siding has a 1½-inch poll (the widest point) with a tongue configuration on one edge and a rabbet on the other. This is a specialty-type siding that usually has to be special-ordered from the manufacturer.

The wood siding described above is available in several grades of wood. They include Nos. 1, 2, and 3 Common; C and Better, Supreme, Choice, and Quality are available in Idaho white pine species. No. 1 Common usually is specified by quality architects and builders.

WOOD SIDING CLASSIFICATIONS. The different types of siding described above are often put into three classifications: board, bevel, and drop siding. In general, these classifications have the following characteristics:

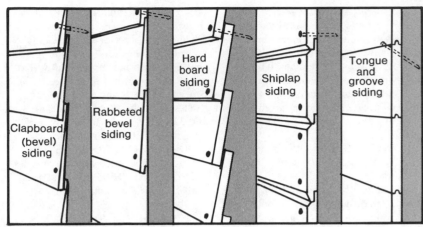

Horizontal wood siding looks like this when it is installed. These types of siding are for horizontal application, although shiplap and tongue-and-groove can also be applied vertically.

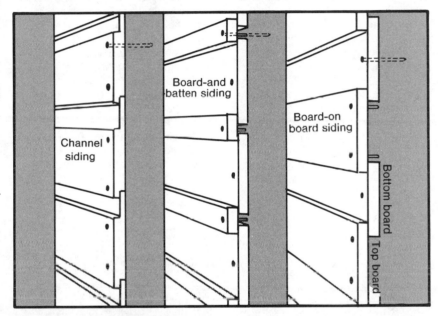

Vertical wooden siding looks like this when it is applied. Channel siding is sometimes called reverse board-and-batten siding. Wide boards are best to use for this type of siding design.

Board siding has square edges and the thickness is maintained at ¾ and ²⁵⁄₃₂ inch. The larger thickness is used for clapboard-style installation. Board siding sometimes is slightly beveled along the top and back of the board so the siding may be set tight on sheathing when using the product as clapboards.

Board siding is most often installed vertically with batten strips to cover the joints. Boards 8 to 11 inches wide are used for siding; 1×3 strips are used for battens.

Bevel siding usually is available in random lengths of 4 to 16 feet. The thickness varies to width: Nominal 4-, 5-, and 6-inch widths have ⁷⁄₁₆-inch butts; 8- and 10-inch widths have ⁹⁄₁₆-inch butts; 6-, 8-, 10-, and 12-inch materials also have ¹¹⁄₁₆-inch butts if a deeper shadow line is desired. Some bevel siding has two grooves, or dadoes, cut into the back. One groove is a water barrier; the other groove is used to align the siding. The back of the siding also is milled so that the boards will lay perfectly flat against the sheathing to which they are fastened.

Drop siding is usually ¾ inch thick at the butt and has been milled so it will go over the framing members, or studs, without a sheathing backing. If this siding is used over sheathing covered with building felt, the siding should be protected by a roof overhang to prevent moisture buildup behind the siding next to the sheathing or felt.

HOW IT'S SOLD. Wood siding is sold by the square (100 square feet) or by the piece.

The better the wood and the more complicated the design, the more costly the siding will be.

Trim for wooden siding (casings, jambs, etc.) is always priced separately and may be found in the molding departments of building material retailers.

SPECIAL ORDER. Most retailers will special-order special types of siding; the transportation costs will be paid by the retailer if you can wait four to six weeks for the special shipment to be delivered with a regular order of siding materials.

If you can't find the wood siding product you want, try writing to the Consumer Information Director of the following manufacturers. These same firms also will help you with any special installation problem:

Potlatch Wood Products, Div.
Box 5414
Spokane, Wash. 99205

California Redwood Association
617 Montgomery St.
San Francisco, Calif. 94111

Southern Forest Products Assn.
Box 52468
New Orleans, La. 70150

Vermont Weatherboard Inc.
Wolcott, Vt. 05680

Wood shingles and shakes

The same shingle and shake products used for roofing may be used as siding. Siding shingles, or wall shingles, come in 16-, 18-, and 24-inch lengths. Shake sizes are 18, 24, and 32 inches in length. Greater exposure widths may be used for wall covering than for roof covering.

Shakes have a different weather ex-

posure recommendation than shingles for wall use. For single courses, figure 8½-inch exposure for shakes 18 inches long; 11½ inches for 24-inch-long shakes, and 15 inches for shakes that are 32 inches long. For double courses, figure 14 inches for 18-inch shakes; 20 inches for 24-inch shakes, and 22 inches for 24-inch shakes, if straight-split shakes are used.

HOW THEY'RE SOLD. See the notations for wooden roofing shingles.

SPECIAL ORDER. See the notations for wooden roofing shingles.

Stucco siding repairs

Stucco is a concrete mixture; it should be applied in new construction over metal lath by a professional builder. The techniques and equipment necessary for a quality stucco job are beyond the skills of most weekend do-it-yourselfers.

However, if your stucco siding is damaged, you may be able to patch it. The mixing formula is:

1 part Portland cement
3 parts clean sand
Hydrated lime equal to 10 percent of volume of the cement and sand.
Water to make a stiff mixture; apply with a trowel.

You also can buy premixed stucco at some home centers and lumberyards. If you can't find it in either place, try a hard materials retailer. The Portland Cement Association, Old Orchard Road, Skokie, Ill. 60076, can be helpful with mixing and installation techniques.

Wooden shake siding produces interesting textures; it is installed much the same way as roofing shingles are.

The appearance of stucco can be created with a texture paint, which is troweled onto a flat wooden surface, as shown here. Repairs in stucco can be easily made with a mixture of Portland cement, as explained in the text.

7

PAINTING PRODUCTS

Paints, stains, and painting equipment are constantly changing. This year's hot new product often makes an unscheduled appearance at next year's inventory-clearance sale. But this is good news for you and the paint business. Manufacturers are constantly improving paint formulas so that paints last longer, wear better, and are easier to apply. You can even apply some of the new finishes over wet surfaces—a convenience unheard of several years ago. Equipment gets better, safer and even cheaper—such as foam plastic paint brushes that are so inexpensive you can throw them away after one use. But regardless of the finish or equipment you use, the key to a successful paint job is still preparation of the material to be painted. If the surface is not in top condition, no paint on the market can do its job efficiently.

Pricing of paint products

Unlike many other home maintenance and improvement products, paint has a wide price range—often $10 or more per gallon—and from a buyer's position, making a decision can be quite confusing indeed. An inexperienced paint salesperson will sometimes credit the price difference to the oil in the paint or the color or the high cost of petroleum products that are often used in modern paint formulas. These reasons have a thread of truth. But the real story concerns the quality of the paint pigment and its hiding ability.

You almost always can base a paint-buying decision on price alone: the higher the price, the better the quality. So perhaps you don't need too much quality? Perhaps. But be a smart buyer and figure it this way: A lesser quality exterior paint will protect and decorate your home for about 4 to 5 years, while a higher-quality paint (costing $5 to $10 more) will protect and decorate for about 8 to 10 years. By purchasing the better paint, you automatically reduce your labor time by delaying repainting for 4 to 5 years; the better paint will have greater hiding ability, and it will offer more protection. You also have a hedge against price increases later on: a lower-quality paint selling for $10 per gallon now probably will be selling for $12 or more per gallon four years from now, when you have to repaint. By spending a few dollars more now for the expensive spread, you'll end up saving money in the end, plus postponing the labor of applying the paint.

Take advantage of paint sales that are held during mid-summer and late fall in most communities. You often can buy high-quality, brand-name paints for one-third to one-half off the regular retail price. These sales are especially planned to meet the private label and no-name paint competition. The retailer figures that you, the shopper, will pay a few dollars more for brand-name paints than for private label or no-name paints.

Paint Formulas and Coverage

Basically, paint has a three-part formula: the pigment, which gives the product color and body; an oil or water vehicle, which carries the pigment in suspension; and thinners, which give the pigments and vehicles the right consistency for easy spreading.

Paint is classified in these types:
• *Oil-base and alkyd-base paints* and stains are thinned and cleaned up with mineral spirits or turpentine. In stores, the products are sold as either "oil-base" or "alkyd-base."

Oil-base paints have a slow drying time compared to latex paints. Alkyd-base dries somewhat faster than oil-base, but slower than latex.

The dried surface of both oil- and alkyd-base paints ranges from high gloss to semigloss to flat. The higher the gloss, the better resistance to wear and to cleaning and scrubbing.
• *Latex paints* and stains are thinned with water. The products also are known as "acrylics" and "vinyl" paints. Important features of this type include: easy clean-up with water, fast-drying (30 minutes to an hour), and lack of odor. Most of these paints can be applied over damp surfaces, a factor that may affect your choice.

Latex paint has a flat to semi-gloss finish when dry. Durability is excellent; the paint will withstand lots of rubbing and scrubbing.
• *Polyurethane paint* is thinned with mineral spirits. On the showroom shelf it is called "synthetic," "plastic," and "urethane." This paint is available in colors or clear, and has a gloss or satin finish (satin is a semigloss). The polyurethanes are usually more wear-resistant than the oils and latexes.
• *Shellac* is thinned with alcohol. It is available in an orange or clear mixture and is easy to apply. Shellac dries to a glossy finish only. Its big disadvantage is that it is easily damaged by water; the finish turns white.
• *Varnish* has a resin base and is highly resistant to wear and tear. Spar varnish—for use on exterior surfaces—remains flexible but dry to withstand heat and cold. Synthetic varnishes include urethane, epoxy, and vinyl and amino resin. Urethane is ideal for decks, outdoor furniture, and porch floors. Epoxy can be used

on masonry. Vinyl and amino resin are designed for paneling, molding and trim, and furniture.

• *Stain*—in colors and tones—is used to darken light wood. Stain may be water- or oil-base. It usually isn't thinned.

• *Primers*—water- or oil-base—should be used over new wood, plaster, and other materials that have never been finished. The temptation, of course, is to thin the finish coat and use it as the primer. This may not produce satisfactory results: Primers have ingredients that seal surfaces properly, making a perfect base for the finish coats. The finish will wear longer over a quality primer than over a thinned finish paint.

• *Metal paint* is formulated especially for use on metals such as galvanized steel. Metal surfaces should be primed only with metal paints, although any finish paint may be applied over a metal primer. Metal paint helps deter rust; don't use it on wood.

• *Cedar shake paint* is for natural wood surfaces. It dries to a flat finish, and is formulated to deter sap and discolorations from bleeding through the finish coat. The color selection is somewhat limited.

• *Dripless paint* (thixotropic) is available in polyurethane, urethane, and epoxy formulations.

HOW IT'S SOLD. Exterior and interior paints and stain are sold in pint, quart, gallon, and five-gallon containers. Exterior paints should be used only outside; interior paints should be used only inside. Stain may be used both inside and outside, but remember to check the label on the container before you apply it to any type of surface.

Retailers who stock paint usually have mixing equipment that can be used to blend a wide range of colors into a white base color. All the colored paint for a job should be mixed at one time so that there is no color variation from one container to another. When you buy paint—in ready-made colors or for blending—make sure that the manufacturer's batch numbers that are stamped on the container are the same or in sequence. Batches can vary slightly in color from one production run to another.

When checking colored paint in the store—either freshly mixed or premixed—remember that all paint will dry slightly darker. The showroom

Exterior Paint Selector
Always read the label before buying or applying paint.

TYPE OF PAINT	GENERAL USE
Oil	All surfaces and primed metal.
Latex	All surfaces and primed metal. Do not use over oil-based paint unless so noted on the label of the container.
Acrylic	Same as latex.
Alkyd	All surfaces. May be used over alkyd and oil paints unless otherwise noted by the manufacturer.
Primer	All new materials. All worn materials. Do not use as a metal primer.
Masonry	Epoxy, latex, rubber, alkyd, and Portland cement mixtures may be used over masonry surfaces.
Stain	All surfaces excluding some metals.
Porch and deck enamels	May be labeled epoxy, rubber, oil, alkyd, latex, or polyurethane.

Interior Paint Selector
Always read the label before buying or applying paint.

TYPE OF PAINT	GENERAL USE
Oil	All surfaces and primed metal.
Latex	All surfaces. May require two coats. In flat, semigloss, and gloss finishes.
Acrylic	All surfaces and primed metal.
Alkyd	See exterior alkyd. Plaster and gypsumboard must be prime-coated.
Primer	On all surfaces except metal. Must be used on one-coat systems over new material.
Masonry	See exterior masonry.
Texture	All surfaces. Best for surfaces with hairline cracks and blemishes.
Metal	All metals and some primed woods. See manufacturer's recommendations on label.
Polyurethane	All finishes and porous materials.
Urethane	Same as polyurethane. Primer usually required.
Epoxy	All materials including metal and glass. Special mixing may be required; check container label for instructions and use.

Primers for Metal

TYPE OF METAL	TYPE OF PRIMER
Aluminum	None. If top coat of finish won't stick, try zinc oxide.
Galvanized iron and steel	Zinc oxide.
Iron and steel	Zinc chromate. Use three coats.
Copper	None.
Brass	None. May be finished with lacquer or polyurethane to maintain shine.

color chips are fairly accurate, but don't expect a perfect match.

SPECIAL ORDERS. Many home centers and hardware outlets will special-order finishes. But if they won't, you may be able to find what you want at specialty paint and wallpaper stores. If you still have problems or if you have any special finishing questions that can't be answered by the retailer, contact the Consumer Information Director at any of the following companies:

Glidden Coatings & Resins Division
SCM Corp.
900 Union Commerce Building
Cleveland, Ohio 44115

Valspar Corporation
1101 Third St.
Minneapolis, Minn. 55415

Minwax Co. Inc. (stains)
72 Oak Street
Clifton, N.J. 07014

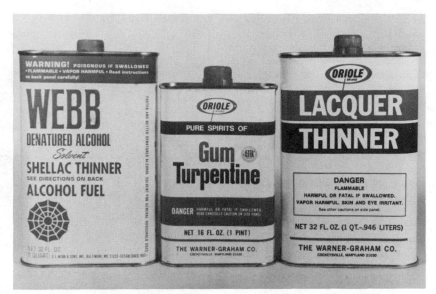

Basic paint thinners include alcohol for shellac, turpentine or mineral spirits for oil-based paint, and lacquer thinner for lacquers. Always use the thinner recommended by the manufacturer on the label of the paint container.

Estimating Paint Needs

A coverage estimate is printed on the labels of all paints and stains. The stain coverage figure is fairly accurate; the paint coverage figure should be reduced by 30 square feet. For example, if the coverage figure is 400 square feet per gallon, drop this figure to 370 square feet. The coverage figures are determined by manufacturers who have applied their product under optimum conditions. You seldom will be working under the same conditions, and will not get as much coverage as you might expect. The conditions described below explain this.

The amount of paint needed depends on the dryness and type of surface to be painted. The number of coats that are applied to the surface are another estimating factor. If it takes one gallon of paint to cover a wall, the second coat of paint over the same wall will take about ¼ gallon less. A third coat will take about ½ gallon less. Wooden surfaces that have not been painted in 10 years will take more paint than those that have been painted in the last four to six years.

Textured siding such as cedar shakes, rough-sawn panels, and chipboards will use about 20 percent more paint than lap (drop) siding. Narrow lap siding will take about 10 percent less paint than wide lap siding. Masonry surfaces such as stucco, placed concrete, and concrete blocks will require about 50 percent more paint than wooden siding, since they are very porous.

To estimate the amount of exterior paint you need by guessing, allow one gallon of paint for each room in your home plus one gallon for each gable end. For example, if you have a seven-room house with two gables, you will need approximately nine gallons of paint for one coat.

For a more accurate estimate, add together the areas of the sides in square feet, not including the gables (height × width), plus the areas of the gables (height × width divided by 2), and divide the total by 400. The answer is the number of gallons of paint you'll need for one coat.

To estimate the amount of trim paint needed, allow one gallon for every five gallons of siding paint.

The same procedure can be used to estimate paint needs for interior surfaces: Add the areas of walls and ceilings and divide by 400. Interior trim and molding paint needs are estimated the same as for the exterior.

Paint has light-reflecting qualities that vary with the color. This could be a consideration in deciding what color to use in a specific location. Approximate light reflectance for standard colors:

White:	80%
Ivory:	70%
Yellow:	65%
Buff:	57%
Green:	50%
Blue:	40%
Deep Green:	14%
Rose:	12%

What finish goes where?

Surfaces and finishes must be carefully matched. Below are some guidelines to use when buying finishes:

Masonry: Flat, semigloss, aluminum, latex. A sealer often must be applied first.

Decks and porches: Porch and deck enamel.

Plaster: Flat, semigloss, latex. A sealer or undercoater often is needed.

Gypsumboard: Flat, semigloss, latex. A sealer or undercoater must be applied to new gypsumboard that hasn't been finished.

Kitchens and bathrooms: Gloss or semigloss is best, although flat and latex may be used. A glossy finish is easier to wipe clean than a flat finish.

Paneling: Penetrating wood sealer; shellac; flat, semigloss, or latex paint. An application of hard wax provides effective protection.

Aluminum, steel, vinyl siding: If the surface is weathered, use alkyd, oil, or latex paint. Prime any new or bare metal with Glidden Y-1951 Spread Gel-Flo or similar metal primer before applying a topcoat. If the surfaces have weathered so that they are lightly chalked and have no gloss, clean them thoroughly by scrubbing with a stiff brush and plain water before any paint is applied.

Note: Vinyl siding formulas are changed frequently by the manufacturers. If possible, tell the retailer the brand name of the siding so the right paint may be specified. Otherwise, the finishes noted above probably will perform to your satisfaction. If the siding is new and unweathered, and you have any doubt about latex adhering to the surface, prime the surface with an alkyd or oil primer before the latex topcoat is brushed on.

Changing paint colors from a dark paint to a light paint requires two coats of the lighter paint; sometimes three coats are needed over red, green, and dark or royal blue colors.

All enamels and semigloss paints should have an undercoater.

For natural wood tone, apply a stain; then cover the stain with two coats of varnish or shellac. Apply a top coat of wax.

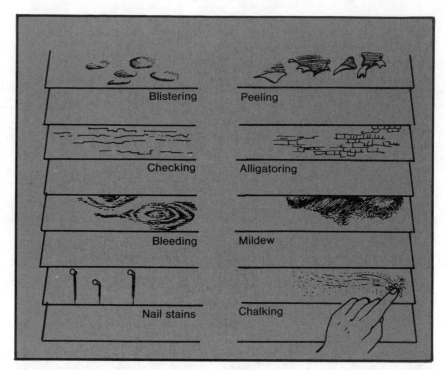

Paint failures are seldom caused by the paint itself. Moisture usually is the reason for peeling, checking, blistering, and mildew. Improper application can usually be blamed for alligatoring, checking, bleeding, and stains. Chalking, however, is a *normal* condition of paint; it shows that the paint film is doing its job.

Special problems

Contrary to popular belief, paint failures are not caused by the paint, unless it is a cheap mixture. Most paint failure problems can be avoided by (1) proper preparation of the surface and (2) the proper application of the paint, according to the manufacturer's recommendations on the label. Common paint troubles include these:

Paint fading: Exposure to the sun is the prime cause of fading. Poor-quality paint fades faster.

Blistering: Moisture vapor coming from inside the house is the usual cause. Ventilate bathrooms, laundry areas, and kitchens to solve this problem. Blistering also can be caused by applying paint to unseasoned wood or to wet wood.

Sagging: Too much paint applied to the surface causes sagging. Also, paint applied over a glossy, slick surface will sag; dull the gloss with abrasive before painting.

Wrinkling: If the top film of paint dries before the undercoater or bottom film of paint it will wrinkle.

Alligatoring: Too many layers of paint film applied to the surface cause alligatoring, as will a combination of incompatible paints, such as an enamel under a flat paint.

Checking: A topcoat applied over a wet undercoat will cause checking.

Brushes

Choosing between nylon or pure bristle brushes is the basic buying question. If quality is assured, either type will do a good job—but with one exception: Do not use a pure bristle brush in water-based paint. If you do, the bristles will quickly turn into a lumpy mess and the brush will spread paint like a rag mop.

Natural, or pure bristle, brushes cost more than nylon brushes. They may be used in all oil-base paints such as alkyd, varnish, and enamel, as well as with shellac.

Nylon brushes may be used in both oil and water paints; do *not* use them in varnish, enamel, or shellac.

Pure bristle and nylon brushes are sold in a wide variety of sizes and shapes. Here is a selection guide:

Wall brushes are your best choice for straight, flat areas such as wall surfaces, siding, and panels. These tools are made in 3-, 4-, 5-, and 6-inch widths (lengths vary). Buy the biggest brush you can handle comfortably; you'll probably find a 4-inch brush easiest to use.

Window trim brushes, or sash tools, have angled bristles along the tip edge so the brush may be stroked into the corners of window mullions without getting paint on the window glass. Sash tools also have a small handle that lets you control the stroke better for fine trimming. These brushes are available in widths from 1 to 3 inches. The 1½-inch size can handle most trim jobs.

Round, pencil-like sash brushes may be easier for you to handle than the flat ones. This shape does a neat job on round objects such as stair-step spindles. The size of the brush should be about the size of the spindles or railings that you will be painting.

Varnish and enamel brush should be between 2 and 3 inches wide. A 2½-inch brush splits the difference and will handle most varnishing and enameling jobs.

Masonry brushes are similar to wall brushes; widths range up to 9 inches. Since masonry surfaces take a lot of paint, you want to buy a brush that will hold a lot of paint. Therefore, the more bristles in the brush, the better. However, a 9-inch brush may take too much effort. A comfortable size for most homeowners is 7 inches.

Oval brushes are made especially for round and curved surfaces. They also are used for making stencils and stippling.

Throw-away brushes are very low-priced (three for $1, for example) and it makes good sense to use them if you have a small or touch-up paint job. When you are finished with the project, just throw away the brush. This may sound wasteful, but the cleaner and your time required to remove the paint from the bristles (especially epoxies and varnish) cost more than the brush.

Buying brushes

When buying paintbrushes, check three parts carefully: the ferrule, the plug, and the bristles. The ferrule is the metal band around the bottom of the handle that holds the bristles in place. A quality brush has a rust-resistant metal ferrule that is fastened to the handle with rivets, small screws, or roundhead brads. A poor-quality brush lacks these features. If you tap the ferrule of a poor brush against the palm of your hand, the ferrule will loosen and wiggle. Later, when you're painting, the loose ferrule will let the bristles fall out.

To check the plug, spread the bristles in half. You will see a wood or plastic plug inserted in the ferrule at the base of the bristles. This plug helps support the bristles. If the plug fills more than half of the ferrule, it is too large; paint will load in the base of the brush, causing problems.

To check the bristles, lay the brush flat on a countertop. Hold the bristles flat with one hand and pull the handle straight up; hold it for a moment or two, and then release the bristles. If they spring straight back instantly, you have a quality brush. If the bristles stay more or less bent, the brush is not a quality product. When you're painting, poor-quality bristles will fan out and mat together. Bristles on a good brush will hang together when they are wet with paint.

Nylon bristle brushes of good quality have *exploded tips* that have been enlarged to carry more paint and do a smoother job; such tips are usually colored off-white or brown. Synthetic bristles can be used in both oil and water paints; they're generally less expensive than natural bristle brushes.

Pure bristle brushes have tiny flags at the tips of the bristles. It looks almost as if the bristle has been split by a very sharp knife. The flags increase the ability of the brush to smooth out the final stroke. The flags also permit more paint to be loaded into the brush.

A good-quality paint brush is a worthwhile investment. If you take care of it (clean it thoroughly with thinner and wrap it in newsprint) it will last several lifetimes.

HOW THEY'RE SOLD. Paintbrushes are priced and sold as individual items. Inexpensive throw-away brushes are sold at three for $1, or two for 50¢, or one for $1 and the second one for 1¢, or some similar pricing method.

Quality brushes go on sale once or twice annually at about 10 to 15 percent off regular prices. Since you have to buy brushes to apply paint, the retailer tends to discount the paint more than the brushes.

SPECIAL ORDER. Paintbrushes are available in all sizes, shapes, and price ranges, so special orders are not necessary. However, if you have a problem with paintbrushes, the following manufacturers may be able to answer specific questions. Write the Consumer Information Director.

Baker Brush Co. Inc.
4051 South Iowa Ave.
Milwaukee, Wis. 53207

Tip Top Industries Inc.
151 West Side Ave.
Jersey City, N.J. 07305

Foam plastic brushes (foreground) do a good job applying any finish, and they are so inexpensive you can afford to junk them when the project is finished. Shake painters (background) are napped pads with a very short pile designed for painting rough or striated surfaces. The handle is threaded to accept an extension pole for painting walls and ceilings.

Rollers and Roller Covers

It's difficult to choose between paint rollers and paint brushes since both tools perform equally well. One difference is that a brush is easier to control than a roller. Brushes are much better for small areas—windows and trim—while rollers are excellent for painting large flat surfaces such as walls and ceilings; the wide swath the roller makes gets the job done fast with satisfactory results.

Rollers have three parts: a handle, the frame onto which the roller cover slides, and the cover itself. A quality roller frame is made of wire because wire is easier to keep clean than a solid frame. The handle also has a female thread connection for an extension pole that is used for painting ceilings. This method eliminates the use of a ladder except for trim work at the wall and ceiling junction.

Special rollers are available for trimming corners, windows, molding, and rounds such as pipe and spindles.

The covers that carry and apply the paint are the important part of rollers; they are manufactured from mohair, polyurethane foam, Dynel, lamb's wool, and acetate. The roller cover should be matched to the paint and the surface to be painted.

A brush and roller combination makes an excellent painting team: The brush handles tight quarters, while the roller is quickest on large, flat surfaces. Roller covers usually show size (here: 9 inches), nap or pile height (here: ⅜ inch), what paint the cover should be used with (here: flat latex paints), and the type of surface it's suited for (here: smooth).

Mohair covers are for enamels and varnish. The covers have a short nap to give a smooth finish.

Dynel-nylon covers are for water-base paints. If the label says so, you may be able to use Dynel covers for oil-base paints.

Lamb's wool are fairly expensive and should be used for oil-base paints only.

Polyurethane covers are for all paints.

The nap lengths of roller covers range from about ¹⁄₁₆ to 1½ inches. The short nap is used for smooth surfaces, while the long nap is for rough surfaces.

The nap is fastened to either a paper or plastic base. If you will be applying lots of water-base paint, buy the plastic base since it won't absorb the paint and soften.

For stippled effects, buy rollers that have a carpet-like nap to create a special design. The trick to using this cover is to run the roller so the strokes don't overlap.

HOW THEY'RE SOLD. Rollers and roller covers may be purchased together or separately. Packaged roller kits usually include the roller frame, one or two roller covers, a metal or plastic paint tray, and an extension handle. You can also buy a roller and tray combination without the covers and handle.

Roller covers are packaged in a plastic wrap. This is usually clearly marked as to roller width, type of nap, and the type of paint the roller should be used with. Standard roller widths are 7 and 9 inches; trim and other special roller tools take smaller and odd-shaped covers that are

plainly labeled on the cover package.

SPECIAL ORDERS. Roller equipment seldom needs to be special-ordered since it can be found in many types of stores including drug, grocery, variety, and general merchandise outlets. Special questions or information about roller products should be directed to the Consumer Information departments of the following manufacturers.

E-Z Paintr Corp.
4051 South Iowa Ave.
Milwaukee, Wis. 53207

Bestt Rollr Inc.
1800 Morris St.
Fond Du Lac, Wis. 54935

Wooster Brush Co.
604 Madison Ave.
Wooster, Ohio 44691

Painting Equipment

The equipment category includes ladders, dropcloths, scrapers, wire brushes, and all the other products and tools needed to prepare and paint surfaces. Here is a rundown on the more important items, and how they are merchandised and sold.

Ladders—both folding stepladders and two-piece extension ladders—are rated according to capacity. A household ladder, Type III, has a weight rating of 200 pounds. Type II ladders, commercial grade, are rated at 250 pounds. Type I ladders, industrial grade, are rated at 300 pounds. For most home improvement and repair jobs, buy a commercial- or industrial-grade ladder that can support you and your materials.

For length information, see the Ladder Selection Guide.

Ladders, when opened, should have a three-rung overlap; that is, the top should extend at least three feet above the eaves of your house. This lets you step off the ladder onto the roof instead of climbing over the gutter or eaves onto the roof, which can be very dangerous.

Scaffolding should be rented rather

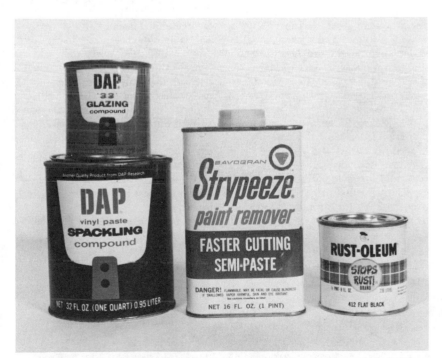

Paint supplies needed for most interior/exterior projects include glazing compound for window mullions; spackling compound for chips and holes in plaster and gypsumboard walls (available pre-mixed as shown above, or in ready-to-mix powder); paint remover for furniture, trim, molding paint, and stain removal; and metal paint for metal priming and finishing (gutters, downspouts, railings, and the like).

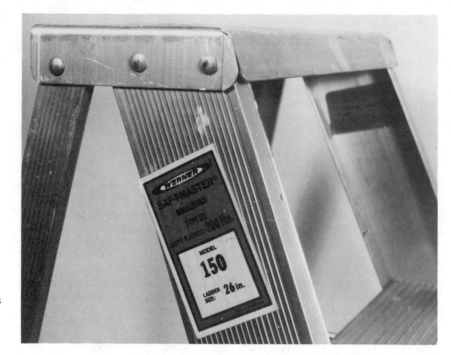

Quality ladders are rated by weight capacity. This Type III stepladder has a 200-pound rating, which is adequate for household uses, unless you weigh 300 pounds. Extension ladders for safe use outdoors should have a commercial (250-pound) or industrial (300-pound) rating.

than purchased since it is expensive and the chances are you won't use the planks often. In any case, working on scaffolding is extremely dangerous; always use great caution. Ladder jacks to support scaffolding may be rented with the scaffolding.

The big difference between metal and wooden ladders and scaffolding is weight. The metal equipment usually is lighter in weight and easier to handle. It you buy a wooden ladder, don't paint it to protect the wood. Paint hides defects in the wood—a dangerous situation. If you want to protect the wood surfaces, coat the ladder with a clear sealer or apply linseed oil and wipe it dry.

A two-inch-wide flat *scraper* is the right tool for most paint removal, especially peeling paint. If the surface needs a great deal of attention, a two- or three-inch pull scraper is the best buy. Use a metal file to sharpen the edges of a pull scraper.

Hot scrapers (electric-powered) are good tools for removing several thicknesses of paint, but since they work slowly they're not practical for an area much larger than one square yard.

Propane torches can be used to remove old paint film, but this is not recommended because of the fire hazard. Only an experienced do-it-yourselfer should use a torch; the problem is not with the surface being cleaned but with the framing members and insulation behind the surface. These materials can catch fire and you won't know it until the house is ablaze.

Wire brushes are the best tools for removing flaking paint from all types of surfaces, including metal.

A fine to coarse assortment of *steel wool* is the best buy for removing rust from metal.

Sandpaper is used to remove roughness from a surface that is to be primed or topcoated, for example, to

feather the edges of a small area that has been scraped bare. An electric-powered belt sander can be used to smooth larger areas.

Paint remover, usually associated with furniture refinishing, can be used to remove exterior paint. However, it should be used on a small area at a time since it evaporates very rapidly and looses its paint-softening ability.

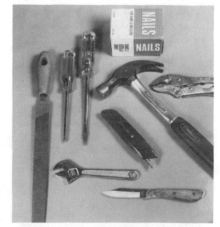

Basic surface-preparation tools and supplies include a screwdriver and an adjustable wrench for removing hardware, a file for sharpening scrapers, a hammer to drive in popped nails, pliers to pull nails, a utility knife to break paint seals around windows, a paring knife to cut plastic and paper, and nails to renail loose boards.

Ladder Selection Guide		
FROM GROUND TO HOUSE EAVES (FT.)	LADDER LENGTH (FT.)	WORKING LENGTH (FT.)
9½	16	13
9½–13½	20	17
13½–17½	24	21
21–25	32	29
25–29	36	33
29–32	40	37

Using paint remover for large jobs may cost too much.

If you do a lot of painting, buy the canvas *drop cloths*. For small and occasional jobs, the plastic cloths work fine. But be careful walking on plastic; it becomes very slippery.

A rimless *paint bucket* is the best buy. Make sure the handle is securely attached. Buy a ladder hook for the handle while you're in the store.

The 1½-inch width of *masking tape* is the most useful, although some jobs may require a wider or narrower tape; for example, use ½-inch tape on mullions.

Roller trays are metal or plastic; both are recommended. The tray should have a metal grid for the bottom of the tray; this prevents the roller from skidding as it picks up paint.

Glazing compound for window mullions is better than linseed oil putty

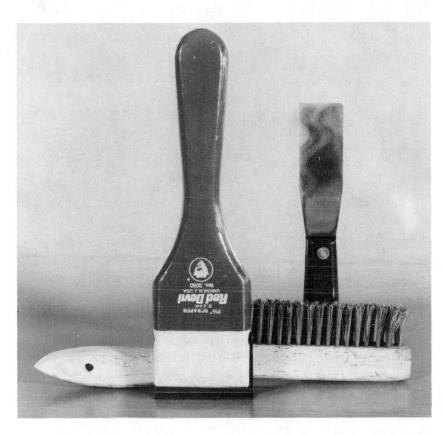

Basic paint-removal tools include a pull scraper, wire brush, and stiff-bladed putty knife. The pull scraper is sharp and efficient enough to take paint off down to the bare wood. The wire brush and putty knife and best used for peeling and flaking paint.

Steel wool is an excellent abrasive for removing finishes softened by paint remover or heat. Use coarse wool (left) to get the bulk of the finish off; then use fine wool (right) for smoothing and polishing. Steel wool can be purchased in an assortment—fine to coarse—or in individual pads.

Steel Wool Selector

RECOMMENDED USE	TYPE	GRADE NUMBER
Removing paint, varnish, lacquer, enamel	Medium	1
Final finish stripping	Medium or fine	0
Wood smoothing before finish is applied	Fine	00
Deglossing between finish coats	Extra fine	000
Stain removal; deglossing between coats	Super fine	0000
Furniture refinishing	Degreased	All grades

Sandpaper (Abrasive) Selector

GRIT NUMBER	GRIT	GRADE	GRIT TYPES AVAILABLE
40	Coarse	1½	Flint, garnet, silicon carbide, emery.
50	Coarse	1	Same as 40.
60	Coarse	½	Same as 40 plus aluminum oxide.
80	Medium	0 (1/0)	Same as 60.
100	Medium	00 (2/0)	Same as 60.
120	Medium	3/0	Same as 60.
150	Fine	4/0	Same as 60.
180	Fine	5/0	Same as 60.
220	Very fine	6/0	Garnet, aluminum oxide, silicon carbide.
240	Very fine	7/0	Aluminum oxide and silicon carbide.
280	Very fine	8/0	Same as 240.
320	Super fine	9/0	Aluminum oxide and silicon carbide.
360	Super fine	—	Silicon carbide.
400	Super fine	10/0	Silicon carbide.

Sandpaper, or abrasive paper, is marked to identify the coarseness of grit (here 100 medium), type of grit (aluminum oxide), and type of coat (open). Open-coat paper, with the granules not closely packed, is best used for finishes that will gum and clog the grit. Closed-coat paper, with the granules tightly packed, is for final smoothing and sanding. Coarse grit (low numbers) is best for removing lots of material fast; fine grit (high numbers) is best for smoothing materials just before applying the finish or for sanding between coats of finish. The type of grit determines the price of the paper; flint paper costs less than its oxide and carbide cousins.

Flexible sanding block has abrasive attached to a plastic core. Wash the block in water when the abrasive coating becomes clogged with residue. The blocks come in a range of grits for both wood and metal sanding.

because glazing compound will not dry hard. If a pane of glass has to be replaced, the glazing is easy to remove with a putty knife.

Caulking compound, to make a seal around doors, windows, and other joints, is available in bulk or cartridge form. Use the cartridges; they are much easier to handle and less messy. Caulking compound is formulated for different jobs. The standard types include:

Latex-based caulking is often called painter's caulk. It is quick drying, may be used with water-based paints, and sticks to almost anything.

Polyvinyl caulking is similar to latex; it will adhere to almost any surface including surfaces that are already painted.

Silicone caulking is very expensive, but it can be used on all surfaces. It is long-lasting and pliable; some silicone caulking is guaranteed for up to 20 years against cracking, shrinkage, and fall-out.

Butyl rubber caulking is used between metal and masonry, and metal and wood. It is fairly costly, but for the price you get a long-lasting caulk that withstands temperature extremes without cracking.

HOW THEY'RE SOLD. Painting accessories are usually priced and sold as individual items and seldom in quantity.

Ladders are sold by the linear foot; so is scaffolding.

Caulking is sold by the cartridge for use in a gun. As pointed out, cer-

tain types of caulking are more expensive than others. Oil-base caulking is the least expensive; it usually has to be replaced every three years or so.

Glazing compound may be purchased in half-pint, pint, and quart containers. You usually get a small discount for quantity.

Scrapers, wire brushes, drop cloths, and masking tape are sold individually, priced by size and quality.

Hot scrapers are sold individually. Propane torches are sold in kits or separately. Special fittings for torches, such as flame spreaders, may be purchased separately or as special packages.

SPECIAL ORDERS. Paint accessories are seldom special-ordered by any retailer because of the abundance of these products in the marketplace. One exception is ladders: a home center or hardware store may be able to order a special-size ladder for you, but be prepared to pay freight costs.

If you can't find the ladder equipment you need for a specific project, contact the Consumer Information Director of the following manufacturers:

W.W. Babcock Co. Inc.
36 Deleware Ave.
Bath, N.Y. 14810

Michigan Ladder Co.
12 East Forest Ave.
Ypsilanti, Mich. 49187

Special finishes

Enamels, stains, shellac, penetrating resin, wax, and natural varnish and polyurethane are *special finishes* that are used mainly for finishing furniture and fine woods. These products may be purchased individually or as parts of a *system;* systems, such as those marketed by Formby, Minwax, and Carver-Tripp, contain matched paint remover, cleaner, stain, and wax in one package.

Working with these finishes is a world unto itself; consult the paint retailer for information on what finish to use on your projects. There also are many reference books on the subject; consult them before you buy any tools or materials.

Speciality finishes are sold at most home centers, hardware stores, and specialty paint outlets. Some hobby shops stock them, too.

Masking tape and newspaper combine to protect surfaces from unwanted paint drips and spills. The tape also masks off glass, metal, paneling, and other materials to protect them and provide a sharp paint edge after the paint has dried.

Check the labels on caulking compounds. Many containers look alike, but they contain such different products as concrete patch, subfloor adhesive, paneling glue, and even asphalt roof coating. Some caulking manufacturers make their products in colors so matching paint is easier.

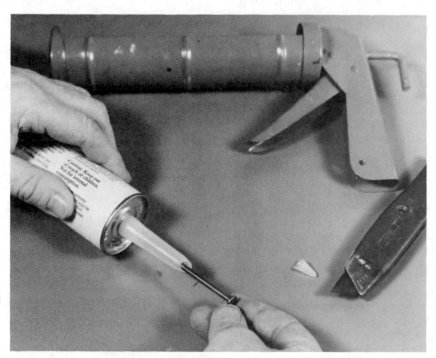

Break the seal of the caulking after cutting off the plastic tip. The seal, which can be broken with any sharp object such as a nail, lies inside the plastic nozzle in front of the metal end cap. If you don't break this seal, pressure from the caulking gun can break the paper cartridge, causing an awful mess.

8

SPECIALTY PRODUCTS

The basic building products discussed in this chapter include:

Gypsumboard
Fiber and chip board panels
Doors
Windows and window shutters
Ceiling tile systems
Floor tile
Metal products
Wallpaper
Builders' hardware

If you can't find what you want, ask a salesperson for help. Sometimes these specialty products are stuck away in a corner or shelved in a back storeroom.

Gypsumboard

Known better by its tradename "Sheetrock," gypsum wallboard or just gypsumboard, is available in 4×8- and 4×9-foot sheets in standard thicknesses of ⅜, ½, and ⅝ inch. It also is called "dry wall construction," to distinguish it from lath-and-plaster construction which is "wet."

Gypsumboard is fire-resistant. It is made from gypsum (plaster of Paris) that is covered with heavy kraft paper. On one side, the paper is a soft gray; on the other side, which usually faces the room, it is off-white.

The product is manufactured with different types of edges: square, beveled, tapered, round, and tongue-and-groove. You are most likely to find only the square and beveled or tapered edges in stock; the others may be special-ordered.

The beveled and tapered edges allow room for the joint tape and joint compound so the buildup will not protrude above the face of the panel.

Gypsumboard Nail Estimator

SIZE OF BOARD	NAIL SIZE REQUIRED	NO. OF NAILS PER 1,000 SQUARE FEET
⅜ x 4 x 8	1⅛ in.	5¼ lbs.
½ x 4 x 8	1⅜ in.	5¼ lbs.
⅝ x 4 x 8	1⅞ in.	6½ lbs.

Gypsumboard Tape Estimator

AREA (sq. ft.)	JOINT PRE-MIX (gal.)	JOINT POWDER* (lbs.)	TAPE (ft.)
100– 200	1	12	120
200– 400	2	24	180
400– 600	3	36	250
600– 800	4	48	310
800–1,000	5	60	500

* Gypsumboard powder for tape is mixed with clear, clean water.

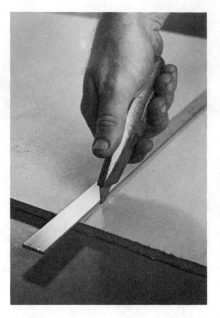

Left: To cut gypsum wallboard, score one side with a sharp knife and then snap the board over a straight edge to break it. Then cut the back paper cover with the knife. *Right:* To seal joints in gypsumboard, fill the beveled edges with joint compound and smooth it with a wall knife. Then embed joint tape in the compound; apply another coat of compound over the tape and smooth it with the wall knife. When the compound dries, sand it smooth and level with the surface of the board.

Gypsumboard also is available in ¼- and 1-inch thicknesses and in 2×4-foot panels. You also can buy decorated gypsumboard; the panels are covered with a laminate similar to wallpaper.

For bathrooms, laundry areas, and kitchens where water and moisture may be a problem, you can buy gypsumboard with a water-resistant green covering instead of the kraft paper; it may be painted or used as a base for wall tile.

Gypsum laths are made from the same process as gypsumboards; the standard sizes are 16 × 48 inches and 16 × 96 inches, with thicknesses of ⅜ and ½ inch. The ⅜ × 16 × 48-inch sizes generally are sold six to a package, although some retailers may break the package and sell you single pieces at a slightly higher price. Gypsum laths are used instead of wooden or metal laths for plaster walls and ceilings.

Gypsumboard also is available mixed with fiberglass particles to make it more fire-resistant. This product probably will be stamped with a flame spread rating or a class number, indicating fire-resistance.

Installation products

Gypsumboard is applied to ceiling joists first, then the wall studs, with special wallboard nails (see Chapter 2), joint compound and joint tape, which may be plain or perforated. Joint compound is sold premixed by the bucket, or you can buy joint compound in powder form and mix it yourself. If the gypsumboard is decorated with a special laminate, colored nails are used.

Gypsumboard may be installed both horizontally and vertically over framing.

To break a piece of gypsumboard, score the material deeply with a utility knife and snap it over a straight edge such as a length of 2×4.

The outside corners of gypsumboard can be covered with a metal trim molding, which you nail through the gypsumboard into the corner framing members. The metal is then finished over with joint compound and tape. Inside corners are finished with just joint compound and tape.

HOW IT'S SOLD. Gypsumboard is sold by the sheet; the thicker the board, the more it costs. Lath is priced by the bundle or by the piece. Nails, metal outside corners, joint compound, and joint tape are sold by weight and length.

SPECIAL ORDERS. Most retailers will special-order gypsumboard for you at no extra charge. However, be prepared to wait as long as six weeks for delivery.

If you can't find the product you want, or need any special installation help with gypsumboard, contact the Consumer Information Director at the following firms:

U.S. Gypsum Co.
101 South Wacker Drive
Chicago, Ill. 60606

Gold Bond Building Products Div.
National Gypsum Co.
2001 Rexford Rd.
Charlotte, N.C. 28211

Fiber and Chip Board Panels

These lightweight panels, sometimes called strawboard, can be used for unlimited applications, such as closet lining, wall paneling, garden sheds, and cabinet backs. They should not be exposed to the weather without being sealed with a penetrating sealer or paint. Even then, the material doesn't weather well, although it probably will give service for a year or two.

Cedar closet lining panels are made from cedar chips and shavings; they make a closet smell like an old-fashioned cedar chest.

HOW THEY'RE SOLD. Panels are available in ¼- and ½-inch thicknesses by 4×8 feet. Some retailers sell 2×4 precut panels.

They are sold by thickness, and by length and width.

SPECIAL ORDER. Most retailers will not special-order these panels for you unless you are buying a large quantity. On special order, you probably will have a four to six week wait for delivery; you may have to pay part of the freight costs. Get the total cost estimate before you decide.

If you can't find these products in your area, or need special installation information, contact the Consumer Information Director at these companies:

Duraflake Co.
Box 428
Albany, Ore. 97321

MacMillian Bloedel Building
  Materials
6640 Powers Ferry Rd.
Atlanta, Ga. 30339

Weyerhaeuser Co., Wood Products
  Group
Box B
Tacoma, Wash. 98401

Doors

Exterior doors
Exterior doors come in three types: flush panel, panel, and glazed (with glass). There are two types of door cores: solid and hollow; solid core doors are generally used for exterior doors because they are stronger. Exterior doors also are available with steel and hardboard faces. Both types are difficult to tell from wooden doors when finished. Some brands are available prefinished.

Flush panel doors have wood, hardboard, or metal fastened to a frame and core of wood. As a rule, solid cores are made of blocks of wood laminated together, similar to a butcher block. The core may also be made of particleboard.

Panel doors—sometimes called raised panel doors—are made of styles and rails into which panels are fitted; the panels may be wood, glass or sometimes plastic.

Glazed doors include French doors and doors with multiple glass insert panels.

SIZES. Door sizes are stated in this way: 2/8 × 80; 3/0 × 78, 2/0 × 76. The first number is the width of the door in feet and inches; the second number is the length of the door in inches. In the example above, a 2/8 door is 2 feet, 8 inches wide, or 32 inches wide, by 80 inches long. A 3/0 door is 36 inches wide; a 2/0 door is 24 inches wide.

There are two ways to measure the wall opening for the door. If the opening is rough, that is, it hasn't been cased, allow 1½ inches at the top and side jambs and at the bottom for the casing and fitting in a typical installation. Be sure to check any door manufacturer's instructions; they may call for a special measurement. If the opening is finished, that is, it has been cased, measure from the inside jamb across to the opposite inside jamb and from the inside top header to the threshold. If you are replacing a door, simply measure the old door for the correct new door measurement.

Interior doors
Interior doors in stock usually are limited to flush panel and raised panel doors with hollow core construction. The choice of styles includes single doors, single doors with a cutout for locksets, and pre-hung doors. Special types may be ordered; delivery usually is within several days.

Hollow cores are made up of a roughly two-inch framework of wood with strips of wood spaced throughout the length; the filler may also be cardboard or hollow wooden discs. Hollow core doors are usually reinforced with a wood block at the lockset location, providing a solid surface through which the lockset is attached to the door.

PRE-HUNG DOORS. Pre-hung doors are hung, or hinged, in a framework that includes the header, side jambs, and casings. One side of this framework dovetails into the other side. When the door is installed, the frame is separated and one side is fastened to the stud framing around the door opening. Then the other side of the frame is fastened on. The door is finished by installing a lockset; sometimes the lockset is installed on the door. Pre-hung doors in stock often are limited to flush panel styles. The panel usually is lauan wood (a type of mahogany), which can be sealed and left natural, stained, or enameled.

JAMB KITS. The top and side jambs and thresholds for many door styles are available pre-cut in kits.

Wooden jambs are manufactured in two basic sizes: 5¼-inch widths for lath and plaster walls, and 4½ inches

Standard doors include both flush and raised panel designs, shown here. Only a few of these styles are usually stocked by a retailer. Some glazed doors are available with an optional plastic grid to make a mullioned effect.

Left: A pre-hung door is easier to install than a single door because the pre-hung door is already hinged in the framework, which is assembled. You start installation by fastening the framing in place around the rough

opening. *Middle:* To square the door frame in the rough opening, force shim shingles between the frame and the wall. Once it's square, the door frame is nailed to the studs in the rough opening. Make sure the door is

vertical by using a plumb line. *Right:* The door casing is mitred together and nailed to the wall surface as the final step in installing a pre-hung door.

for gypsumboard walls. Metal jambs are made 5¼ inches wide for lath and plaster; 6¾ and 8¾ inches wide for concrete block, brick, and brick veneers. Standard metal jamb sizes in stock at home centers and hardware stores are 5½ and 5⅝ inches; these will handle most needs of a do-it-yourselfer.

Exterior and interior doors are *handed,* that is, left- or right-handed. To identify a door's handedness, stand on the side of the door that opens *toward* you. If the door is hinged on the right side, it is a right-handed door and will be stamped RH. If the door is hinged on the left side, it is a left-handed door, stamped LH.

Standard door thicknesses are 1⅜ and 1¾ inches, although you can buy thicker and thinner doors. Locksets are sold by door thickness. Before you buy a lockset, be sure to measure the thickness of the door.

HOW THEY'RE SOLD. Doors are sold as single units. If the door is pre-

hung, the price includes the hinges, framework, and, sometimes, the lockset.

Jamb kits are sold as a single item; so are interior and exterior thresholds. Hinges and locksets are sold as single components. Door casing and jamb material is sold by the linear foot.

SPECIAL ORDER. Although most home center stores and lumberyards carry only a few styles of doors, they will special-order any exterior or interior door you pick from their catalogs. You usually don't have to pay transportation costs, and, sometimes, the retailer will even have the door delivered from the manufacturer right to your home within 48 hours. On special orders, be sure to take the size of the door opening to the store. This will save you and the retailer lots of time figuring.

If you can't locate the style or type of door you want, including wood, steel, or patio doors, write to the Consumer Information Director of these firms. The company also will help

you with special installation problems.

Jessup Door Do.
300 East Railroad St.
Dowagiac, Mich. 49047

Ideal Millwork Co.
Box 889
Waco, Tex. 76703

CECO Corp.
5601 West 26th St.
Chicago, Ill. 60650

Andersen Corp.
Bayport, Minn. 55003

C-E Morgan, Combustion Engineering Inc.
601 Oregon St.
Oshkosh, Wis. 54901

E.A. Nord Co. Inc.
Box 1187
Everett, Wash. 98206

Windows

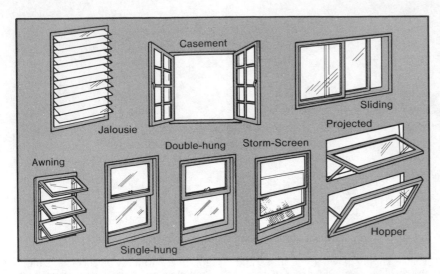

Standard wood frame window types are illustrated here. Metal frame windows also are available in many of these same styles.

Windows are fully assembled when you buy them; some are pre-hung in their frames with the casings; others are assembled with hardware and weatherstripping.

Types of standard windows readily available for do-it-yourselfers include: double-hung; casement; fixed; horizontal sliding; awning and hopper; and jalousie.

Sometimes, glass blocks are used for light instead of windows, especially in basement areas. Hire a professional to set glass blocks.

General specifications

Wooden windows usually have jambs (including tops) the same width as the wall from the siding through the face of the wall covering. The jambs are milled from standard one-inch (nominal) boards, and the jamb liners are used to shim the window to fit the space. Sills also are included with the window package. They are cut from two-inch (nominal) lumber and are pitched about 3 in 12 for water drainage. The sash are usually $1\frac{3}{8}$ inches thick; combination storm and screen units are $1\frac{1}{8}$ inches thick.

Metal windows are similar to wooden windows in sizes.

Double-hung windows have two parts: an upper and lower sash. They may have a single pane of glass or multiple panes of glass in each sash; the panes are called *lights*.

Glass Selection Guide

TYPE OF GLASS	RESISTANCE TO BREAKAGE	FOR D-I-Y INSTALLATION	COST
Standard single	Bad	Yes	Low
Standard double	Fair	Yes	Low
Tempered	Good	Yes	Medium
Plate	Fair	Yes	Medium
Safety	Good	Yes	High
Wire	Good	No	High
Insulation	Good	No	High
Blocks	Good	No	High
Tile	Bad	Yes	Medium

Note: Most paint and wallpaper stores stock these types of glass and cut pieces to order.

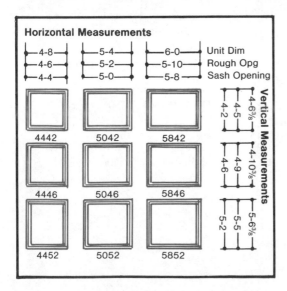

Horizontal Measurements

Standard picture window designs are shown at left. The horizontal dimensions of the windows are given directly above in the illustration, and the vertical dimensions are listed at the right. The unit numbers that identify each design are given under each window. Use these numbers when ordering. Compare the dimensions of your windows with the sizes shown here to find the exact size and the unit number to ask for. The chart below lists the size of the pane of glass that fits each of these standard windows, assuming a 1-inch rabbet is provided all around the frame.

Unit Number	Dimensions of a 1-in. Glass Rabbet	Order this 1-in. Glass Size
4442	$49 \times 46\frac{1}{2}$	$48\frac{1}{2} \times 46$
5042	$57 \times 46\frac{1}{2}$	$56\frac{1}{2} \times 48\frac{1}{8}$
5842	$65 \times 46\frac{1}{2}$	$64\frac{1}{2} \times 46$
4446	$49 \times 50\frac{1}{2}$	$48\frac{1}{2} \times 50$
5046	$57 \times 50\frac{1}{2}$	$56\frac{1}{2} \times 50$
5846	$65 \times 50\frac{1}{2}$	$64\frac{1}{2} \times 50$
4452	$49 \times 58\frac{1}{2}$	$48\frac{1}{2} \times 58$
5052	$57 \times 58\frac{1}{2}$	$56\frac{1}{2} \times 58\frac{1}{8}$
5852	$65 \times 58\frac{1}{2}$	$64\frac{1}{2} \times 58$

Double-hung windows provide more ventilation than any other type: one-half of the window may be opened. The windows are locked in window channels and move only up and down; one style has easily removable sash for cleaning.

Double-hung window hardware, sometimes furnished by the window manufacturer, includes the sash lifts and window locks.

Casement windows are hinged along one edge and open out with a crank-and-gear mechanism or a simple adjustable rod. Hardware usually is furnished by the manufacturer; it includes the crank and gear, hinges, and sash locks.

Fixed windows are large picture windows that don't open. Since they are usually glazed with insulation glass, they don't need storm windows.

Horizontal sliding windows may be likened to a standard double-hung window that is tipped on it side. The sash move horizontally in guides or tracks. In multiple windows, several sash may be opened; in single units, one sash is fixed and the other is movable.

Awning and hopper windows are hinged at the top and open outward like an awning. A rod holds the window in different open positions. A hopper window is hinged at the bottom and opens outward at the top; it also has a rod that holds the window open. The jambs of these windows are usually at least $1\frac{1}{16}$ inches thick; the sill is at least $1\frac{5}{16}$ inches wide if multiple units are framed side-by-side.

Jalousie windows have a series of glass panels or slats that run horizontally across the window from its side frames. A crank-gear device opens and closes the panels. Wooden-framed jalousie units are generally preferred over metal units because the insulation value of wood is greater than that of metal.

Rough opening size, that is, the actual size of the hole in the wall, varies with the style of window. Tell the retailer the exact dimensions of the rough opening, and he will tell you what window frame to buy and how much space there will be between rough frame and window.

As a rule of thumb, however, allow $1\frac{1}{16}$ to $1\frac{1}{2}$ inches between the rough framing and the window for top, bottom, and side jambs; this space will be filled with shims to hold the window square and level in the opening.

HOW THEY'RE SOLD. Windows are sold individually. If you order a number of windows, you may be able to get a discount from the retailer; ask for it. The styles of windows that a retailer stocks may be limited.

Window hardware usually is included with the window units. If not, the hardware is sold as single items.

Window jambs and casings are sold by the linear foot. Some jambs come in kits priced as a unit, rather than by individual pieces.

SPECIAL ORDER. Most retailers will special-order any style of window

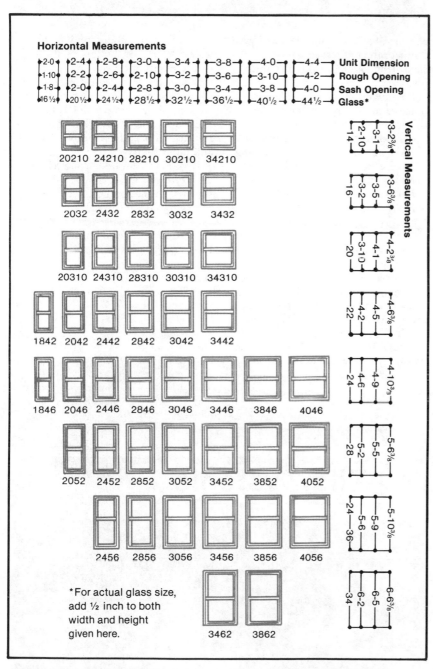

Horizontal Measurements

Unit Dimension	Rough Opening	Sash Opening	Glass*
2-0	1-10	1-8	16½
2-4	2-2	2-0	20½
2-8	2-6	2-4	24½
3-0	2-10	2-8	28½
3-4	3-2	3-0	32½
3-8	3-6	3-4	36½
4-0	3-10	3-8	40½
4-4	4-2	4-0	44½

20210 24210 28210 30210 34210

2032 2432 2832 3032 3432

20310 24310 28310 30310 34310

1842 2042 2442 2842 3042 3442

1846 2046 2446 2846 3046 3446 3846 4046

2052 2452 2852 3052 3452 3852 4052

2456 2856 3056 3456 3856 4056

3462 3862

*For actual glass size, add ½ inch to both width and height given here.

Vertical Measurements

3-2¾ / 3-1 / 2-10 / 14

3-6¾ / 3-5 / 3-2 / 16

4-2¾ / 4-1 / 3-10 / 20

4-6¾ / 4-5 / 4-2 / 22

4-10¾ / 4-9 / 4-6 / 24

5-6¾ / 5-5 / 5-2 / 28

5-10¾ / 5-9 / 5-6 / 24-36

6-6¾ / 6-5 / 6-2 / 34

Window sizes are identified by four- or five-digit numbers, which the retailer uses in ordering. Here is a typical window schedule which you can use for comparison and ordering. For example, the small window at top, left, number 20210, has the horizontal dimensions listed directly above, and the vertical dimensions listed to the left.

for you. You can pick the styles and sizes from a specification catalog. Delivery normally is within three days, but this time may be extended if the order is especially large or involves special styles or sizes. In this event, expect to wait from up to four weeks for delivery. If you can't find the windows you want in your community, try contacting the Consumer Information Director of the following companies. Also, if you have any special installation problems—such as heavy condensation, replacing windows in an old house, excessive heat loss or gain through windows—these firms will be able to help you.

Norandex Aluminum Building Products
7120 Krick Rd.
Cleveland, Ohio 44147

Andersen Corp.
Bayport, Minn. 55003

R-O-W Sales Co.
1315 Academy
Ferndale, Mich. 48220

Marvin Windows
Box 100
Warroad, Minn. 56763

Window shutters

Wooden shutters are usually prehinged; the louvers can be purchased fixed or movable. Wooden shutters

	Standard Sizes of Pre-hinged Shutter Sets			
		WINDOW WIDTH (in.)		
HEIGHT OF WINDOW (in.)	24–28	30–32	34–36	36–40
15–18	6 × 18	7 × 18	8 × 18	9 × 18
18–21	6 × 21	7 × 21	8 × 21	9 × 21
21–24	6 × 24	7 × 24	8 × 24	9 × 24
24–27	6 × 27	7 × 27	8 × 27	9 × 27
27–30	6 × 30	7 × 30	8 × 30	9 × 30
30–33	6 × 33	7 × 33	8 × 33	9 × 33
33–36	6 × 36	7 × 36	8 × 36	9 × 36

also are available unfinished and prefinished; the unfinished ones are sanded smooth and ready for finishing.

Pre-hinged shutters include the hinges and usually the hasp locks. Single shutters require hinge hardware, mounting hardware, and hasps; pre-hinged shutters require mounting hardware, which sometimes is furnished by the manufacturer.

For *sizes,* see the chart above.

HOW THEY'RE SOLD. Pre-hinged shutters are sold as sets of two or multiples of two. Single shutters are sold as individual items. Hinge and hasp hardware is sold by the item. Brass, chrome, and stainless steel hardware is available. Most shutters can be trimmed up to three inches in height and two inches in width.

SPECIAL ORDER. Many retailers will special-order shutters for you.

However, you will probably find a wide selection of shutters available in your community if you spend some time shopping on the telephone. Don't overlook the home furnishings sections of department stores, interior decorators and shops catering to interior decorators, and window shade and blind shops.

If you can't locate the shutter size and style you want, contact the Consumer Information Director of the following manufacturers:

Pinecroft Industries Inc.
Hamlet, N.C. 28345

American Wood Corp.
Box 298
Commerce, Tex. 75428

Maywood Inc.
Box 30550
Amarillo, Tex. 79120

Ceiling Tile Systems

Ceiling tiles and panels are available in a seemingly endless variety of styles and designs. Your biggest problem probably will be selecting a tile pattern, not the system to install it. Fortunately, all ceiling tiles and panels are on a module measurement (see chart); you buy only one standard size in the module you choose.

Tile and panels are either plain or acoustical; acoustical tiles and panels will absorb about 60 percent of the airborne sound that strikes them. Most tiles are washable and some are scrubbable; some may be painted, in-

Ceiling Tile Selector	
TYPE OF TILE	SIZE/INSTALLATION
Mineral fiber	Tiles: 12 × 12 in.; 12 × 24 in.; 24 × 24 in. Panels: 2 × 2 ft.; 2 × 4 ft. 12 × 48 in. Planks: 5^{3}/₁₆ × 48 in.; 6⅝ × 48 in.; 8^{3}/₁₆ × 48 in. Tiles go on wood or metal furring or are glued to the ceiling surface. Planks and panels ride on grid system.
Wood fiber	Tiles: 12 × 12 in.; 12 × 24 in.; 24 × 24 in. Panels: Not available Tiles go on wood or metal furring or are glued to the ceiling surface.
Fiberglass	Panels: 24 × 24 in.; 24 × 48 in.; 24 × 96 in. Designed for grid systems. Panels also available in 4 × 16 ft. for beamed ceilings.

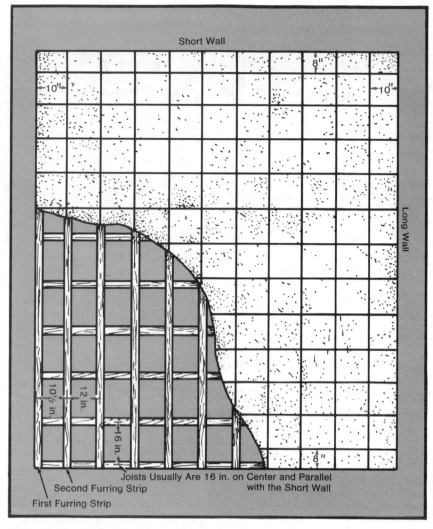

Short Wall

8"

10"   10"

Long Wall

10½ in.   12 in.

16 in.

8"

Joists Usually Are 16 in. on Center and Parallel
with the Short Wall

Second Furring Strip

First Furring Strip

Furred ceiling tiles are stapled to furring strips that have been nailed at
right angles across the joists. Here is
a typical ceiling layout; use it to lay
out your ceiling for 12×12- or 12×24-
inch tile. Note how tiles have been cut
for installation around perimeter.

cluding some acoustical tiles. Some
are fire-rated and UL-listed. Tiles are
edge-matched and have square,
grooved, beveled, or tongue-and-
groove edges. Some panels have insulation qualities that are described on
the package.

Estimating tile needs

To determine the number of tiles or
panels to cover a ceiling, lay out the
room on a sheet of squared graph
paper, using one or more squares to
represent the tile or panel. For example, for 12×12-inch tile, use one
square; for 2×4-foot panels, use 4
squares wide by 8 squares long—or
any configuration that will give you
an accurate count and grid layout of
the room.

You also can estimate the number
of tiles or panels by the square foot:
Multiply the length and width of the
room to get the number of square
feet. Then divide the room area by
the number of square feet in a ceiling

tile or panel package to get the number of packages to buy.

Installation

There are only three ways to install
tiles and panels: on furring strips,
with adhesive, or on metal grids to
make a suspended ceiling. If the ceiling is to be fastened to furring strips
with staples, use 1×3- or 1×4-inch
strips that are fastened to the ceiling
joists with nails.

If the ceiling is gypsumboard or
plaster that is in good repair, the tiles
may be fastened to the surface with
ceiling tile adhesive; this is a good
method, because the tiles simply slide
into place. Tiles may be leveled
slightly by simply adding more adhesive to the backs.

At least one manufacturer (Armstrong) sells a metal furring installation system in kit form. The metal
strips are nailed to the ceiling joists
and tiny clips snap into the furring to
hold the tiles in position. The furring

can be installed with slightly irregular
spacing, making the job much quicker
and easier than by using wood furring
strips. These kits are fairly expensive,
but the time and effort you save is
probably worth it.

Ceiling panels are installed in a
grid system that is suspended from
the ceiling with hanger wire. At first
glance, this system seems complicated, but it actually goes up quickly
when manufacturer's instructions are
followed exactly.

The basic parts of a suspended ceiling system are wall angles, main tees,
and cross tees. Wall angles are fastened to the walls at the height at
which you want the face of the ceiling
panels. The main tees are suspended
from the ceiling at the height of the
wall angles with wire and screw-eyes,
and the cross tees interlock with the
main tees at two- or four-foot increments. The tees can be cut with
straight aviation snips or a hacksaw.

Here's how to install a suspended

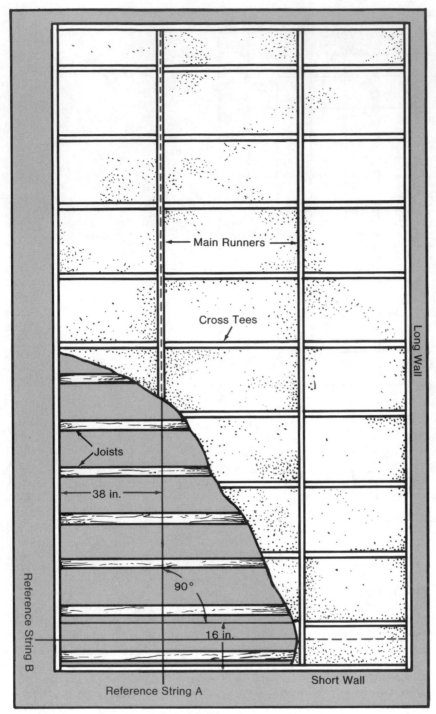

Main Runners

Cross Tees

Joists

38 in.

90°

16 in.

Reference String B

Reference String A

Short Wall

Long Wall

Suspended ceiling panels are installed in a metal grid system. Here's a typical example of how the grids and panels are laid out. The key to a straight, level job is the reference string (see text).

ceiling level: stretch a nylon string between opposite wall angles. Then suspend the hanger wires from the ceiling and bend them at the string line so the hangers match the holes in the main and cross tees. Once this level is established for the whole ceiling, the grid is installed and the panels are slipped into place. A four-inch clearance usually is needed for panel installation between the grids and the ceiling surface. If insulating panels are used, they may be compressed into even less clearance space. Check this with the retailer.

HOW THEY'RE SOLD. Ceiling tiles and panels are sold by the carton. Retailers sometimes will break a carton and sell you single tiles or panels; if they do the tiles will be priced individually.

Furring strips are sold by the linear foot. Adhesive is sold in quart, gallon, and five-gallon containers. Staples are sold by the package; $9/16$-inch staples usually are specified for most ceiling tile installations. Grid systems are sold by the piece: main tees, wall angles, cross tees. The main tees are 12 feet long; the wall angles are 10 to 12 feet long; the cross tees are 2 and 4 feet long. Hanger wire is sold by the package; screw-eyes are sold by the package.

SPECIAL ORDER. Ceiling tile and panels are so plentiful that you shouldn't have any difficulty finding what you want. Most retailers will special-order a design not in inventory. Expect a brief wait for the product—a week or so. You generally don't have to pay freight charges on special tile orders.

If you have a problem finding the tile you want, or have any special installation questions that a retailer can't answer, write the Consumer Information Director of the ceiling tile and panel manufacturers below.

Armstrong World Industries, Inc.
Lancaster, Pa. 17604

Owens-Corning Fiberglas Corp.
Fiberglas Tower
Toldeo, Ohio 43659

Celotex Corp.
1500 North Dale Mabry
Tampa, Fla. 33607

Floor Tile

Floor tile is easy to install—probably easier than ceiling tile because you don't have to work overhead. There are hundreds of tile designs available. Floor tiles—commonly known as resilient tiles—are manufactured from asphalt, vinyl, and rubber. Other floor coverings include: hardwood parquet blocks and carpet tile.

SIZE. Most asphalt and vinyl tile measures $\frac{1}{8}$-inch thick by 9×9 or 12×12 inches. Rubber tile measures from $\frac{1}{8}$ to $\frac{3}{16}$ inches thick by 4×4, 9×9, 12×12 inches. Larger sizes may be available through special order.

Room layout

The room to be tiled should be sketched out on graph paper. Let one square of the grid represent one tile. This plan will give you an accurate count for buying tiles, and will also serve as a cutting diagram; by positioning the tiles *on paper,* you can save yourself countless hours of cutting and fitting actual tiles.

Another way to estimate tiles is to find the area of the room by multiplying width times length. Then, divide the area of the room by the square footage of tile in a carton. If the figure comes out in a fraction, buy the next larger whole number of cartons. You'll need extra tiles for cutting, and scrap, and odd-shaped corners.

Installation

Tiles are cemented to the flooring. Tiles with adhesive backing are self-sticking; other types have to be set in a bed of floor mastic (adhesive). In any case, the floor must be perfectly clean and free of grease and wax. If the floor is of wood, it must be smooth with the nails *set,* that is, below the surface. If the floor is uneven wood, a hardboard underlayment must be installed. New tiles can be installed over old tiles if the old ones are firmly bonded to the floor surface. If not, they must be stripped from the floor, all mastic removed, and the floor sanded or smoothed and then cleaned.

HOW THEY'RE SOLD. Floor tiles are sold by the carton. Some retailers sell single tiles priced by the piece. Prices depend on the type and design of the tile. For example: asphalt tile is less costly than vinyl or vinyl-asphalt. Parquet blocks are more expensive than resilient tile. Carpet tiles cost about the same as resilient tiles.

SPECIAL ORDER. Most retailers will special-order any type or design of tile you want, if the tile is part of the brand-name line that the retailer carries. But, an Armstrong tile dealer probably won't order a GAF-brand tile for you; you will have to find a GAF dealer. Most special orders are filled within a week; you generally won't have to pay freight.

If you can't find the tile you want, or have any special installation problems, contact the Consumer Information Director of the tile manufacturers listed below.

Armstrong World Industries. Inc.
Lancaster, Pa. 17604

GAF Corp., Building Products
140 West 51st St.
New York, N.Y. 10020

Azrock Floor Products
Box 531
San Antonio, Tex. 78292

Carpet Selector				
TYPE OF FIBER	FADE RESISTANCE	STAIN REMOVAL	CLEANING	STATIC SHOCK RESISTANCE
Wool	Fair	Fair	Good	Poor in low humidity
Acrylic	Fair	Good	Fair	Fair
Nylon	Fair	Fair	Good	Good
Polyester	Good	Good	Fair	Poor in low humidity
Polypropylene	Good	Good	Good	Good

Floor Tile and Sheet Goods Selector		
TYPE	PROPERTIES	COST
Asphalt	Excellent product, but hard to keep clean and waxed. Don't use in areas where grease is present, such as a kitchen.	Low
Vinyl asbestos	Excellent durability; easy to install; resistant to wear.	Medium
Solid vinyl	May be laid without adhesive; if mineral-backed, it may be used below grade. Burns easily.	Medium to high
Roto sheet vinyl	May be laid without adhesive. If mineral-backed, may be used below grade. Burns easily. Easy to install; cuts with scissors.	Varies
Cushioned sheet vinyl	In several grades; wear-resistant and very easy to install. Burns quickly.	Varies
Sheet vinyl	This is solid vinyl. Several grades can be laid over most any floor including existing resilient flooring material. Must be installed by a professional.	Medium to high
Parquet block	Usually self-sticking and easy to install. Wears well; pre-finished.	High
Carpet tile	Wears like carpet; fairly durable. Installs without adhesive, but is usually taped at perimeter of room with double-faced tape. Burns easily.	Medium

Metal Products

Most home centers, hardware stores, and lumberyards stock do-it-yourself metal products—especially aluminum. The metals are available in sheets, rods, bars, channels, angles, and tracks for all sorts of projects.

Heavy metals, such as galvanized steel and lead, are not carried by these retailers. Retailers also don't deal in gold, silver, and other precious metals. You will find heavy metals at welding shops; precious metals may be purchased at hobby shops and jewelry stores.

Metals Selection Guide

METAL	CLASS	PRODUCTS AVAILABLE	TOOLS NEEDED
Aluminum	Nonferrous	Sheets; tubes; embossed sheet; tracks; bar; angle; channel; colored metals	Rivet tool; snips; hacksaw; pliers
Galvanized steel	Ferrous	Sheet; angle; rod; tubes; channel; ducting	Hacksaw; metal drills; metal punches; metal vise for bending
Copper	Nonferrous	Rod; sheet; tubes	Hacksaw; metal drills; snips; pliers
Brass	Nonferrous	Rod; sheet; tubes	Snips; pliers; metal drills; metal punches
Wrought iron	Ferrous	Rod; pre-formed rod; railings; fittings	Hacksaw; welder; metal drills; metal punches; wrenches; hammer
Bronze	Nonferrous	Rod; sheet; tube	Snips; pliers; hacksaw; metal drills; vise
Mild steel	Ferrous	Rod; sheet; bar	Hacksaw; metal drills; metal punches; pliers
Cast iron	Ferrous	Rod; bar	Hacksaw; metal drills; metal punches

Wallpaper

Some home centers and lumberyards stock wallpaper, but seldom in quantity. These retailers usually have wallpaper books from which you can select the paper you want. The retailer will order it.

Wallpaper is attached to the wall by (1) mixing paste separately and applying it to the back of the paper or (2) moistening the pre-pasted back of the paper with water. Paint and wallcovering dealers, general merchandise stores, or shops that specialize in wallcoverings usually stock larger varieties of paper, and have access to distributors who will deliver your order in several days.

HOW IT'S SOLD. Wallpaper types include: standard papers, foil, flock, burlap, and fabrics, as well as lining paper. Lining paper is used to smooth the wall before the paper is applied; it does the same job as a coat of primer paint that is put on before the top coats. All types of paper are sold by the roll or the double-roll.

Wallpaper Adhesive Selector

TYPE	ADHESIVE
Standard	Wheat or stainless paste
Strippable	Liquid strippable or wheat paste
Backed burlap	Vinyl adhesive
Plain burlap	Wheat or stainless paste
Vinyl	Vinyl adhesive
Backed cork	Vinyl adhesive
Fabrics	Stainless paste
Flocks	Vinyl adhesive
Murals	Vinyl adhesive
Foils	Vinyl adhesive
Borders	Vinyl adhesive
Hand prints	Vinyl adhesive

Flexible Wallcovering Estimator for Single Rolls

PERIMETER OF ROOM (in ft.)	ROLLS NEEDED FOR 8-ft. Ceiling	ROLLS NEEDED FOR 9-ft. Ceiling	ROLLS NEEDED FOR 10-ft. Ceiling	YARDS NEEDED FOR BORDER	ROLLS NEEDED FOR CEILING
28	8	8	10	11	2
30	8	8	10	11	2
32	10	10	10	12	2
34	10	10	12	13	4
36	10	10	12	13	4
38	10	12	12	14	4
40	12	12	14	15	4
42	12	12	14	15	4
44	12	12	14	16	4
46	14	14	14	17	6
48	14	14	16	17	6
50	14	14	16	18	6
52	14	14	16	19	6
54	14	16	18	19	6
56	16	16	18	20	6
58	16	16	18	21	8
60	16	18	20	21	8
62	16	18	20	22	8
64	18	18	20	23	8
66	18	20	20	23	8
68	18	20	22	24	10
70	18	20	22	25	10
72	18	20	22	25	10
74	20	22	22	26	12
76	20	22	24	27	12
78	20	22	24	27	14
80	20	22	24	28	14
82	22	24	26	30	14
84	22	24	26	30	16
86	22	24	26	30	16
88	24	26	28	31	16
90	24	26	28	32	18

SPECIAL ORDER. Most wallcoverings are available on a special-order basis. Expect a short wait before you receive the products you want; you generally do not have to pay freight.

If you can't find the wallcovering you want, or have any special installation problems, write the Consumer Information Director of the companies listed below.

North American Wallpapers Ltd.
1055 Clark Blvd.
Bramalea, Ont. Canada L6T 3W4

Imperial Wallcoverings Inc.
23645 Mercantile Rd.
Cleveland, Ohio 44122

Birge Company
390 Niagara St.
Buffalo, N.Y. 14240

Builders' Hardware

This vast catagory contains more products than could be listed in this book.

Builders' hardware is in two classifications: construction hardware (heavier products for door hinges, locksets, joist hardware, and deck hardware), and cabinet hardware (lighter items, such as cabinet pulls, latches, and escutcheon plates).

Most home centers carry only a limited inventory of basic builders' and cabinet hardware. For a wider selection, try a hardware outlet or specialty cabinet shop. Before you go shopping, determine exactly what type and size of hardware you need.

Here is a list of classifications:

Barn
Bench and table
Cabinet
Closers and
  operators
Closet
Deck and patio
Door (folding
  and sliding)
Door accessory*
Drapery
Drawer
Garage door
Gate
Joist and timber
Locks and keys
Mixer shelf
Padlocks
Revolving shelf
Security
Screen and storm
Window

HOW IT'S SOLD. Hardware is sold by the piece or package.

SPECIAL ORDER. Some home centers and most hardware outlets will special-order hardware for you. You can expect to wait four to six weeks and you probably will have to pay the freight charges.

If you can't find what you want, write to the following hardware distributors—not manufacturers. The distributors have a large variety of hardware items; a manufacturer usually makes and sells only a few items.

Ace Hardware Corp.
2200 Kensington Ct.
Oak Brook, Ill. 60521

American Hardware Supply Co.
Box 1510
Butler, Pa. 16001

Hardware Wholesalers Inc.
Nelson Rd., Box 868
Fort Wayne, Ind. 46801

Our Own Hardware Co.
Box 720
Minneapolis, Minn. 55440

---

* Bolts, knobs, plates, silencers, and stops.

9

LAWN AND GARDEN PRODUCTS

Many home centers want to be one-stop shopping centers; so among the nuts, bolts, concrete, and plywood you are likely to find lawn and garden products, such as fertilizer, grass seed, chemicals, lawn mowers, and lawn-care tools. Some home centers even stock bedding plants, such as tomatoes, and lettuce, as well as balled trees on a seasonal basis. The prices of these goods usually are lower than those at nurseries and specialized lawn and garden outlets. The best bargains are available in late fall and winter, after the growing season and before new merchandise arrives on the showroom floor for the spring sales push. During the winter months, you might even be able to negotiate special prices on last year's merchandise. It's worth trying; talk to the store manager.

Lawn feed and weeder

The key to understanding fertilizer and fertilizer with weed killers is the label on the package, which explains what the chemicals in the package will and will not do. Before making a buying decision, compare labels even if a salesperson is handy to discuss the features of the products. The basic nutrients in most fertilizers are nitrogen (N), phosphorous (P), and potash (K). The strengths of these chemicals in a fertilizer are indicated by a ratio on the label: 5-10-5 or 27-3-3 or 20-5-5. The first example means five parts nitrogen to ten parts phosphorous to five parts potash. Since you probably won't recall the chemical names at point-of-purchase, buy by the numbers. Here's a good way to remember what they mean: The first number (nitrogen) makes the grass grow UP, green and thick. The second number (phosphorous) makes the grass grow DOWN to build a healthy root system. The third number (potash) makes the grass grow AROUND by spreading the root system. Therefore, *up, down, and all-around* is the catch-phrase to remember when choosing a fertilizer.

Here are several examples. A starter fertilizer that is used for a new lawn may be labeled 18-24-6. The second number is the key: the 24 (phosphorous) builds a good, healthy root system necessary to establish the new lawn. A fertilizer applied to an established lawn in the spring may have a 31-4-4 formula. Here the key is 31 (nitrogen) for green, thick grass. The 4-4 provides food for the roots, but the roots don't require much feeding since they are already established in the earth.

The same formula appears on plant food chemicals. Each can or bottle of chemical food—usually liquid—has the numbering system, which, over-simplifed, means *Up, Down, and All-Around.*

Fertilizer and crabgrass killer combinations give the grass a healthy dose of nutrients, while "controlling" the crabgrass and other weeds. The word "controlled" is used by manufacturers because the chemical may not rid the lawn of all crabgrass or weeds; it holds them at an acceptable level.

Fertilizer with crabgrass controllers must be applied before the crabgrass germinates. The proper time varies according to growing seasons. For example, crabgrass germinates sooner in Georgia than Maine. A good rule of thumb to use, if you can't find out germination times in your area, is: apply the controllers from March to April 1. After this time, crabgrass controller is absolutely worthless because the crabgrass seeds have germinated.

Fertilizer with dandelion controllers must be applied when dandelions are growing because the chemical has to touch the growing plant in order to stop its growth.

Weeds are divided into two classifications: broadleaf (dicot) and grassy (monocot). They are then subdivided into annual or perennial, and, further, according to growth style, such as clumps or patches.

Annual weeds come up just once each season; the plant then dies and the same plant will never grow again. Typical annual weeds include crab-

The numbers on bagged fertilizer are the key to lawn feeding. The first number represents nitrogen, which makes the grass green. The second number represents phosphorous for root growth. The third number is for potash, which increases the root system. This number on this pack, 30-4-4, shows that the fertilizer has been formulated to promote lots of green grass with some help to the root system. If you are trying to establish a lawn, the second and third numbers should be large, and the first number small, for example, 5-10-10.

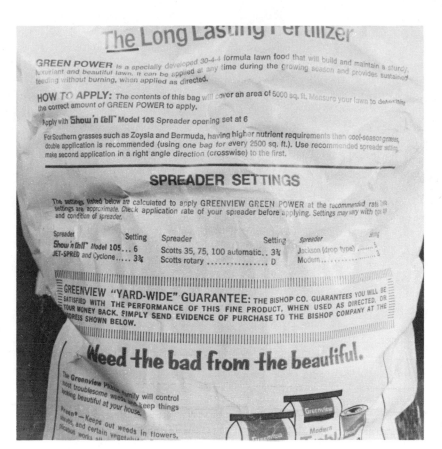

Lawn spreader settings are indicated on most bags of fertilizer. Match your setting to the number shown for your brand of spreader. You should feed a lawn in the early and mid-fall months. If the soil is extremely poor, a fertilizer feeding about mid-July will aid the lawn.

Turn the knob or adjust the lever to match the spreader setting with the recommendation on the fertilizer bag. The knob or lever changes the size of the opening in the bottom of the spreader for proper distribution. Never spread fertilizer by throwing it onto the lawn by hand; this causes streaking in the grass because all grass roots do not receive the same amount of fertilizer. Mark the route of the spreader across the lawn with a lime wheel attached to the spreader or with stakes and string. Do not overlap distributed fertilizer; streaks in the grass will appear if you do.

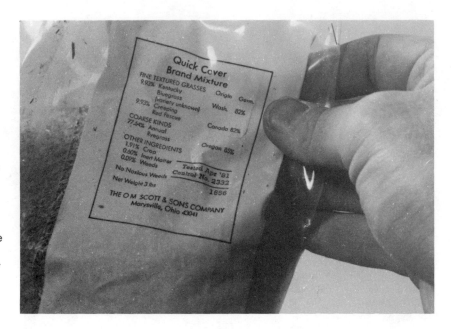

By law, grass seed packages must be labeled to show the mixture of seeds and other ingredients. This product has a large amount of ryegrass, an annual, for quick covering of bare spots in the lawn. The ryegrass will not grow again after a fall frost. Notice the amount of "other ingredients": This brand has a very low percentage. Poorer brands may have large amounts of worthless inert matter—pecan hulls, corncobs, sand—and weed seed.

grass, barnyardgrass, goosegrass, and foxtail. Perennial weeds grow year-after-year, that is, the same plant blooms again and again. Typical perennial grassy weeds include redtop, bentgrass, coarse fescue, and timothy.

Fertilizers with chemicals are available to control all of these weeds; the specific weeds are usually listed on the bags.

Lawn disease preventers are available with or without fertilizer; they may be used on mixtures of bluegrass and fescue, perennial ryegrass, St. Augustine, and bahia grasses. They prevent leaf spot and other fungus diseases.

Lawn insect-control products take care of such pests as cutworms, lawn moth larvae, and flea beetles; they are available with or without fertilizer. For the West Coast, the products contain chemicals to stop Japanese beetles, European chafer, sod webworms, and May and June beetles.

A moss control/fertilizer is available for use in the extreme western sections of Oregon and Washington.

Spread fertilizers according to the directions on the package. Some manufacturers build in a margin of error for fertilizers; others don't. If too much fertilizer is spread on the grass, the grass will burn brown from the chemicals. Therefore, resist the temptation to apply more fertilizer than recommended. Set your spreader as recommended by the manufacturer, even though the amount of chemical being distributed may seem skimpy.

Different types of nitrogen (the first number on the label) have different methods of release and different performance characteristics. The types are listed on the label along with the correct spreader settings.

Ammoniacal nitrogen is released quickly and is absorbed almost immediately by the grass; it produces very fast greening.

If this chemical is not spread according to the manufacturer's recommendations, it can burn the grass and turn it brown.

Water soluble nitrogen is released at varying rates by rain and sprinkling systems. The chemical starts to work about three days after it has been spread and continues to release nitrogen gradually for about three weeks or more. This type of nitrogen is safer than ammoniacal; it also provides good, extended greening.

Water insoluble nitrogen is slow to release; the breakdown starts about two or three weeks after spreading and continues for several months. The chemical is converted by soil microorganisms.

Some manufacturers use only one type of nitrogen; others mix a combination of all three, which is explained on the label.

Understanding grass seed

By law, grass seed must be labeled to show ingredients. By reading the analysis of the contents you can determine what is a bargain and what is not.

The list of ingredients is divided into three categories: Fine Textured Grasses, Coarse Textured Grasses, and Other Ingredients. The germination percentage—the percentage of seeds that will grow in a prescribed time in a laboratory—is also listed. The higher this percentage, the better; 85 percent is a good base figure. A standard lawn mixture should contain at least 50 percent fine grasses and at least 40 percent annual ryegrass in the coarse-grass category. The big problems are found in the other-ingredients category. There should be a very low, or zero, percentage of crop seed, and a low percentage of inert matter, which is nothing more than pecan hulls or seed husks. It is useless filler and does nothing except fill up the package. The less inert matter, the better the seed. Weed seed contents are also given in percentages; the lower the figure, the better. If it does not contain noxious weeds, the mixture is a quality one. The noxious weeds are listed by seed count on the package.

A large bag of seed at a low cost may look like a bargain, but the package may be filled up with ryegrass seed, which weighs more than the bluegrass and fescue seeds you want, as well as other ingredients, especially inert matter, which only adds to the weight. So, when buying grass seed, look for high percentages of fine textured grasses, and low or zero percentages of other unwanted ingredients.

Lawn and garden chemicals

Chemicals to make lawns, gardens, and plants grow better are now stocked by many home centers and hardware stores. Many of these products are in liquid form and must be diluted with water. Others are in pellet and powder form. All are labeled to show what they're good for: to help the growth of vegetables, flowers, shrubs, or trees; to kill insects that eat away at vegetables and flowering plants; to keep dogs, rabbits, and other animals off the plants; to remove tree stumps; to heal tree wounds; to kill all vegetation.

Like all chemicals, these products are carefully labeled by manufacturers; follow the directions carefully for mixing and application.

Buying a lawnmower

The size of your lawn is a big factor in determining which basic type of lawnmower you should buy—rotary or reel—as well as deciding what power source to use: hand, gasoline engine, or electric motor. If your lawn is very small, a hand-driven reel mower will be adequate. If your lawn is small to medium-large, a rotary-type electric mower might be a good choice. For large to extra-large lawns, a gasoline-powered rotary or reel mower, or even a riding mower with either a rotary or reel attachment, may be in order.

Hand-driven reel mowers have five or seven cutting blades that revolve vertically. This mower is best suited to small, flat lawns that are planted with a thin-bladed grass such as fescue.

Reel power mowers are more costly than rotary power mowers, whether the engine is mounted on the mower, or a riding mower pulls the reel or a gang of reels. However, reel mowers—hand or power—usually outlast their rotary relatives since the engine driving the reels doesn't work as hard and the blades of a reel mower stop dead when the blades hit a solid object. The big disadvantage of a reel mower—especially a powered one—is blade height: the blade has to be carefully adjusted if the ground over which the reel blades and cutter bar runs is uneven. Badly set blades can scalp the ground and cut the grass unevenly.

Rotary power mowers are the real workhorses among lawnmowers. This type has a single blade that turns horizontally to cut the grass.

Rotary mowers may be powered by an electric motor or a gasoline engine. If the lawn is small to medium-large, an electric rotary mower is a good buy. A 100-foot extension cord (buy at least No. 12 wire) will reach from lot-line to lot-line. For 5,000-sq.-ft. lawns or smaller, a 14- or 18-inch-wide blade is adequate. Electric motors are rated in amps instead of horsepower: the more amps the motor can use, the more power the motor puts out. A 12-amp motor, for example, is the approximate equivalent of

Chemicals for Common Lawn Diseases

DISEASE	CHEMICAL TO APPLY
Leafspot. Red-brown spots or purple-black spots on the leaves of Kentucky and Merion bluegrass.	Thiram, captan, or cycloheximide spray. Don't mow grass short; avoid adding too much nitrogen to the soil.
Rust. Red powdery deposits on leaves.	Zineb, cycloheximide, or thiram. Plant the lawn with Merion bluegrass or red fescue to help eliminate the problem.
Brown patch. Appears mostly on fescue, bluegrass, ryegrass, St. Augustine, and bentgrass.	Fungicides containing mercury compounds. Do not apply when the temperature is below 80°F.
Fading. Yellow patches in lawn.	Thiram, captan, or cycloheximide spray.
Grease spot or cotton blight. Moldy spots ringed by blackened blades of grass.	Zineb spray. Avoid excessive watering or keeping the lawn wet for long periods of time.
Dollar spot. Bleached spots about the size of a silver dollar.	Spray with chemicals containing cadmium compounds.
Snow mold. Leaves have a white appearance. Disease usually occurs in small areas, scattered throughout the lawn.	Spray with chemicals containing mecurial fungicides. Use fertilizers with a low nitrogen content; cut the lawn after the first frost.
Fairy ring. Large arcs and circles of dark grass surrounding yellowish or dead grass.	Cover the ground affected thoroughly with mercurial fungicides.
Slime mold. Black, bluish, or yellow mold on the leaves.	All-purpose fungicide.
Stripe smut. Blackish strips running the length of the leaves.	No chemical control. Plant grasses other than Merion bluegrass to help stop the disease.

Chemicals for Common Lawn Pests

PESTS	PESTICIDE
Grubs: Japanese; Oriental; garden; European; Asiatic	Diazinon or sevin
Ants	Diazinon or carbaryl
Sod webworms	Diazinon or carbaryl
Clover mites	Dicofol or tetradifon
Chinchbug	Diazinon or carbaryl
Billbugs (Zoysia grass)	Diazinon
Japanese beetle grubs	Diazinon

Note: Apply chemicals to lawns according to the instructions on the label.

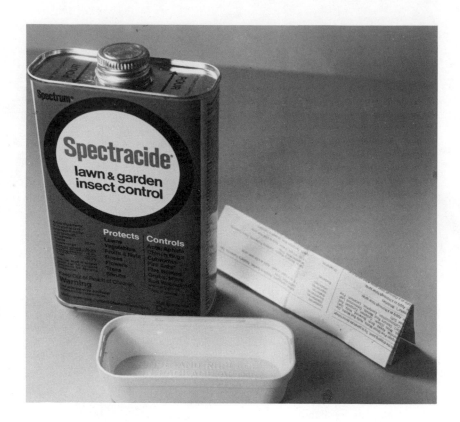

Lawn chemicals formulated to control lawn diseases and insect pests are available in liquid and powder form, packaged in metal containers and glass bottles. Read the labels and instructions carefully and follow them accurately; don't overdo the application.

a 2-horsepower engine. Electric motors have an advantage over gasoline engines: they start easily in any weather and require no fussing with liquid fuels and oil lubricants. The big disadvantage, however, is the power cord, which can be easily cut by the blade. Also, a short cord can limit the range of the lawnmower.

Gasoline-powered mowers include three varieties: push-type, self-propelled, and riding units. If your lawn is from 5,000 to 10,000 square feet, buy a mower with a 20- to 22-inch blade. If the lawn is flat, the push-type will give you a good workout. If the lawn is hilly, you may want to consider a more costly self-propelled model; you have to walk behind this mower, but the mower pulls itself along. If the lawn is more than one acre in size, a riding mower with a rotary blade or reel attachment should be considered. And, if the lawn is hilly, buy at least a 16-hp engine to stand up to the terrain.

Gasoline engines are rated in horsepower. For a small lawn, a 3-hp engine is adequate. For an average lawn with some slope to it, a 3½-hp engine is recommended. For large lawns and lawns with severe slopes and hills, a 4- to 5-hp engine is needed. The engine size is the same

for both rotary and reel mowers.

If you're buying a rotary mower, look for these features:

1. Blade deck: Should be low enough to go under obstructions such as fences and low-hanging shrubs.
2. Blade adjustment: Should be adjustable by means of a lever or levers on the wheels or by unbolting the wheels so they can be raised or lowered. A single blade setting is not desirable for general lawn maintenance.
3. Discharge chutes and rear deflectors that will contain any objects flipped by the spinning blade: Deflectors are standard on most mowers for safety reasons.

If you buy a self-propelled lawnmower, choose front-wheel drive if the lawn is flat. If the lawn is hilly, buy a rear-wheel drive, since it offers more traction.

Brand-name lawnmowers usually cost more than the "no-names" or "never-heard-ofs," but the slightly higher price often is worth it since the mowers are sold with a full warranty, replacement parts are easy to buy, and repairs are easier to make. You can often buy replacement parts, such as blades, sparkplugs, and filters, at

home centers and hardware stores.

However, if you do select an off-brand mower, make sure the engine has a brand-name such as Briggs & Stratton, Clinton, Tecumseh, or Kohler. If you spend a little time maintaining these engines, they will usually outlast the other mower parts, and, best yet, replacement parts for these engines are readily available.

Riding mowers or tractors are a major investment because the prices are generally very high in comparison with push-type and self-propelled mowers.

Features you should consider include a low profile to go under trees and shrubs, and close to fences and retaining walls; easy parts replacement (equipment-mounting bars, air filters, batteries, plugs, etc.); flexibility to convert into plows and other lawn and garden tools; a transmission with a low gear to provide plenty of torque for cutting, plowing and cultivating. Also consider the turning radius, and the stability of the machine on hills and slopes.

Other power tools
GRASS TRIMMERS. These units have a whirling nylon string that whacks grass and weeds right down to the ground. They are gasoline-,

electricity-, and battery-powered. The electric models are adequate for average lawns. The gasoline-motor trimmers are best for large lots, where power cords won't reach conveniently. These units have two-cycle engines that require fuel mixed with oil. The battery-operated models are useful for short time periods, but the batteries must be recharged fairly often.

Some trimmers may be converted into edgers by simply tipping them over along one side. For a professional edging job, however, a motor-driven edger is recommended.

LAWN BLOWERS. *Lawn-blowers* generate wind velocities to 100 mph or more—enough power to clear leaves, grass clippings, dirt, and snow from lawns, walks, driveways, and other areas. They are either gasoline- or electric-powered. As a rule, the more power, the greater the wind rating.

CHAIN SAWS. *Chain saws* are designed for both tree trimming and tree cutting. The 10-inch models are recommended for trimming operations, while the 12- to 16-inch models are best for cutting tree trunks, big limbs, and firewood.

Chain-saw features you should consider include automatic chain oiling, and an automatic, built-in chain-sharpener, and safety features such as double insulation (for electric saws), a chainbreak to prevent saw kickback, vibration-insulation for hand protection, and a nose guard on the tip of the chain blade to help prevent saw kickback.

SPECIAL ORDER. Fertilizers, chemicals, and lawn and garden tools are so plentiful at a variety of stores that you shouldn't have any difficulty finding the products you want.

Specialized garden centers and nurseries usually have the most complete stock, while home centers and hardwares may carry only the essentials.

Retailers are usually reluctant to special-order a single item for you, although it's worth asking. Expect to wait four to six weeks, and pay any freight charges.

Here is a list of lawn and garden product manufacturers, classified by their specialties. Address your questions to the Consumer Information Director of each manufacturer.

Fertilizers and Seed:
Lawn Diseases
The O.M. Scott Co.
Marysville, Ohio 43040
Toll-free phone: 1-800-543-TURF

Lebanon Chemical Corp.
The Bishop Company Division
Lebanon, Pa. 17042

Garden Tools Equipment
Ames, McDonough Co.
Box 1774
Parkersburg, W.Va. 26101
Toll-free phone: 1-800-624-2654

Black & Decker (U.S.), Inc.
701 East Joppa Rd.
Towson, Md. 21204

Lawn Mowers
Jacobsen Mfg. Co.
1721 Packard Ave.
Racine, Wis. 53403

Lawn-Boy
Outboard Marine Corp.
McClure St.
Galesburg, Ill. 41401

Chemicals
Dow Chemical Corp.
2020 Dow Center
Midland, Mich. 48640

Spectrum Home & Garden Products
Agricultural Division
CIBA-GEIGY Corp.
Greensboro, N.C. 27409

10
DECKS AND PATIOS

Decks are wooden structures that are raised off the ground. Patios are made of almost any type of building material laid on the ground—concrete, brick, stone, wood, sand and gravel, asphalt, concrete block, ends of sawn logs, or even railroad ties.

Decks and patios are fairly easy for a do-it-yourselfer to construct, although patios probably are easier because all the work takes place on the ground. Some deck designs require

working from a ladder or scaffolding.

Decks and patios can be any size you want them to be. The standard size is 8 × 10 feet, but consider a larger size if you have the space. The standard size seems to shrink considerably when it becomes filled with furniture and people. In any case, use standard-size building materials; they can save you money and time. For example: 2×8-inch dimension lumber that is often used for deck joists is

available in standard lengths of 8, 10, 12, 14, 16, and 20 feet. By designing a deck in any of these modules, you save the time and waste of sawing the 2×8s to a different size.

Decks are more adaptable to homes built on sloping or uneven building lots. Patios are ideal for flat lots. The reason is obvious: It's easier to place concrete, brick, stone, and other materials on flat ground; it's easier to build up and over sloping ground.

Deck and Patio Design

If you are looking for deck or patio designs to match the architecture of your home, you'll find plenty of ideas in books and magazines. If you have a problem lot, consult an architect or landscaping architect. The cost of having a deck or patio designed is not as great as you might think. Money you save by building the structure

yourself will more than offset any fees, and when the job is completed, you'll have a well-designed deck or patio tailored especially to your needs.

Since deck and patio construction often is subject to local building codes, make sure the structure will conform to the codes *before* you spend any time on design and money on materials. If you intend to light the deck or patio, local electrical codes must be considered. If the area is fenced, you may have to conform to building codes that restrict heights. If the area will include a swimming pool, local codes definitely must be consulted. If your deck will stand more than two or three feet off the ground, consult an architect or engineer for information about the weight and stress loads that will be imposed on the materials you plan to use. The span tables in this chapter will give you an idea of how structural members are placed. If you decide to have a building contractor construct the deck or patio, get at least three bids before signing any contract. It's smart, too, to check the reputation of the contractor you pick with the local Better Business Bureau. Examine some samples of his work and talk to some of his customers. Be sure to get

bottom-line costs for the project. Also, set firm completion times and payment dates in any contract.

Sketch your project on graph paper; then stake the outline on the ground. From this, you can accurately determine the quantities of materials you need.

Wooden deck construction uses standard size dimension lumber throughout. The support posts frame the railings, benches, and stairs. This deck is on buried concrete footings.

Patio is constructed of mortared used bricks. These materials are appropriate to the rustic siding of the house. The bricks are laid on a concrete base; the joints of the bricks were mortared after they were laid out in a simple alternating-pair design. The level of the patio matches the floor level inside the house.

Deck materials

Decks have several component parts that must be considered before you buy any materials.

Decking is the lumber (2×4s or 2×6s) that forms the floor of the deck. There will be a ⅜-inch space between decking pieces to permit

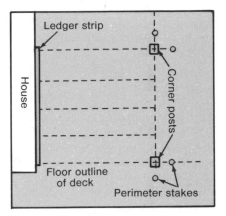

Lay out a deck with string and perimeter stakes, which are moved until the structure is square. The corner posts stand where the lines cross. Joists are nailed around the perimeter to the posts and the ledger strip; the space inside the perimeter is filled with joists on 16- or 24-inch centers. Strings can also mark the form placement for patios.

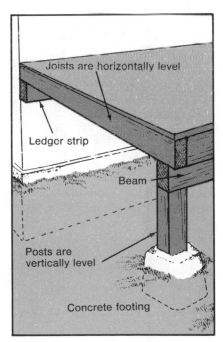

Side view of a deck shows how the deck is supported on a ledger strip attached to the house. The support posts must be absolutely plumb (vertically level) to support the superstructure, as well as furniture and people.

drainage; allow for this measurement in lumber calculations.

The best woods to buy for decking are redwood, cedar, and cypress. These woods will not rot or decay; they never need finishing or refinishing. The second decking choice is pressure-treated lumber—usually structural lumber, such as fir, spruce, and hemlock. The third choice is untreated lumber, such as fir, spruce, and hemlock, but this material should be coated with a quality wood preservative before it is put into place. For lumber sizes, pricing, and other information, consult the chapter in this book on lumber and plywood.

Joists support the decking; they may be 2×6s, 2×8s, and 2×10s in redwood, cedar, cypress, fir, spruce, and hemlock, or almost any grade of construction lumber. Sizes larger than those mentioned seldom are used since the superstructure of the deck doesn't need any greater support. The spacing of joists is critical to provide support for the live weight loads; check the span charts in this chapter.

Ledger strips are 2×6s or 2×8s nailed or bolted to the house joists, or attached to masonry with masonry bolts. They support the deck joists.

Beams support the joists and transfer the weight load to the support posts. Wood types can be the same as those mentioned for joists.

Posts support the decking, joists, and beams. Standard 4×4-inch posts may be used for light- to medium-heavy superstructures. For heavy superstructures, timber-type posts are needed.

Footings are supports or the foundation for the entire deck structure. The footings go into the earth and are usually reinforced concrete. Sometimes concrete blocks are used to support a lightweight deck structure. The footings should be placed below the frost depth; you can find out the frost depth by phoning the National Weather Service in your area. A standard depth is from 36 to 42 inches in most sections of the country; it may be less in the south, southeast, and southwest, where heavy freezing is not commonplace.

Deck height

The base point is the doorway through which people will walk out onto the decking. Therefore, the deck should be the same height as the floor in the house or an easy step down—one to five inches—from the threshold of the door.

When you determine this height, make a mark on the house exactly at the top surface of the decking. You will use this mark to estimate the materials you need.

For slightly raised decks at ground level, you can place the joists directly on the footings. Posts and beams are not needed for this deck design.

Deck fasteners

All framing members should be fastened with galvanized steel carriage bolts and washers, or with lagbolts and washers. The size of the lumber will determine the size of the fasteners. See the chapter on fasteners for details about these products.

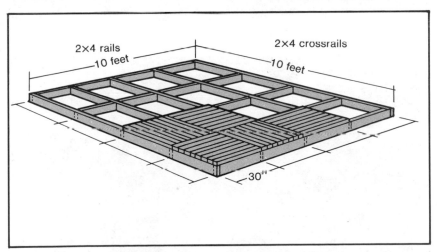

Ground level deck is made with an egg-crate framework over which decking is nailed. The frame can sit on concrete footings or concrete blocks.

The same frame could be used for a concrete patio: the concrete is placed in the framework, screeded, and troweled smooth.

Decking should be fastened to joists with either galvanized or coated nails, or with aluminum nails. If you use aluminum nails, drill pilot holes; aluminum nails bend very easily.

The joists may be suspended from any ledger strips with galvanized joist hangers, which are described in Chapter 2. The hangers will provide more strength and support than bolt assembly or toenailing the joists to the ledge strips.

Footings

Footings are easy to place; simply dig a hole below frost depth and fill it with concrete. Standard footings are 15×15 inches, or 12 inches in diameter. The concrete should be reinforced with ½-inch steel reinforcing rods placed vertically one inch in from the perimeter of the concrete, and in the center of it. If post anchors will be used for support, the anchors are placed in the top of the footing before the concrete hardens. You have some margin for error when placing the anchors, but they should be centered and level.

If the footings will stand above ground you will have to build forms for the concrete the same size as the hole. Plywood, boards, or fiber cylinders available from ready-mix concrete companies may be used to make forms (see chapter on concrete and lumber). When the concrete hardens, the forms are removed or stripped from the work.

If you purchase ready-mixed concrete, all holes and forms must be ready when the concrete arrives for the pour. If you mix the concrete yourself from pre-mixed concrete mix, you can build the forms one-by-one, place the mixture, let it harden, strip the forms, and then use the forms for the next position. In this case, coat the insides of the forming materials with form oil for easy stripping.

One bag of pre-mixed concrete mix yields about ⅓ yard of concrete. For a sand/gravel/cement mix, use a 3 to 1 ratio: three bags of sand and gravel to one bag of cement. Mix the dry ingredients thoroughly and then add enough water to make a fairly stiff mixture.

Spans for Decking

SIZE	RECOMMENDED LUMBER GRADES	SPAN WITHOUT SUPPORT
2 × 4	Construction Common Construction Heart	24 in.
2 × 6	Construction Common Construction Heart	36 in.

Based on non–stress-graded redwood with a live load (people) of 40 pounds per square foot.

Beam Spans for Decks

SIZE	LUMBER GRADE	6	8	10	12
4 × 6	Construction Common Construction Heart	4½	4	3½	3
4 × 8	Construction Common Construction Heart	6	5	4½	4
4 × 10	Construction Common Construction Heart	7½	6½	6	5½

WIDTHS (feet)

Based on non–stress-graded redwood with a live load (people) of 40 pounds per square foot. Recommended wood grades are construction heart and construction common.

Typical Joist Span Loads

JOIST SIZE	SPACING (on center)	JOIST LENGTH (feet)
2 × 6	16 in.	6
	24 in.	5
	36 in.	4
2 × 8	16 in.	9
	24 in.	7
	36 in.	6
2 × 10	16 in.	13
	24 in.	11
	36 in.	9

Based on non–stress-graded redwood with a live load (people) of 40 pounds per square foot. Recommended wood grades are construction heart and construction common.

Concrete footings support most decks. The footings extend below the frost line and are reinforced with steel rods. The footings do not have to be formed for most installations; placing concrete and rods into a hole is adequate. If the footing extends above the ground, as shown here, only the exposed part of the footing has to be formed. The metal post anchor was set into wet concrete.

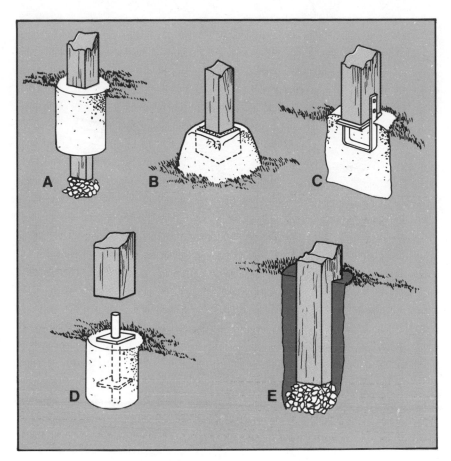

Deck footing construction types include: (A) The post runs through a concrete collar and sits on a bed of gravel for drainage. (B) A wood nailing block is inserted into a block of wet concrete. The post is nailed to the block after the concrete sets. (C) A post anchor is inserted into the wet concrete; the post is bolted to the anchor. (D) A drift pin, made of a piece of heavy reinforcing rod and two metal plates, is inserted into wet concrete. The bottom of the post is drilled to fit over the pin, which prevents the post from drifting. (E) Simple post-in-the-hole construction can be used for very light decks. The wood should be treated with wood preservative and set on two inches of gravel for drainage.

Pre-cut stair stringers are set on a concrete pad and nailed to a framing piece fastened to the deck's outside joist. The treads are 2×12s nailed to the stringers; three lengths of 2×4s could be substituted for the 2×12s. (See next page.)

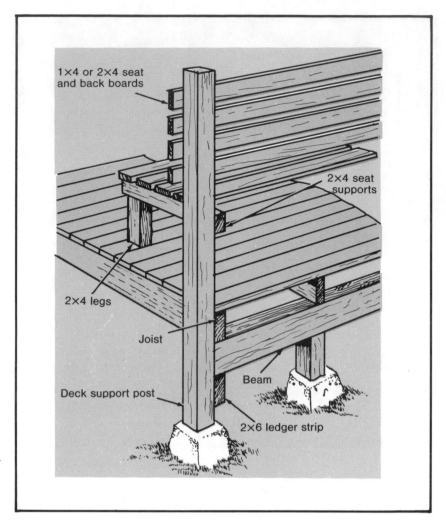

1×4 or 2×4 seat
and back boards

2×4 seat
supports

2×4 legs

Joist

Deck support post

Beam

2×6 ledger strip

Deck benches are built on support
posts. The seat support should be fastened to the post with a lag or carriage bolt; other bench parts are
nailed with galvanized or aluminum
nails. Beam and ledger construction
supports decking.

To order ready-mix, give the retailer the diameter and depth of the
footing. The retailer will calculate
your needs from this information.

Railings, seats, and steps

These components should be considered as part of the design, instead of
being added later. This will save you
money and time.

Railings, seats, and benches are
usually built on the post supports that
extend up beyond the decking. The
additional support pieces are made
from the same materials used for
decking and the posts, if the posts are
4×4s.

Posts and other framing can be
supported by special hangers and
brackets described in the chapter on
fasteners.

Spindles for railings may be metal,
lengths of 2×4s spaced at two-foot intervals, or wrought iron railings that

are available in kits. The railings
themselves can be 2×4s or 2×6s of
the same wood as used for the decking and joists.

Benches are built with 4×4s for
legs and 2×4s or 2×6s for the seat.
Fasteners are countersunk and the
holes filled with matching wood filler.

Steps may be cut from 2×12s. Construction is easier if you buy precut
step stringers, or carriages, which are
available in two-, three-, four-, and
five-step increments. The step treads
can also be made of 2×4s or 2×6s;
nail the treads to the stringers with
hot-dipped galvanized or aluminum
nails, both of which deter rust and
corrosion.

Deck finishes

If the deck is constructed of redwood,
cedar, or cypress, the wood does not
have to be finished to protect it from
the weather, although it may be fin-

ished if you wish. But if it is finished,
the wood must be maintained by refinishing every three to five years.

A good finish for redwood, cypress,
or cedar is a clear penetrating stain;
this protects the wood but leaves a
natural appearance. If the wood is fir,
hemlock, or spruce, use a pigmented
penetrating stain. It will color the
wood slightly while protecting it from
the elements. Stain is also available in
colors.

Porch and deck enamel may also
be used. It is available in gray, green,
and maroon. The enamel actually is a
pigmented varnish, and the surfaces
have to be refinished every three to
five years. Clear spar varnish makes
an excellent finish.

Under no circumstances should a
deck be painted with standard house
paint. This product does not provide
a surface hard enough for the heavy
foot traffic a deck endures.

Patio Materials

A patio surface can be almost any solid material, but for all-round use, easy maintenance, and permanence, concrete or bricks are the best. The second choice is flagstone. Third-choice products would be pea gravel, asphalt, or discs cut from logs.

Design factors

Unlike decks, which almost have to be square or rectangular, patios can be round or free-form, as well as square or rectangular. A patio should be designed in relation to the house and located to take advantage of doors and windows. A patio with a southern exposure will be in the sun during the months of its greatest use. If it faces east, it will be in shade during the afternoon; if it faces west, it will be in the shade during the morning hours. A patio on the north side of a house may be out of the sun all day long. Keep in mind that fencing, trees, and awnings also affect the amount of sunlight the patio receives.

Brick and stone patios.

Laying brick and stone takes more patience and muscle than skill. Since these materials are dry, you can schedule the project in stages and do just as much as you want at one work session.

Brick and stone should be laid over a bed of sand and small gravel, which permits easy leveling of the units. The sand bed should be at least three inches thick. A four-inch layer is better, if your budget permits. You can order sand by the cubic yard or by weight from a hard-materials dealer; it will be dumped near the job site for easy access.

Unmortared patio joints should be tight, with no cracks. Fill the joints with sand after the bricks are laid. Mortared joints should be ½ to ⅜ inch wide; any joint less than ½ inch will not hold the mortar: it will crack and fall out.

Type MW (medium weathering) bricks should be used for patios. These masonry units will withstand weather and wear well. MW bricks also withstand the freezing conditions to which most patios are subjected. Used hard bricks are a good buy, if they are clean; don't use soft bricks.

A 200-square-foot patio—10 by 10 feet—is a standard size. Here is an estimate from which you can figure the materials you will need for a brick patio:

A 200-square-foot patio uses 920 standard-size bricks. A four-inch sand base requires 12 cubic yards of sand. You will need one cubic yard of sand to fill the joints after the bricks are laid.

See the chapter on concrete and masonry for more product information.

FORMS AND GRADING. Even if the area on which the patio will be laid is fairly level, you should grade, or smooth, the ground slightly to accept the sand base. By filling the valleys with dirt from the hills, you will save sand and the base will be easier to work. The perimeter of the patio should be formed with redwood, cedar, or cypress boards or dimension lumber; these forms should be set into the ground and left in place after the patio is finished. The forms keep the patio blocks together. Another way to make the edge is to set a border of bricks on end around the perimeter; bury the bricks about half their length. This method works well, but requires more time.

If the lot is not level and much grading must be done, you can build the patio in terrace fashion with several levels. Another solution, of course, is to build a deck.

Wood forms also may be used to cut the patio into halves or quarters; the forms may be left in place when the bricks have been laid.

Brick patios laid without mortar do not have to be sloped for drainage; the sand in the cracks absorbs the water on the brick surface. If the joints are mortared, the patio should slope slightly away from the house; a three-inch drop in ten feet is adequate.

To mortar patio bricks, use a pre-mixed mortar mix. Add water to the product until the mixture is fairly thin—almost soupy. Then fill the joints with a triangular pointing trowel. Scrape off as much excess mortar from the brick faces as possible, and let the joints dry. Then scrub the bricks with a stiff broom; most of the mortar will be brushed away. To remove any remaining mortar, use a good-quality concrete cleaning solution; most are muriatic acid-based. These products are sold in plastic containers at most home centers and hardware stores.

Flagstone patios

Laying flagstone takes more muscle than laying bricks, but the technique is similar. The forming materials are available at home centers; the stones sometimes are stocked by home centers, but you're most likely to find them at a hard-materials retailer or an outlet selling lawn and garden supplies. To estimate your needs, look under the chapters on lumber and plywood, and masonry and concrete.

The procedures for laying flagstone must be carefully scheduled.

1. Plan the job on graph paper and figure the quantities of stone materials needed. Buy the stone.
2. Lay out the job on the ground with stakes and string. If leveling is necessary, do it at this point. Allow about two inches for a sand base, or 1½ inches for the concrete base; two inches for the thickness of the stone. Since the thickness of the flagstone may vary slightly, you can make the adjustment with the amount of sand used.
3. Plan to do the job in sections; quarter sections are best since they constitute about one day's work for an average-sized patio measuring 10 × 10 or 10 × 15 feet.
4. Place and level the sand in the quarter. Fit the stones in the form, mark them, and remove them from the form.
5. Mix enough concrete to fill the quarter section 1½ inches deep over the sand. The concrete ratio should be 3 to 1: three bags of sand and gravel to one bag of cement. Add water until the mixture is fairly soupy, since the sand base will absorb the water from the concrete quickly. Place the concrete in the form and level it, or screed it, with a 2×4. You'll find it easier to rent a cement mixer for this project; you usually can't mix enough concrete by hand at one time to fill a quarter form.
6. Replace the marked stones in

the forms and imbed them in the concrete by tapping them lightly with a wooden mallet or rubber hammer.

7. When the base of the patio has hardened—in about a week—fill the joints between the stones with pre-mixed mortar mix, using a pointing trowel.

8. Keep the joints wet for several days by spraying with a garden hose; this helps the concrete cure to a tough and durable surface.

Concrete patios

There are four basic steps involved in laying a concrete patio:

1. Grading the ground level and smooth.
2. Building and assembling the forms.
3. Placing the concrete.
4. Finishing the concrete.

GRADES. The earth should be fairly level for concrete. If the soil is sandy in your area, no special base is needed, although the sand should be tamped with a tamper that you can buy or rent. If the soil is clay, spread a layer of sand or gravel about two inches thick over the area so that the patio will drain properly.

If the grade has to be filled, use a combination of sand, gravel, and crushed stone (slag) for the base. The base, however should not be more than four inches thick. If it has to be thicker, level the earth as best you can and place the concrete over the earth; this will provide a better base than the fill. Sand, gravel, crushed stone, and slag may be ordered from a hard-materials dealer. It is sold by the cubic yard or by weight.

FORMS. Dimension lumber (2×4s or 2×6s) should be used for forms. If the forms are to be left in place, use redwood, cedar, or cypress. If fir, hemlock, or spruce is used, buy pressure-treated lumber or coat the

wood with preservative. Do not paint the forms. Lumber sizes for forms and other data may be found in the chapters on lumber and plywood, and concrete and masonry.

CONCRETE. Already mixed concrete is your best concrete source if the patio will be any size larger than 6 × 6 feet. The material is sold by the cubic yard; a minimum order is usually five yards, although you generally can pay a surcharge on orders for less than five yards. To order ready-mixed, give the retailer the length, width, and depth of the patio; he will figure your needs.

When the truck pulls into your backyard and dumps the concrete, you will have to be prepared to work extremely fast. Therefore, all grading and forming work must be completed before the concrete is ordered and delivered. The exception is if you quarter the patio area with permanent forms and fill one quarter at a time with hand-mixed concrete.

If you decide to mix the concrete yourself, rent a concrete mixer. Tub mixing by hand is extremely time-consuming. A good patio mix is 3:1 or 4:1 ratio: three sand/gravel or four sand/gravel to one cement. Rental fees for cement mixers are in the $20 per day category.

FINISHES. A concrete patio surface can be finished in several ways.

Smooth concrete is the easiest. Use a large wooden float to rough-smooth the surface; then use a steel trowel, called a *finishing trowel,* to complete the job. Both tools are sold at home centers and hardware stores and are inexpensive.

Rough surface concrete is easily created by pulling a push-broom carefully across the wet concrete surface after the surface has been rough-smoothed with a wooden float. A rough surface may be created by using only a wooden float to strike the surface level.

For an exposed aggregate surface, leave the surface of the poured concrete about ⅜ inch lower than the top edge of the form boards. Level the concrete and float the surface.

Spread the large aggregate (gravel) by hand over the wet concrete surface; distribute it as evenly as you can.

When the concrete has hardened enough so that it will support you standing on a 2 × 2-foot square of plywood, brush the surface of the aggregate and the concrete with a stiff-bristle broom. Do not use too much pressure—only enough to expose the aggregate no more than ¼ inch.

When the concrete hardens in a day or two, spray the surface with a garden hose and brush the aggregate again with the stiff-bristle broom. If the broom dislodges a lot of the aggregate, let the concrete set another day or so and try again.

The surface should be washed and brushed until there is no glaze or haze of cement left on the particles of aggregate.

CONCRETE COLORS. Patios may be colored with special concrete pigments at the time the concrete is placed. This procedure and the materials you need are described in the Concrete and Masonry chapter.

SPECIAL ORDER. Bricks, stone, concrete, cement, sand, lumber, and other materials for decks and patios are available in most communities at home centers, hardware outlets, and hard-materials dealers. To special-order any of this material would be almost prohibitive because of freight costs.

If you need special construction help, here is the best source of information in America:

Portland Cement Association
Old Orchard Road
Skokie, Ill. 60076

11

ENERGY-SAVING PRODUCTS

The energy crisis has stimulated manufacturers to turn out a flurry of products touted to save oil, electricity, gas, and, ultimately, your money. Many of these products, however, have failed to perform as advertised. The products that *have* proved their value over the years—and how to buy them—are described in this chapter.

Insulation, storm doors and windows, weatherstripping, and caulking compound are the primary products that seal your home from cold and heat. Secondary heating sources such as wood- and coal-burning stoves, fireplaces, electric and kerosene heaters, and solar heating devices can take some of the load off expensive oil and gas systems. Set-back thermostats, window shades, and solar film are a few of the products that may be added to basic systems to reduce energy consumption.

Insulation Products

Wall, floor, and ceiling insulation is manufactured from six basic materials: fiberglass, rock wool, polystyrene, vermiculite, perlite, and cellulose. Each has its own R-Value, which indicates its resistance to heat passing through the insulation: the higher the R-Value of the product, the better the insulating qualities.

The following R-Values are based on a 1-inch thickness. Fractional R-Values printed on some insulation packages are rounded off at the next highest number.

Product	Approx. R-Value
Fiberglass	3.3
Rock wool	3.3
Polystyrene	3.5
Vermiculite	2.1
Perlite	2.7
Cellulose	3.7

Here's a descriptive shopping guide to these products.

Fiberglass insulation
Fiberglass insulation is available in batts, rolls (called blankets), and chucks for loose-fill application.

Batts and blankets are about 16 inches and 24 inches wide (to fit framing members spaced 16 and 24

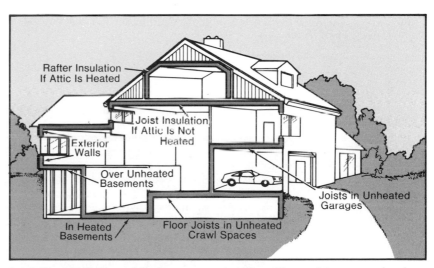

Insulation installation guide shows where insulation may be added to help lower heat costs and provide more living comfort. When applying insulation with a moisture vapor barrier, always make sure that the barrier faces the warm side of the room.

inches on center), and about 3½ and 6 inches thick.

Fiberglass products are faced with either kraft paper or aluminum foil, which serve as moisture vapor barriers. This barrier prevents the moisture inside the room from penetrating the insulation. If the insulation be comes wet, it loses its insulating efficiency. There is no difference in the efficiency of kraft paper- or aluminum foil-backed insulation. Kraft paper is designed for use where there is no danger from heat; aluminum foil is meant to be used next to heat sources such as heating ducts, hot

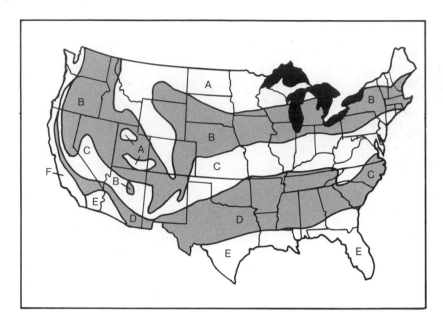

Area	Ceiling Value	Floor Value	Exterior Wall Value
A	R-38	R-22	R-19
B	R-33	R-22	R-19
C	R-30	R-19	R-19
D	R-26	R-13	R-19
E	R-26	R-11	R-13
F	R-19	R-11	R-11

How much insulation? Different areas of the country require different insulation R-Values. Find the zone where you live, and then refer by zone letter to the chart for the R-Value required.

Loose fill insulation between framing. Assuming there is a vapor barrier under the loose fill, simply add more loose fill or *unfaced* batts or blankets over the loose fill. The batts or blankets may be laid across framing members, instead of between them, if you wish.

Foil or paper-faced insulation between joists: If there is a vapor barrier facing up (toward the attic), the additional insulation must have a vapor barrier and it must face up also. But before the new material is added over the old, slash the vapor barrier on the old insulation with a utility knife or a kitchen knife. This increases the R-Value of both layers.

Foil- or paper-faced insulation between rafters with the foil facing toward you: The installed insulation has to be removed. Insert an unfaced blanket or batt between the rafters and reinstall the old insulation—foil or paper facing you—over the unfaced material.

In new construction, six inches of insulation sometimes is specified for walls. Wall framing usually is 2×4 (nominal) studs, which actually measure 1½ × 3½ inches. Since insulation should never be compacted (it loses its efficiency), the question is how to install six inches of insulation in a 3½-inch space. One answer is to use

water pipes, and fireplaces. The aluminum foil, however, must not be installed next to an open flame or extremely high temperatures. The moisture vapor barrier is *always* installed facing the warm side of the wall or ceiling. For example: In an unheated attic, the vapor barrier faces downward toward the heated rooms below. In walls, the vapor barrier faces toward the rooms—not to the outside. In a crawl space, the vapor barrier faces the floor or subflooring.

ESTIMATING. To determine the amount of fiberglass batts or blankets needed to insulate a wall or ceiling, first find the number of square feet in the area by multiplying the length by the width or height.

Then determine the spacing of the framing members. They probably will be 16 or 24 inches on center—from the center of one member to the center of the adjoining member. Buy insulation to fit this width. If the framing is on 16-inch centers, multiply the area by .90. If the framing is on 24-inch centers, multiply the area by .94. This gives you the number of square feet of insulation needed to fill the area, allowing for the width of the framing. For example, if the width of the area is 10 feet, and the length of the area is 12 feet (the area is 120 square feet), and the framing is on 16-inch centers, multiply 120 by .90, and divide the product (108 square feet) by the number of square feet marked on the insulation package to find out how many packages to buy.

INSTALLATION DATA. Fiberglass batts and blankets generally can be installed in unfinished areas, such as an unheated attic, a basement, and crawl spaces, where there is open framing. It can be used in any new construction, but it is impractical to install it behind finished walls, since you have to remove the wall covering.

Fiberglass batts and blankets may be added to installed insulation to increase its thickness and, therefore, insulation value. Typical situations are these:

Insulation can be suspended between joists under crawl spaces with a lacing of rot-proof string. You can also use wire hangers or furring strips.

2×8s, which measure 7¼ inches wide, for the framing members in the walls. Another way is to use a new product called Foilpleat Type C-4 insulation, Many, but not all, home centers and lumberyards carry this insulation. It is extremely thin (125 square feet fits in a 1-cubic-foot package) and has R-Values of 10 in walls, 10 in ceilings, and 19 in floors.

INSTALLING INSULATION. A staple-gun with ⅜-inch staples is the best tool to use for installing faced blanket and batt insulation. The staples should be spaced about every three inches; the wires should be spaced about every two feet. If the insulation is not faced, hangers may be used to support it. The hangers are 16-inch lengths of wire with pointed ends. The wire is flexed and inserted, under tension, between the framing members; the tension supports the insulation. If the insulation is laid between floor joists, no fastening is required. However, the edges of the insulation should be butted tightly.

SAFETY. Fiberglass insulation in any form gives off a fine dust that can be uncomfortable if it settles on your skin.

When installing insulation, wear shirt buttoned at the collar and

Exposed foundation walls can lose up to 10 percent of the heat circulating in the house. Rigid insulation panels will stop this loss. They should be applied to the outside of the foundation, according to the manufacturer's (Dow Chemical) recommendations and procedures.

Insulation is fastened with ⅜-inch staples driven in to framing members by a staple gun. Insulation has ¾-inch-wide tabs along its edges for staples. The tabs should be flush with the edges of the framing.

sleeves, a breathing mask and safety glasses. Take a break for fresh air every 20 minutes. When the work day is finished, bathe in cool water first, and then warm water; this prevents the fiberglass particles from getting into the pores of your skin and causing itching.

LOOSE-FILL ROCK WOOL. This is the same material that's used in the manufacture of fiberglass blankets and batts, but in chunk form. By law, the R-Value by inch is printed on the package. Coverage information also is on the package, and you can determine how many bags of loose fill are needed by dividing the square footage of the area you're insulating by the coverage figure on the package. Loose fill may be added to existing loose fill, or over blanket or batt insulation. If the blanket or batt has a vapor barrier, this material must be cut before the loose fill is placed. Then, the loose fill must be covered with a vapor barrier. Polyethylene sheeting in 4-mil thicknesses is generally used for a vapor barrier in this case.

Vermiculite insulation

This product is granular, loose fill and it generally costs less than its rock wool cousin. It is installed the same way as rock wool, and it has a lower R-Value per inch.

Perlite insulation

Perlite insulation is loose fill; the small pellets are similar in consistency to vermiculite. It does, however, have a slightly higher R-Value per inch. It is installed the same way as rock wool and vermiculite; estimating is also the same.

Polystyrene boards

Polystyrene boards, or rigid insulation, comes in 16×48-inch panels and is installed behind wall paneling. The product is 16 inches wide so it can slip between furring strips. It is usually held in place with adhesive; the DAP brand of subflooring adhesive is usually specified. It comes in cartridges for use with a standard caulking gun.

Other forms of rigid insulation include a 24×96-inch blue-colored polystyrene panel that may be used under wall paneling and as an addition to wall sheathing. Insulation fiberboard sheathing is another rigid insulation product that is used in new construction as the basic wall sheathing. It is manufactured in 4×8- and 4×10-foot sheets.

Another type of paneling insulation is a mineral wool blanket 16 inches wide that is encased in a plastic wrapper.

Cellulose insulation

This product looks like ground-up newspaper. If properly treated with chemicals, this product offers an insulation value that equals or exceeds fiberglass and rock wool. Be sure to check for fire ratings and the Underwriters' Laboratory (UL) listing on the package; if it doesn't have either one or the other, you'd be wise to pass it by.

Urethane foam

Urethane foam insulation is banned by codes in many locations. If it can be used in your area, the product must be installed by a professional with special equipment. You can use small aerosol containers of foam for minor insulating jobs such as around windows and doors.

Pipe wrap

This is a form of roll insulation that comes in 2- to 12-inch widths. The product may be fiberglass or a vinyl foam laminated to foil facing. Pipe wrap helps prevent heat loss from hot water pipes—especially those that run through unheated crawl spaces. Pipe wrap also is used on cold water pipes: it stops dripping caused by water condensation. Rolls of the material vary in price and length. Standard lengths are 25, 50, 75, and 100 feet.

Insulation values

Insulation values of materials should be taken into consideration when calculating the total R-Value of an insulated wall or floor. The R-Values of the common materials shown below are for one-inch thickness, unless otherwise noted.

Air	R- .94
Gypsumboard (½ in.)	R- .79
Plywood (¾ in.)	R- .93
Carpeting (padded)	R-2.09
Asphalt shingles	R- .44
Brick (4 in.)	R- .85
Concrete block (8 in.)	R-1.10
Floor tile	R- .04
Polystyrene board	R-4.00
Polystyrene sheet	R-4.00

HOW IT'S SOLD. Insulation is sold by the square foot. A roll of 3½-inch insulation contains 89 square feet; the 6-inch variety comes in 50-square-foot rolls. Loose fill is sold by the bag, with coverage per bag based on R-Value per inch.

Insulation panels are sold by the panel in large sizes and by the square foot for packages of small panels. For example, polystyrene boards or panels are usually packaged six square feet to the unit.

Pipe insulation is sold by the roll; the wider and longer the measurement, the more it costs. You generally get a small price break by buying a larger quantity.

Many retailers regard insulation as a loss leader, so if you are in the market for insulation, be sure to check newspaper ads for sales. Don't be afraid to ask the manager of a home center or lumberyard when the next insulation sale will be held. You may be able to save money by waiting for a few weeks or months. Some retailers will discount insulation prices if a large quantity is purchased at one time, but you have to ask for this discount.

Insulation products also are subject to tax credits by the Federal government and some state governments. Be sure to save the cash register receipt when buying these materials, and consult the tax instructions for the specific credits that you may receive.

SPECIAL ORDER. Insulation products are so plentiful in most communities that special-ordering usually is not necessary. If you have difficulty locating insulation products, or have any special installation questions, write the Consumer Information Director of the following firms:

Johns-Manville Corp.
Ken-Caryl Ranch
Denver, Colo. 80217

Owens-Corning Fiberglas Corp.
Box 901
Toledo, Ohio 43601

Frost-King
Thermwell Products Co. Inc.
150 East Seventh St.
Paterson, N.J. 07524

Storm Doors and Windows

Storm windows and doors are vital to energy-saving and comfort both during the heating season and in the cooling season, especially if your home is equipped with window or central air conditioning.

Storm doors and windows create an air space between the prime door or window and the storm unit. Since air space has an R-Value of .94 per inch, this adds considerable insulation. The storm doors and windows also lower drafts to make your home more comfortable and energy-efficient.

Storm doors

Several types of storm doors are available; thermal barrier with interchangeable storm and screen panels is a good buy. The door material can be aluminum, galvanized steel, or wood; most materials are prefinished. All the necessary door hardware is included in the door package. Storm doors come in two types: regular doors that have to be hinged to the jambs of the door opening, and pre-hung doors, which are hinged to a metal framework that's screwed to the door casing or under the door casing.

MEASUREMENT. To find out what size storm door you need, measure the door opening from the top header to the threshold. Then measure from one side jamb to the other side jamb at the inside of the frame. Do not measure from casing to casing. You also will need to know whether the door is right- or left-handed. Stand on the side of the prime door that opens toward you. Note on which side the prime door is hinged. Tell the retailer this so you will go home with a storm door that is properly hinged.

The key to hanging a storm door is to make sure that the door is level in the opening, regardless of how much out-of-square the opening is. After the door is partially secured in the opening, set a carpenter's level on the edge of the storm door to make sure it's vertically level. If the door is not plumb, it will rack and bind in the opening when it is opened and closed.

Storm windows

Storm windows with single glazing (one pane of glass), have aluminum or wood frames. If they are combinations of screens and storms, the frame will have a triple-track and be extruded from aluminum. The frames are sold pre-primed or uncoated; the pre-finished color choice usually is white, black, or a bronze-brown.

MEASUREMENT. If there are old storm windows or screens already on

Leveling is important for storm window and door installation. The storm unit must be level in the opening or it won't open and close properly.

the windows, simply measure them to find the size of replacements. If not, measure from the top header of the window to the sill and from the inside jamb to the opposite jamb. Do not measure out over the casings; stay within the framework of the window opening.

Most home centers and lumberyards stock a standard size of storm windows. Below is a chart for matching purposes:

Standard Storm Window Sizes (inches)

Width	Height
24×38	32×46
24×46	32×54
24×54	36×38
28×38	36×48
28×46	36×54
28×54	40×38
32×38	40×36
32×42	40×54

INSTALLATION. Leveling is the key to installing storm windows. After you fit the window into the frame, place a level along the storm window outer frame or along the dividing strip that runs across the window at its center. This is important with single-glazed windows, but doubly important with combination windows on tracks. If the windows are not level in the framework opening, the windows and screens won't raise and lower properly. Don't worry about the

squareness of the prime window frame. Just make sure the storm window is square in the frame.

HOW THEY'RE SOLD. Storm windows and doors are sold individually and are priced according to finish and quality.

SPECIAL ORDER. Most retailers will special-order sizes of storm doors and windows not in stock. If your special size is regularly made by the manufacturer, no special costs are involved. If the window has to be specially made to your specifications, expect to pay double the stock price and be prepared to wait up to eight weeks for delivery. You may even have to pay the freight costs.

If you can't find the storm doors or windows you want for your home, or have any special questions concerning installation, contact the Consumer Information Director of the following firms:

Season-All Industries Inc.
Indiana, Pa. 15701

Wartian Lock Co.
20525 East Nine Mile Rd.
St. Clair Shores, Mich. 48080

S-B Manufacturing Co. Ltd.
11320 Watertown Plank Rd.
Milwaukee, Wis. 53226

Alcan Building Products Div.
100 Erieview Plaza
Cleveland, Ohio 44114

Weatherstripping

Air leakage around an entrance door through the cracks between the door and frame and the door and threshold is equal to a six-inch-square hole cut in the center of the door panel. Weatherstripping instantly stops this leakage during the winter months when the furnace is on and in the summer when the air conditioning is running. Best of all, the cost of weatherstripping is very moderate; you can install most types yourself with simple hand tools—usually just a hammer and screwdriver.

The following is a list of the standard weatherstripping types, with a brief description of how each works.

Spring metal weatherstripping

comes in rolls and is generally packaged with the nails needed for installation. The metal may be aluminum, brass, stainless steel, or copper-coated. The V-shaped strips press against the frame as the door or window is shut to block air leakage.

Adhesive-backed foam weatherstripping is packaged in rolls. To install it, the covering is stripped off the adhesive, which is then pressed in place along the jambs of a window or door where the frame meets the jamb. When the window or door is closed, the frame presses against the foam, compressing the foam and sealing out the air. The product is manufactured in several thicknesses and lengths. It

is very easy to install and works efficiently for about two to three years before replacement is needed. It is inexpensive.

Felt weatherstripping is tacked to the jambs of doors or windows; the doors or windows compress the soft felt material, forming an air seal. Felt is very inexpensive; it comes in several widths, thicknesses, and lengths, and is generally sold in a package which may contain the nails for installation. Felt with an adhesive backing is available at a higher price. Felt comes in three standard colors: black, grey, and brown.

Felt or vinyl in a metal stripping combines the rigidity of a metal

Foam insulation weatherstripping with a self-sticking seal goes against the jamb or the stops of the window or door. You just peel off the strip that protects the adhesive and stick the weatherstripping on. This product compresses when the window or door is closed to form an air seal.

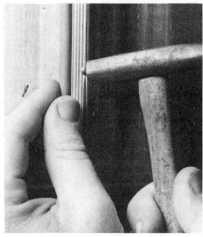

Tubular gasket weatherstripping with a metal strip is nailed to the jambs of the door or window. The door or window frame then closes against the gasket, which compresses to seal out the air.

spline with the softness and sealing ability of felt or vinyl. The product is sold in rolls of various widths, thicknesses, and lengths. Brads for installation to window and door jambs usually come with the material.

Tubular-gasket weatherstripping is an excellent choice for irregularly shaped window and door jambs and frames. It is usually applied to the exterior of the windows or door with brads. The gasket is a hollow vinyl tube which is soft and flexible. The weatherstripping is available in white and gray and in strips and rolls in a range of widths and diameters.

Tubular-gasket weatherstripping with foam has a tubular gasket filled with an insulating foam. Since the product is more rigid than the unfilled gasket, it will hold its shape longer.

J-strip metal weatherstripping comes in two pieces: One piece is nailed the edge of the door; the other is nailed to the door jamb. When the door is closed, the two pieces interlock to form a weathertight seal. J-strip usually is extruded brass. The nails for installing it often come in the package. Several widths and lengths are available.

Thermal thresholds provide weatherstripping at the bottoms of doors. There are two basic types: sweeps and plastic gasket inserts. Both types are available in standard door widths. They may be cut to size with a hacksaw. The sweeps are usually felt that has been encased in a strip of metal or plastic. The strips are nailed to the inside bottom of the door; the felt in the strip presses against the threshold when the door closes and forms a seal.

Thermal thresholds with plastic gasket inserts fasten directly to the floor under the bottom edge of the door. As the door closes, it compresses the plastic gasket, forming the seal. The old threshold must be removed to install the new one. When the plastic inserts wear out, they may be replaced with new gasketing material that comes in strips or rolls.

Casement gaskets for casement windows are slipped onto the edge of the window frame; no fasteners are used. The weatherstripping is extremely thin so the window may be closed tightly. The weatherstripping compresses against the window frame.

Jalousie weatherstripping fits over the edges of the glass jalousie window louvers. The clear material requires

Thermal thresholds have a plastic gasket that runs down the center of the aluminum threshold. This gasket compresses when the door is closed to provide an air seal; replacement gaskets are available. The old threshold must be replaced before the new thermal model is installed with screws.

no fastening devices. Sold in rolls, this weatherstripping is about ¾ inches wide; it may be trimmed to fit with scissors.

HOW IT'S SOLD. Weatherstripping is usually sold by the package, although some of it—rigid strips, for example—is sold by the piece of linear foot.

SPECIAL ORDER. There are so many different styles, widths, lengths, and thicknesses of weatherstripping at most home centers, lumberyards, drug stores, and variety outlets that you shouldn't encounter any difficulty in finding a weatherstripping product to fit your needs. However, in the event you can't find what you want, the retailer may order the product for you. Expect a wait of several weeks for delivery; you may have to pay freight costs, which won't be much because weatherstripping is lightweight. For special information about weatherstripping products, try contacting the companies listed below.

Macklanburg-Duncan Co.
4041 North Santa Fe Ave.
Oklahoma City, Okla. 73125

Mortell Co.
550 Hobbie Ave.
Kankakee, Ill. 60901

Schlegel Corp.
400 East Ave.Box23113
Rochester, N.Y. 14692

Caulking Compounds

For an average three-bedroom home with about 1,500 to 1,800 square feet of space, you'll need about six cartridges of caulking to seal cracks around windows, doors, chimneys, in siding, and between dissimilar materials (wood and stone) to prevent air and insect infiltration. If you buy an inexpensive caulking compound, such as an oil-based product, you can expect to spend money and time cleaning and refilling the cracks about every three years. If you buy a quality caulking—such as butyl, silicone, or polyurethane—the life of the job will increase to about 20 years before replacement is necessary.

Caulking compounds are described in the Painting chapter. For exterior use, consider the more expensive caulking compounds such as nitrile and neoprene rubber for stationary masonry cracks; polysulfide; hypalon (needs a primer); and the others mentioned in that chapter.

HOW IT'S SOLD. Caulking is sold by the cartridge. Some types are sold in bulk form in one-gallon and five-gallon buckets; they are loaded into special caulking guns with a plunger on the gun. The bulk product is messy to use, and you probably don't need the quantity at one time to make it worth the investment.

SPECIAL ORDER. Caulking compound is widely available; you seldom have to special-order it. If you do, the retailer will place the order, but expect to buy a 12-tube carton in order to get a price break, and to wait from four to six weeks for delivery.

For information about special caulking and special caulking problems, contact the Consumer Information Director of the following companies:

DAP Inc.
Box 277
Dayton, Ohio 45401

GX International
2610 Northeast Fifth Ave.
Pompano Beach, Fla. 33064

Coplanar Corp.
1631 San Pablo Ave.
Oakland, Calif. 94612

Dow Corning Corp.
Midland, Mich. 48640

Other Energy Savers

Retailers' shelves are loaded with many other energy-saving products, some of which are worth consideration, especially those used in the maintenance of furnaces and air conditioning.

Hot-air furnaces: All forced-air heating systems have an air-filtering system; the filter, located near the blower fan, must be changed at least at the start of every heating season and usually several times during the season.

Note the arrow printed on the edge of the filter, which indicates the direction of airflow through the filter. Always install the filter so that this arrow points the right way. Home centers, hardware stores, and some drug and variety outlets stock a wide range of filter sizes.

Oil furnaces have a fuel filter that must be cleaned or changed at the start of every heating season. This is a job for a professional; home centers and lumberyards do not stock the parts that are necessary for maintenance.

Central air conditioners use the same air filter as the furnace to which they are attached.

Window air conditioners usually have a washable filter behind the airflow grille work. If the filter is not washable, you usually can find replacements at an appliance outlet, rather than a home center, hardware store, or lumberyard.

Furnace flue energy savers are devices that prevent heat from escaping up the chimney when the furnace is off. Several models are available; all are installed in an existing flue pipe, or replace a section of the pipe.

Set-back thermostats, or programmed thermostats, are easy to install; simply remove the old thermostat and connect the new one to the existing wires. An automatic thermostat may be set to turn the furnace or air conditioning on and off at any interval.

Clean furnace filters mean full furnace efficiency; change them at least three times a year—more if dusty conditions exist. Install filters in the correct airflow direction, as printed on the filter.

Air conditioner filters are washable in household detergent and water. Rinse and dry before replacing.

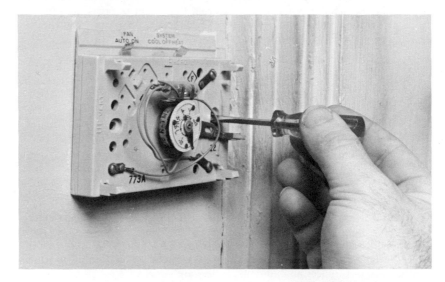

Set-back thermostats that automatically control heating and cooling can reduce utility bills. The new models are extremely simple to install: Just remove the old thermostat and wires from its terminals and connect the new thermostat to the wall and wires. Keep all thermostats free of dust; a light brushing twice a year will improve their efficiency.

An attic fan cools a house more cheaply than an air conditioner. The new models are designed for do-it-yourself installation; complete instructions are furnished by the manufacturer. This typical model comes in 24-, 30-, and 36-inch sizes to cool 1,200, 1,700, and 2,300 square feet of floor space.

Heaters and Fireplaces

Using supplemental heaters helps to lower utility bills, but remember that you have an initial investment in the supplemental heater. The question is: Will the cost of the supplemental heater and its heat reduce the utility bill enough to pay for itself? The answer usually is yes, but you should make some cost comparisons and estimate the payback period before buying.

Supplemental heaters

Supplemental heaters that are powered by electricity, kerosene, or the sun are not intended as prime heat sources. They will take the chill from the room and help lower power costs, but heating a room with them alone may be impossible.

Electric heaters are available with or without a blower system to circulate the warmed air produced by their resistance cables. These heaters are rated in watts: The higher the rating, the more electricity consumed and the more heat put out. As a basis of comparison, 1,000 watts will deliver about

3,500 BTUs of heat. A BTU stands for British Thermal Unit. Electric heaters are portable, there is no fuel odor, no liquid refueling, and the initial cost of an electric heater usually is less than that of a kerosene heater. Electric heater hazards are low if the heater is not plugged into an overloaded power circuit.

Kerosene heaters may be the most efficient heating source invented: all heat from the burning fuel is radiated into the room. In some states, the use of kerosene heaters is restricted, so check the retailer and local codes in your community to make sure heaters may be used in your home.

Kerosene heaters are rated by BTU output, and the more BTUs, the more heat. Standard models are rated from about 9,000 to 15,000 BTUs. Finding fuel for the heater is a problem in some areas; find out if there is a source before buying a kerosene heater. No. 1 clear kerosene is generally required for most standard brands of kerosene heaters. The price of packaged kerosene in home centers

can be as much as $5 per gallon. Some gas stations sell kerosene at about $1.50 per gallon, but make sure it's No. 1. No. 2 clogs burners.

Do not expect a kerosene heater to warm an uninsulated area such as a garage, basement, or enclosed porch. It will remove the chill from the area, but the room won't be toasty warm. In an insulated room that has a prime heat source the heaters are extremely efficient; they may cut your heating costs by as much as 50 percent.

Passive solar heaters look something like a room air conditioner. When you set the heater in a sun-swept window area, the unheated air in the room moves into collector plates in the solar heater where it is heated and then recirculated into the room. Standard units will heat a 700-square-foot room. The units are available for window or roof mounting.

Coal- and wood-burning stoves

A fire in a coal- or wood-burning stove, fireplace, or fireplace insert is

Kerosene space heaters are good supplements for a furnace, but they cannot supply enough heat to be the prime heat source. Before buying a space heater, make sure it complies with the codes in your area. If you buy a kerosene heater, make sure that you also have a fuel source for No. 1 clear kerosene. Heaters should be labeled with a BTU and UL rating for your protection.

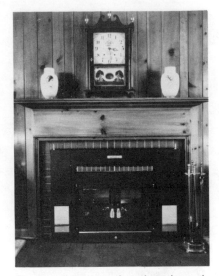

Fireplace inserts and coal- and wood-burning stoves are efficient heating supplements, not prime heat sources. Quality heating appliances specify BTU heat output, have UL listings, and generally provide a warranty against defects. Stoves are subject to local codes; check with the codes before making a buying decision.

often more romantic than beneficial. However, an airtight stove or insert can be very efficient; they lose little heat up the chimney. Before buying any of these heating appliances, be sure to check the availability and cost of wood and coal in your community; it could cost more than you're now spending on oil, gas, or electricity.

Quality stoves are rated by the area they are designed to heat, usually from 800 to about 2,200 square feet. Other qualities to look for in stoves include:

- Stove parts should be machined so they fit tightly. The doors should fit snug against door frames; dampers must fit tightly for the stove to be efficient.
- The parts of the stove that are subject to high heat should be cast iron.
- The stove should have an Underwriters' Laboratory (UL) listing. If not, it should be approved by one of several national code groups

such as Building Officials Congress.
- Quality stoves are BTU-rated. Know the heat output before you buy.
- The stove should have a warranty. Don't fall for the old lifetime guarantee pitch. The courts have ruled that there is no such thing as a lifetime guarantee. The stove should be warranted against workmanship and defects for at least one heating season. Some stove companies give a five-year warranty.
- Make sure the stove complies with local codes. They can be very restrictive.

INSTALLATION REQUIRE-MENTS. Wood- and coal-burning stoves must be placed certain distances from combustible surfaces for safety. This is an important buying consideration: The room in which you want the stove located must be large enough to handle it.

Most codes specify that the stove must be placed at least 36 inches from combustible walls, unless a heat shield is used. With the shield, usually 28-gauge sheet metal on ¼-inch stove (mill) board, the stove may be located about eight inches from combustible walls and floors. A one-inch air space should be left between the heat shield and the wall for insulation.

Asbestos no longer may be used as heat insulator; all use of asbestos board has been banned by the government.

The floor, under most codes, must be protected with sheet metal and stoveboard. The base of the stove must extend 18 to 24 inches from the front of the stove and 12 inches from the sides.

The only stove exempt from these requirements is a "zero clearance" stove or fireplace that is designed for use next to walls and other combustible materials.

STOVEPIPE INSTALLATION. According to the codes, stovepipes usually must extend at least three feet above any roof surface and two feet above any part of the house that is

within 10 feet of the chimney opening, such as a ridge of a hip roof.

Most stoves should be installed by a professional. The store where you buy the stove often can recommend a contractor, but if you locate one yourself, be sure to check first with the Better Business Bureau in your community for a reliability report on the contractor.

HOW THEY'RE SOLD. Most energy-saving equipment and appliances are sold as individual items. Filters for furnaces and stoves are often sold by the package.

Wood for wood-burning stoves is sold by the cord; a full cord of stacked wood measures 8 feet long by 4 feet high by 4 feet wide. A face cord of wood is 8 feet long by 4 feet high by the length of the wood; the length varies with the cord, but is usually about 16 inches. A stack of wood is about the same amount as a face cord.

A truckload of wood depends on the size of the truck. A standard pickup truck holds about a third of a cord of wood. A ton of firewood equals about half a cord, if the wood has been air-dried.

The heat produced by burning wood depends on the type of wood. Hickory, oak, and beech woods will produce more heat than cedar, pine, and other soft woods. Always buy seasoned or dry wood when possible. (Seasoned wood is wood that has been cut for at least six months.) Green or wet wood has a high moisture content and is difficult to burn. Split wood costs more than unsplit wood because of the labor involved in splitting it.

SPECIAL ORDER. Most retailers will order out-of-stock energy products for you, provided they handle the brand of the item that you want, but may be reluctant to order small amounts of a product, since the freight costs are too expensive and the profit margins too narrow. Instead of special-ordering, your best bet is to find a retailer who stocks the brand of energy-saving merchandise that you want.

INDEX

METRIC CONVERSION

Conversion factors can be carried so far they become impractical. In cases below where an entry is exact it is followed by an asterisk (*). Where considerable rounding off has taken place, the entry is followed by a + or a – sign.

CUSTOMARY TO METRIC

Linear Measure

inches	millimeters
1/16	1.5875*
1/8	3.2
3/16	4.8
1/4	6.35*
5/16	7.9
3/8	9.5
7/16	11.1
1/2	12.7*
9/16	14.3
5/8	15.9
11/16	17.5
3/4	19.05*
13/16	20.6
7/8	22.2
15/16	23.8
1	25.4*

inches	centimeters
1	2.54*
2	5.1
3	7.6
4	10.2
5	12.7*
6	15.2
7	17.8
8	20.3
9	22.9
10	25.4*
11	27.9
12	30.5

feet	centimeters	meters
1	30.48*	.3048*
2	61	.61
3	91	.91
4	122	1.22
5	152	1.52
6	183	1.83
7	213	2.13
8	244	2.44
9	274	2.74
10	305	3.05
50	1524*	15.24*
100	3048*	30.48*

1 yard =
.9144* meters
1 rod =
5.0292* meters
1 mile =
1.6 kilometers
1 nautical mile =
1.852* kilometers

Fluid Measure

(Milliliters [ml] and cubic centimeters [cc or cu cm] are equivalent, but it is customary to use milliliters for liquids.)

1 cu in = 16.39 ml
1 fl oz = 29.6 ml
1 cup = 237 ml
1 pint = 473 ml
1 quart = 946 ml
= .946 liters
1 gallon = 3785 ml
= 3.785 liters
Formula (exact):
fluid ounces × 29.573 529 562 5*
= milliliters

Weights

ounces	grams
1	28.3
2	56.7
3	85
4	113
5	142
6	170
7	198
8	227
9	255
10	283
11	312
12	340
13	369
14	397
15	425
16	454

Formula (exact):
ounces × 28.349 523 125* =
grams

pounds	kilograms
1	.45
2	.9
3	1.4
4	1.8
5	2.3
6	2.7
7	3.2
8	3.6
9	4.1
10	4.5

1 short ton (2000 lbs) =
907 kilograms (kg)
Formula (exact):
pounds × .453 592 37* =
kilograms

Volume

1 cu in = 16.39 cubic
centimeters (cc)
1 cu ft = 28 316.7 cc
1 bushel = 35 239.1 cc
1 peck = 8 809.8 cc

Area

1 sq in = 6.45 sq cm
1 sq ft = 929 sq cm
= .093 sq meters
1 sq yd = .84 sq meters
1 acre = 4 046.9 sq meters
= .404 7 hectares
1 sq mile = 2 589 988 sq meters
= 259 hectares
= 2.589 9 sq
kilometers

Kitchen Measure

1 teaspoon = 4.93 milliliters (ml)
1 Tablespoon = 14.79
milliliters (ml)

Miscellaneous

1 British thermal unit (Btu) (mean)
= 1 055.9 joules
1 calorie (mean) = 4.19 joules
1 horsepower = 745.7 watts
= .75 kilowatts
caliber (diameter of a firearm's
bore in hundredths of an inch)
= .254 millimeters (mm)
1 atmosphere pressure = 101 325*
pascals (newtons per sq meter)
1 pound per square inch (psi) =
6 895 pascals
1 pound per square foot =
47.9 pascals
1 knot = 1.85 kilometers per hour
25 miles per hour = 40.2
kilometers per hour
50 miles per hour = 80.5
kilometers per hour
75 miles per hour = 120.7
kilometers per hour